THE Myth OF THE Normal Curve

Disability Studies in Education

Susan L. Gabel and Scot Danforth
General Editors

Vol. 11

The Disability Studies in Education series is part of the Peter Lang Education list.
Every volume is peer reviewed and meets
the highest quality standards for content and production.

PETER LANG
New York • Washington, D.C./Baltimore • Bern
Frankfurt • Berlin • Brussels • Vienna • Oxford

THE Myth OF THE Normal Curve

EDITED BY
CURT DUDLEY-MARLING AND ALEX GURN

PETER LANG
New York • Washington, D.C./Baltimore • Bern
Frankfurt • Berlin • Brussels • Vienna • Oxford

Library of Congress Cataloging-in-Publication Data

The myth of the normal curve /
edited by Curt Dudley-Marling, Alex Gurn.
p. cm. — (Disability studies in education; vol. 11)
Includes bibliographical references and index.
1. Special education. 2. Disability studies.
3. Intelligence levels. I. Dudley-Marling, Curt.
II. Gurn, Alex. III. Title.
LC3965.D76   371.9'043—dc22   2010023351
ISBN 978-1-4331-0730-6 (hardcover)
ISBN 978-1-4331-0729-0 (paperback)
ISSN 1548-7210

Bibliographic information published by **Die Deutsche Nationalbibliothek.**
Die Deutsche Nationalbibliothek lists this publication in the "Deutsche
Nationalbibliografie"; detailed bibliographic data is available
on the Internet at http://dnb.d-nb.de/.

FSC

Mixed Sources
Product group from well-managed
forests, controlled sources and
recycled wood or fiber

Cert no. SCS-COC-002464
www.fsc.org
©1996 Forest Stewardship Council

The paper in this book meets the guidelines for permanence and durability
of the Committee on Production Guidelines for Book Longevity
of the Council of Library Resources.

© 2010 Peter Lang Publishing, Inc., New York
29 Broadway, 18th floor, New York, NY 10006
www.peterlang.com

Printed in the United States of America

ACKNOWLEDGMENTS

We have many reasons to give thanks and people to whom we are grateful. To begin with we owe a debt of gratitude to all the contributors who breathed life into this volume. We also wish to thank Scot Danforth for his encouragement and support throughout this project. We are especially grateful to our loving families, whose presence in our lives reminds us how vital it is to fight to make the world a more just and caring place.

Contents

ONE

Introduction: Living on the Boundaries of Normal

Curt Dudley-Marling & Alex Gurn

Charles Murray, co-author of the infamous book, *The Bell Curve: Intelligence and Class Structure in American Life* (Herrnstein & Murray, 1994) has written a new book called *Real Education* (Murray, 2009). *Real Education* builds on the assumption that human behavior—including IQ—distributes along the lines of a bell-shaped, normal curve to make strong claims about the relationship between IQ and the social stratification of American society. In his latest book, Charles Murray argues that, because intelligence is fixed, schools will likely have little impact on the educational achievement of students on the low end of the normal curve, a distribution which Murray presents as an established fact. If, as Murray argues, children at the lower reaches of the normal curve cannot be moved by even the most effective teaching, then there is little reason for states and school districts to invest large sums of money in children "left behind," many of whom are poor children and children of color. Nor is there reason to support policies aimed at expanding college attendance if so many students—and by implication their parents—lack the innate ability to do college work. Indeed, Murray claims that perhaps as few as 10% of the population actually have the innate ability to succeed in college, and it is these academically talented students at the upper end of the normal curve that Murray believes are worth the investment since they will make the greatest contributions to society. These arguments echo themes from *The Bell Curve*, a book that has been severely criticized for its elitism and thinly disguised racism (e.g., Kincheloe, Steinberg, & Gresson, 1996). Using pseudo-science underpinned by unquestioned faith in the reality of the normal curve which holds that human behavior necessarily distributes along a bell-shaped curve, Herrnstein and Murray (1994) concluded that low IQ is the cause of "bad parenting, poor school performance, poverty, crime, teenage pregnancy, accidents in the workplace, divorce, etc." (Kincheloe & Steinberg, 1996, p. 9).

Withering criticism of *The Bell Curve* did not discourage Charles Murray from publishing his follow-up book, and sales rankings from the Amazon.com website indicate there is a substantial audience for his work. And at least some of the people who have read Murray's new book are in a position to affect education policy. According to a recent article in an Indiana newspaper (Francisco, 2009), Murray's *Real Education* has changed the way the governor of Indiana thinks about education. According to the *Ft. Wayne Journal Gazette* (Francisco, 2009), Governor Daniels gave copies of *Real Education* to each member of the Indiana Education Roundtable. The reach of this work —along with *The Bell Curve*—depends, in part, on the ready acceptance of the fundamental idea that underlies these books— that human behavior naturally distributes along the lines of a bell-shaped distribution. Most of the reviews of *Real Education* on the Amazon.com site, for example, readily accept the most important of the "four simple truths" Murray asserts in his book—that half of the population is below average on a range of human abilities—as a simple "fact." The problem is that the "lower half" of the normal distribution for intelligence includes disproportionately large numbers of children of color and the assertion that this is "natural" implicitly supports claims of white superiority.

Although it is likely that the vast majority of people would readily reject the racist subtext of *The Bell Curve* and *Real Education*, the foundational construct of the normal curve is generally taken as common sense. As Dudley-Marling and Gurn argue in their chapter in this volume,

> the concept of normality, in which human diversity is characterized by a bell-shaped curve and "given populations are viewed generally around the idea of a statistical norm" (Waterhouse, 2004, p. 72), is "one of the most powerful ideological tools" (Hacking, 1990, p. 169) of modern society. . . "there is probably no area of contemporary life in which some idea of a norm, mean, or average has not been calculated." (Davis, 1997, p. 9)

In the context of schooling, the ideology of the normal curve affects school placement, grading, college admission, educational policy and research, and the everyday language of teachers.

Challenging the *truth* that half of the population is below average is, for many people, to deny an obvious *fact*. However, as the contributors to this volume argue, there is nothing *natural* (or normal) about the normal curve. Only truly random events distribute along a bell-shaped distribution. Human behavior, however, is always affected by social and cultural factors and is never random. Therefore, there is no reason to expect that any human behavior, including intelligence, will distribute normally and every reason to expect it they will not. Even traits like height and weight, which are influenced by nutrition and diet, will not distribute normally. One place you'd expect to find normal distributions for human behavior would be distributions produced by norm-referenced, standardized tests like the SAT, GRE, or other academic achievement tests, but actual empirical evidences indicates that even these situations do not produce normal distributions (Micceri, 1989).

Collectively, the contributors to this volume make the case that, not only is the normal curve not *normal*, the idea that human behavior distributes along a bell-shaped curve with most people clustered around the mean or average grossly oversimplifies the diversity of human experiences. Beth Ferri, for example, takes up the intersection of race, class, gender, sexuality, disability, etc. to emphasize how overly simplistic—and misleading—the construct of normal is. She concludes that, "When presented with all the factors that intersect to influence individual identity, it is clear how meaningless the notion of normal (normal person, normal disabled person, etc.) actually is." Eileen Ball and Beth Harry make a similar point in their chapter, arguing that there is "no such thing as a homogenous human group." The application of "normal curve thinking" to groups of people (black/white, rich/poor, able/disabled, etc.) ignores all the factors and experiences that make the experiences of individual persons unique. Speaking specifically about the process of "norming" standardized tests by including representative sampling of various groups with whom the tests will be used, Ball and Harry observe that, "While the standardizing process may include a representative percentage of ethnic groups, these may not be representative of those groups." In other words, the lives of members of any group are complicated by race, gender, SES, language, immigration/acculturation status, geographic location, and ability, among other factors. Normative claims that efface the complicated ways people live their lives seriously misrepresent the human experience.

In his chapter, Steven Gelb draws on an analysis by R. J. Williams to illustrate the degree to which the statistical concept of the norm can misrepresent the experiences of individual people.

Williams (1982) computed the possibility of an individual being measured normal on mathematically uncorrelated traits if normality is defined as scoring within the values of 95% of the distribution. On the first score, by definition 95% of the sample would be normal. With two measures the percentage drops to 90% and by the tenth measurement to 60%. If one hundred measurements were carried out only six-tenths of 1% of the sample would still be identified as normal.

The human experience is infinitely complex, yet the concept of the norm presents a circumscribed view of the lived experience of individuals—or groups of people—in ways that mislead and misrepresent. As an alternative, Brent Davis and Dennis Sumara discuss complexity theory, a perspective on human experience that renders the concept of "normal" unintelligible. Like Gerald Campano and Rob Simon in their chapter, Davis and Sumara argue that equating students with scores or positions on a statistical distribution ignores the complex systems of which students are a part. From this perspective, predicting human performance based on test scores, language background, or culture makes no sense. Teachers can expect to understand the learning of individual children, for example, but predicting future performance based on a test score or an educational label—which, in turn, is based on normative assumptions—is foolhardy and destructive. Working from a complexity theory perspective leads to an understanding of diversity leads to an understanding of human diversity that will resonate among those in the Disability Studies community: it's normal to be different. As Davis and Sumara put it, "Among complexity researchers, there is more a counternormative sensibility, whereby diversity is understood to be inevitable and necessary."

Complexity theory offers an intellectually appealing alternative to the simplistic account of human variation provided by the normal curve. But this isn't just a theoretical debate. The normal curve is much more than a theory of human variation. It is an ideology that assigns meaning to difference and human worth affecting people's access to the social goods that people value most (Gee, 2007). To be considered outside the boundaries of normal has consequences. In western cultures difference has long been equated with deviance, and people who are deemed to be different have faced marginalization and discrimination—or worse. In his chapter, Steven Gelb traces the evolution of abnormal in the context of humanity's long fascination with monsters. "In time," Gelb argues, "the concept of monstrosity, first applied to non-humans or fanciful animal-human hybrids found its way into evolutionary science as an explanation for 'abnormal' persons with disabilities." Over time, as most children came under the influence of formal schooling, more and more people have been viewed as living on the boundaries of the normal curve. According to Gelb, "Too much of some things (e.g., activity level) or too little of others (e.g., intelligence) is deemed to be bad."

Being on the wrong side of the mean, being judged to have too little or too much of certain qualities can affect people's quality of life, how they are treated by other people and governmental institutions like schools. Although special education has been portrayed as a benign institution that provides the support individual children and adults require to live more fulfilling lives, being positioned as exceptional (i.e., not normal) always comes with a cost. After all, exceptional is the descendent of "monstrous." Indeed, "exceptional" children and adults are often offered remedial education that denies them access to the rich, engaging curricula experienced by students judged to be more able. As Crawford and Bartolomé note in their chapter, special education classrooms are often plagued by an impoverished curriculum that condemns many students to a lifetime of special education placement (see also, Dudley-Marling & Paugh, 2005). Crawford and Bartolomé cite a study by Crawford (2007), for example, that showed tenth grade history teachers using beginner-level curricular material intended for grades 4 to 8 instead of the state-mandated high school history curriculum. One history teacher used a textbook that was intended for grades 4 to 8.

The infantilization of persons judged to be outside the boundaries of normal is further illustrated by Michael Gill's chapter on sex education for individuals with intellectual disabilities. This chapter traces the various ways in which sex education activities for individuals with intellectual disabilities prescribe what is seen as appropriate or *normal* expressions of sexuality for people who are viewed by society as *abnormal*. Gill also presents the extreme case of sterilization as an illustration of what can happen when some people are treated as less than normal—or worse, less than human.

Living on the boundary of the normal curve can also affect the quality of the lives of parents of children with disabilities. In her chapter, Bernadette Macartney explores the effects of being labeled disabled on two young children and their families living in New Zealand. Macartney observes that, "Normalizing discourses, and the disciplinary mechanisms such as surveillance, diagnosis, and the sorting of people into the categories of normal/not normal in education and society limit the opportunities of children with disabilities and their families to contribute, participate, learn, achieve and feel good about themselves." This point is reinforced by Jan Valle and Susan Gabel who offer a narrative account of the lived experience of a mother of a child with disabilities who describes how the "normative mythology" of motherhood impacted her mothering—and her ability to experience the pleasures of parenthood. In a particularly poignant quote, the mother, Alexandra, shares how conflicted she was made to feel by the discourse of the "good mother" who bears the primary responsibility for her children's physical and mental development. When Alexandra rejects the recommendation to place her son in a segregated special education classroom, she "discovers how daunting it can be to resist normative discourse, despite her legal right to do so."

> It has a way of making you feel *guilty* that maybe you *have* been hurting your child or they *do* convince you at times—you go back and forth, I think. There are days that you want to say, "No. This is all *crazy*. My child is just fine."

As many of the contributors to this book demonstrate, the ideology of the normal curve does harm to individuals with disabilities and their families. But it isn't just individuals who are at risk of being marginalized and pathologized by the concept of "normal." Normal curve thinking has been used to rationalize the marginalization of whole groups of people, perpetuating historic injustices. Donaldo Macedo and Teresa Sordé Martí, for example, document the overrepresentation of Roma children in special education classrooms in Central and Eastern Europe. In a particularly shocking illustration of this trend, Macedo and Martí note that in Hungary, in 2003, the Roma made up less than 7% of the population, yet 98% of the population of students in special education schools were Roma. The overrepresentation of Romani children in special education, by excluding them from mainstream education, "robs them of the opportunity to access equality in society" (Macedo and Martí, this volume). Of course, such exclusionary practices are not unknown in this country where the overrepresentation of poor and minority students in special education has long been a serious concern. Felicity Crawford and Lilia Bartolomé argue that these patterns exist, in part, because of the belief that someone has to fail, and the normal curve makes this seem natural. They conclude that, "The idea that some will fail is substantiated with statistical calculations—suggesting a seemingly irrefutable expectation—that reflect a so-called normal distribution."

Testing practices based on normal curve thinking play a significant role in the overrepresentation of poor and minority students in special education. As Ball and Harry point out, the standards, norms, and percentages on which educational testing is based "are dominated by groups that comprise the majority of the U.S. school population (U.S. Census Bureau, 2009), [therefore] we end up weighting *average* achievement based on the performance of white and middle-class children." Arlette Willis shows how these notions of normal—based on the performance of white and middle-class children—have been used to "reinforce racist, and classist ideologies that have pushed many children of color to the margins of schooling." Yet, Willis observes, reports on the effectiveness of reading instruction, for example, "routinely ignored issues of race, class and gender." Willis makes the important point that "the failures of groups seen to be on the margins of normal should signal a crisis in American education"—the canary in the coalmine, as she puts it. Eileen Ball and Beth Harry make a similar point, arguing that a normal distribution should signal the failure of American education, "that even for children thought to have built-in deficiencies, appropriate, individualized instruction should make a difference; we cannot," they argue, "simultaneously believe in this and in the normal curve."

Yet, the sense that there is something natural—and normal—about school failure prevails, buttressed by tests based on presumably "objective" science. However, one of the more troubling aspects of the ideology of the normal curve is its arbitrariness. Steven Gelb cautions that there is nothing natural—or fixed—about the line between normal and not normal. Gelb concludes that, "the judgment about what constitutes 'too much' or 'too little' of given attributes and where to mark the cutoff between normality and abnormality is entirely arbitrary, and, hence open to contestation." The arbitrariness of the line between normal and abnormal—what's too much or too little of various attributes—is nicely illustrated by Rebecca Rogers and Michael Mancini's chapter that draws on "the tradition of critical discourse studies to describe and interpret how normality is discursively constructed and reproduced across texts and contexts and over time." They argue, for example, that attention deficit hyperactivity disorder (ADHD), is underpinned by notions of normality (i.e., there is some small number of students who are so active that they can't learn in school), yet so many children are identified as ADHD that it seems that it really isn't rare. The use of subjective judgments for determining who is—and who is not—ADHD leads to a diagnosis of a presumably "exceptional" condition that, in practice, isn't exceptional at all.

This raises the question of who benefits from labeling children as exceptional. Rogers and Mancini point to pharmaceutical companies and mental health professionals who have worked to expand their influence and power through the proliferation of categories like ADHD. But perhaps the most significant beneficiaries of normal curve thinking are those positioned at the upper reaches of the normal curve whose disproportionate share of the social and economic goods of society is rationalized by a meritocratic discourse that equates people's place in social and economic hierarchies with their innate talent and ability. In other words, people at the top (or the bottom) of the normal curve deserve to be there.

From the perspective of social Darwinists like Charles Murray, the fact that people of color are overrepresented on the low end of the normal curve has little meaning beyond, "this is just the way it is." It has been proven by "science." For Murray and others the appeal to the normal curve as a phenomenon of nature is legitimated by an appeal to science which, it has been claimed, supports the natural sorting of people along the lines of the bell-shaped, normal curve. In her chapter, Deborah Gallagher traces the rise in the use statistics in regulating human affairs to show that notions of normal and abnormal are human constructions. As she puts it, "The discourse of 'science' and the corresponding practices of contemporary educational research (evidence-based practices) are the enduring heir of the 'taming of chance,' the development of the normal curve, statistical probability, and the subsequent invention of 'normal' people."

Collectively, the contributors to this volume critique, directly or indirectly, the ideology of the normal curve. Some explicitly challenge the assumptions that underpin the normal curve. Others indirectly critique notions of normality by examining the impact of normal curve thinking on educational policies and practices. Many contributors go beyond critiquing normality and the normal curve to propose alternative ways to imagine human differences. Gerald Campano and Rob Simon, for example, offer up practitioner inquiry as part of a project to re-vision students positioning on the lower reaches of the normal curve and illustrating the power of high expectation curricula with students who were deemed unable to perform at "normal" levels. Re-visioning human difference is something we consider in more detail in the concluding chapter. Although each contributor to this volume took up the challenge to confront normal curve thinking differently, all contributors would certainly agree that the hegemony of the normal curve has had a devastating effect on those presumed to live on the boundaries of normal. We hope the readers of this volume find the various contributions as interesting, enlightening, and provocative as we do.

References

Crawford, F. (2007). Why bother? They are not capable of this level of work: Manifestations of teacher attitudes in an urban high school self-contained special education classroom with majority blacks and Latinos. In P. Chen (Ed.), *E-yearbook of urban learning, teaching and research* [American Educational Research Association Special Interest Group] (pp. 12–24) [Online]. http://www.aera-ultr.org/Web%20Site%20Files/Images/PDF%20files/2007_eYearbook_final.pdfCrawford, J.

Davis, L. J. (Ed.) (1997). *The disability studies reader.* New York: Routledge.

Dudley-Marling, C. & Paugh, P. (2005). The rich get richer, the poor get Direct Instruction. In B. Altwerger (Ed.), *Reading for profit: How the bottom line leaves kids behind* (pp. 156–171). Portsmouth, NH: Heinemann.

Francisco, K. (October 11, 2009). Governor's education primer. *Ft. Wayne Journal Gazette.* Available at http://www.journalgazette.net/article/20091011/EDIT05/310119940/11

Gee, J.P. (2007). Social linguistics and literacies: Ideologies in discourses. New York: Routledge.

Hacking, I. (1990). *The taming of chance.* Cambridge, UK: Cambridge University Press.

Herrnstein, R. J. & Murray, C. (1994). *The bell curve: Intelligence and class structure in American life.* New York: Free Press.

Kincheloe, J. L. & Steinberg, S. R. (1996). Who said it couldn't happen here? In J. L. Kincheloe, S. R. Steinberg, & A. D. Gresson (Eds.), *Measured lies: The bell curve examined* (pp. 3–47).New York: St. Martin's.

Kincheloe, J. L., Steinberg, S. R., & Gresson, A. D. (Eds.). (1996). *Measured lies: The bell curve examined.* New York: St. Martin's.

Micceri, T. (1989). The unicorn, the normal curve, and other improbable creatures. *Psychological Bulletin, 105(1),* 156–166.

Murray, C. (2009). *Real education: Four simple truths for bringing America's schools back to reality.* New York: Three Rivers.

US Census Bureau (2009). US Census Bureau. Retrieved October, 2009 from http://www.census.gov/

Waterhouse, S. (2004). Deviant and non-deviant identities in the classroom: Patrolling the boundaries of the normal social world. *European Journal of Special Needs Education, 19,* 70–84.

Williams, R. J. (1956/1982) Biochemical variation: Its significance in biology and medicine. In J. Hirsch and T. R. McGuire (Eds.), *Behavior-genetic analysis* (pp. 22–28). Stroudsburg, PA: Hutchinson Ross.

Two

Troubling the Foundations of Special Education: Examining the Myth of the Normal Curve

Curt Dudley-Marling & Alex Gurn

One of the tasks for developing consciousness of disability issues is the attempt . . . to reverse the hegemony of the normal and to institute alternative ways of thinking about the abnormal. (Davis, 1997, p. 26)

The college professor who seeks to create a fair distribution of marks by grading "on the curve," the Las Vegas gambler who is certain that after a series of losing rolls of the dice, his luck is sure to turn, and the special educator who determines that a child is "developmentally delayed" because she scored two standard deviations below the mean on an intelligence test—all share a tacit belief about the order of the universe. Through their respective behaviors, the professor, the gambler, and the special educator express a shared assumption about how the world works; this assumption is most commonly represented by what most of us have been taught to think of as the "normal" curve. We have all been socialized into the idea that, in the natural order of things, the achievement of students in a college course will cluster around an *average* grade, a very long losing streak in games of chance is rare (i.e., not normal), and certain constellations of scores on intelligence tests are *exceptional*.

In their controversial text, *The Bell Curve*, Herrnstein and Murray (1994) refer to the normal curve as "one of nature's more remarkable uniformities" (p. 557). From this perspective, we can expect most phenomena in nature, including human behavior, to distribute normally. Indeed, it has achieved the level of *common sense* among educators, social scientists, and the general public that a bell-shaped curve describes the distribution of a wide range of natural and social phenomena from income and crime statistics to various human traits (e.g., height, weight) and behaviors (e.g., intelligence, academic achievement, athletic prowess) to the "throw of the dice" (Schroeder, 2003). The conventional wisdom that the academic abilities of school children tend to cluster around "the average," for example, stands behind the organization of schooling around age-graded curricula and whole-class instruction (Thomas & Loxley, 2001/2008). The concomitant notion that construes human differences with reference to the average—or "normal"—is a seminal concept in the field of special education. Davis (1997) observes that

> the concept of the norm . . . implies that the majority of the population must or should somehow be part of the norm. The norm pins down that majority of the population that falls under the arch of the standard bell-shaped curve.... Any bell curve will always have at its extremities those characteristics that deviate from the norm. So, with the concept of the norm comes the concept of deviations or extremes. When we think of bodies, in a society where the norm is operative, then people with disabilities will be thought of as deviants. (p. 13)

Despite its common-sense appeal, a substantial body of evidence indicates that the normal curve is a poor model of social reality that has led to "misguided educational theories, inferences, policies, and practices" (Walberg, Strykowski, Rovai, & Hung, 1984, p. 88). The normal curve adequately describes truly random events like the "throw of the dice"; however, as the Las Vegas gambler may discover, sometimes the dice are loaded (Graham, 1939). Socially mediated human behaviors, for example, do not occur randomly. Human weight, for instance, is influenced by various social, economic, and cultural factors, and, therefore, does not distribute normally (Fashing & Goertzel, 1981). Even the distribution of height among human populations may be skewed by nutritional factors. The effects of social factors on the distribution of phenomena such as wealth, academic achievement, and physical strength are even more obvious. Mistrust of the normal curve as a representation of human affairs has emerged in other fields (see Walberg et al., 1984); however, the myth of the normal curve continues to exert a powerful influence on educational thinking, particularly among special educators.

Thomas and Loxley (2001/2008) observed that "faith in certain kinds of knowledge provides the credence, the believability behind special education's status" (p. 1). However, if one takes a "questioning disposition to this knowledge, serious challenges to the legitimacy of special education begin to emerge" (Thomas & Loxley, 2001, p. 1). The "normalization tendency in society in which given populations are viewed generally around the idea of a statistical norm" (Waterhouse, 2004, p. 72) is a foundational concept in special education. Troubling the normal curve as a representation of social realities will, therefore, have the effect of profoundly unsettling special education theory, research, and practice. At a minimum, challenging the universality of the normal curve will demand alternatives to conceptualizing individual differences in terms of deviations from a statistical mean.

In this chapter we review a body of evidence indicating that the normal curve grossly misrepresents human affairs and, therefore, is a poor model for conceptualizing human difference. We also examine the effects of questioning or troubling the assumptions of normality that are embedded in special education theory, research, and practice. Finally, we briefly consider alternative ways of conceptualizing difference. We begin by briefly reviewing the history of the concept of the normal curve.

Historical Overview of the Normal Curve

The history of the concept of "the normal curve" dates to the early 18th century when French-born mathematician Abraham de Moivre pioneered the theory of probability, formulating the mathematical formula that would later form the basis of the normal curve (Bradley, 1968). Specifically, de Moivre discovered the mathematical expression of the limiting case of a binomial distribution for chance events such as flipping a coin. A generation later, Carl Gauss and Pierre-Simon Laplace applied de Moivre's theory to the distribution of measurement errors in astronomical observations. Gauss and Laplace determined that sightings of stars tended to bunch around the mean of the probability curve of errors, with deviations from the mean resulting from a wide array of minor, independent, and random causes. By calculating repeated observations, astronomers could use the mean to estimate the actual location of stars (Bradley, 1968).

Nineteenth-century Belgian astronomer Adolphe Quetelet appears to have been the first person to propose that the "normal curve of error" could be applied to the social realm of human beings (Hacking, 1990). Convinced that the normal curve would hold for measurements in physical and social domains, Quetelet (1842) sought to determine the average physical and behavioral characteristics of human populations through the use of descriptive statistics. Ultimately, Quetelet hoped to identify a composite of average values across multiple variables that made up the mythical "average man," which, for him, represented an ideal of physical, behavioral, and social form. As Quetelet put it, "deviations more or less great from the mean have constituted ugliness in body as well as in morals and a state of sickness with regard to the constitution" (Quetelet, cited in Porter, 1986, p. 103). From this perspective, deviations from the mean denote errors or imperfections in design that occur in a determinate fashion that approximates a bell-shaped curve. Arguably, Quetelet's appropriation of the normal curve as a model for understanding variation in human behavior conflates variation with deviation and normal with natural, laying the groundwork for social Darwinism and structures of schooling that pathologize difference.

Whereas Quetelet focused on population averages, Sir Francis Galton, cousin of Charles Darwin and a founder of the eugenics movement, turned his attention to variation among human populations, in particular, deviations from the mean. For Galton, the mean represented less than the ideal since clustering around the mean were the undistinguished masses. Galton believed that the tails of the bell-shaped, normal distribution represented strength and brilliance at one end and weakness and feeble-mindedness at the other. He sought to extend Quetelet's application of the normal curve to classify human intelligence, which Galton viewed as biologically determined (MacKenzie, 1981). In *Hereditary Genius* (1869), Galton argued:

> This is what I am driving at—that analogy clearly shows there must be a fairly constant average mental capacity in the inhabitants of British Isles, and that de-viations from that average—upwards towards genius, and downwards towards stupidity—must follow the law that governs deviations from all true averages. (Galton, 1869, p.32, cited in MacKenzie, 1981, p. 57)

Toward this end, Galton employed the normal curve of errors to sort individuals into hierarchically based, quartile ranges based on their deviation from the mean. It was Galton who transformed the normal distribution into rankings so that one tail of the normal distribution would be seen as optimal or desirable and the other tail as abnormal and undesirable (Davis, 1997). Individuals in the lowest quartile were considered abnormal or deficient, while those in the upper quartile embodied progress and perfection. For Galton, the mean and the standard devia-tion provided an objective means for ranking people's mental capacity along a continuum. Arguably, Galton's ideas about the normal distribution stand behind the organization of American education that makes hierarchies out of "any dif-ferences that can be claimed, however falsely, to be natural, inherent, and poten-tially consequential in school" (McDermott, Goldman, & Varénne, 2006, p. 12).

By the late 19th century statisticians were persuaded that natural and social phenomena would always distribute "normally" if a sufficiently large number of observations were obtained (Micceri, 1989). This assumption was challenged, however, by Karl Pearson, a pre-eminent figure in the development of modern statistics, who, on the basis of empirical observations, raised questions about the prevalence of normality among real-world distributions (Micceri, 1989). Despite Pearson's protestations, the tendency to take for granted the normal distribution of observations in the natural and social worlds persisted, partly due to the work of eminent statistician Ronald Fisher "who showed that, when universal normality could be assumed, inferences of the widest practical usefulness could be drawn from samples of any size" (Geary, 1947, p. 241). Following Fisher's insight, "prejudice in favor of normality returned full force" (Geary, 1947, p. 241) and challenges to the universality of the normal distribution as a representation of human variation receded to the background.

For nearly 100 years taken-for-granted assumptions of normality have undergirded educational research and test construction as scholars and administrators in the fields of education and psychology turned to positivist, quantitative science to assert the validity of their scientific claims (Lagemann, 2000). For their part, schools readily embraced the technique of measuring students against standardized norms that "involved new social practices, like standard curriculum, age grading, and examinations, which. . . created the kinds of statistical populations that Galtonian psychology took as its basis" (Danziger, 1990, p. 79). The concept of the normal curve has had a powerful impact on how educators and psychologists think about students, particularly students deemed to be "exceptional." Yet, as we demonstrate below, in the social worlds inhabited by human beings normal distributions are uncommon. Further, even in instances where human behavior distributes more or less normally, the mean offers a poor representation of the behavior of individuals and groups.

The Myth of the Normal Curve

Emerging from the concept of the normal curve are two statistical measures that have shaped understandings of difference in the context of schooling: the standard deviation and the mean. The standard deviation supports the construction of human difference in terms of probability distributions based on assumptions about how various traits and abilities distribute within the general population. Intellectual and developmental disabilities, for example, have been operationally defined in terms of deviations from a statistical construction of average (i.e., the mean). In this case, the mean provides a point of reference for determining who is "normal" and who is not. The mean is also used to support the development of categories of difference. Implicit in the multitude of studies comparing categorical groupings of students with "exceptional needs" to "normal" students is the assumption that the concept of "the mean" represents both differences (from normal) and similarities (shared traits and behaviors within categorical groupings). Studies that reveal statistically significant differences in various traits and abilities between students with learning disabilities and non-disabled students, for example, support the characterization of some students as exceptional (i.e., statistically different from normal) while simultaneously validating a category of exceptionality (e.g., students with learning disabilities who share certain cognitive and behavioral characteristics).

In the following section, we critique the use of the normal curve as a representation of variation within the general population and as a way for representing specific groups and individuals.

The normal curve as a representation of variation among the general population

Sir Francis Galton, one of the first people to advocate the use of the normal curve as a model of human diversity, also provided one of the earliest challenges to the universality of the normal curve. Galton set out to gather a variety of empirical data in order to demonstrate the utility of the normal curve but, as it turned out, he discovered that the data for traits like height, weight, strength, and eyesight failed to produce perfect normal distributions. Ultimately, Galton concluded that the normal curve applied only to homogeneous distributions (Micceri, 1989). Galton found that he could achieve perfectly normal distributions by converting his data to standard scores[1] and averaging these standard scores from different variables together (Fashing & Goertzel, 1981). However, according to Fashing and Goertzel (1981), the normal distributions produced from these average scores, which Galton mistook as evidence of the underlying normality of the variables, merely indicate the presence of measurement error (Fashing & Goertzel, 1981).

Karl Pearson, writing over 100 years ago, offered a more direct challenge to the universality of the normal curve. Based on his extensive observations of various phenomena (e.g., throws of the dice, outcomes of roulette wheel, number of petals in buttercups), Pearson (1900) concluded that a wide range of phenomena—many cited as textbook examples of normality—did not fit a Gaussian, or normal, curve. Pearson expressed regret that statisticians too easily accepted claims of normal distributions on theoretical and not empirical grounds. He concluded:

> If the earlier writers on probability had not proceeded so entirely from the mathematical standpoint, but had endeavored first to classify experience in deviations from the average, and then to obtain some measure of the actual goodness of fit provided by the normal curve, that curve would never have obtained its present position in the theory of errors. Even today there are those who regard it as a sort of fetish…. [However] the normal curve of error possesses no special fitness for describing errors or deviations such as arise either in observing practice or in nature. (Pearson, 1900, pp. 173–174)

David Wechsler (1935) and Lee Cronbach (1970), both major figures in the history of psychological assessment, also cautioned that psychological phenomena are not inherently distributed normally (Fashing & Goertzel, 1981). Geary (1947) went even further, recommending that all statistics textbooks begin with the statement, "Normality is a myth; there never was, and never will be, a normal distribution" (p. 241). Although Geary (1947) conceded this was an overstatement, he argued that researchers should never take normality for granted. Indeed, over time, researchers have identified numerous examples of what Bradley (1977) has called "bizarre distributions" of human behavior that differ significantly from the normal distribution. Human vigilance experiments in which the dependent variable is time to respond to critical signals, human taste thresholds, social conformity, and time to completion for various tasks are just a few examples of human behaviors that have been found to produce dramatically non-normal distributions (Bradley, 1977). In the world of human affairs, significantly non-normal distributions, often the result of uncontrolled-for variables, are quite common (Bradley, 1977). Indeed,

> there are vast areas of research (especially in the behavioral sciences) where the uncontrolled variables are likely to include unknown, or insufficiently known, variables of moderate or even major influence and, indeed, where the experimenter has practically no knowledge as to the shape of the sampled population. (Bradley, 1977, p. 150)

One type of non-normal distribution that is commonplace in the world of human affairs is the right- or positive-skew distribution[2] "in which low or even null performance is most frequent, and high or even moderate performance is rare" (Walberg et al., 1984, p. 87). A former president of the Royal Statistical Society declared that "positive skewness is the most pervasive law-like phenomenon in the social sciences" (Walberg et al., 1984, p. 87). Based on an extensive review of research across a variety of fields of study, Walberg et al. (1984) concluded that "positive-skew distributions characterize many fundamental processes and objects in biology, communication, crime, economics, demography, geography, industry, information and library science, linguistics, psychology, sociology, and the production and utilization of knowledge" (p. 108). This analysis supports the conclusion that the normal curve applies only to truly random events. In the natural world and in the social worlds inhabited by human beings many—and perhaps most—phenomena are not the result of random events and, therefore, do not distribute normally.

Despite widespread challenges to the normal curve as a representation of human behavior, the normal curve continues to exert a powerful influence on educators and psychometricians (Micceri, 1989). It may be that educators and psychometricians have been unduly influenced by the assumption that well-designed, objective tests *necessarily* produce normal distributions that are representative of human behavior. Educators may assume, for example, that learning outcomes are normally distributed because achievement scores are presumed to distribute normally. However, achievement tests are "by tradition, custom, or conscious purpose . . . designed to produce such manifest distributions and are not necessarily indicative of the underlying latent [normal] distributions" (Walberg et al., 1984. p. 88). The second half of this quote bears repeating. Just because objective measures of achievement or ability produce normal distributions does not mean that what is being measured (math, reading, intelligence, and so on) actually distributes normally among human populations.

The tendency of achievement and ability test data to distribute normally is, to some degree, "simply a mathematical and statistical effect" (Sartori, 2006, p. 415). Standardized educational tests rely on summated scaling techniques by which persons taking tests attempt to answer a large number of items and receive total scores corresponding to the number of items they answer correctly. This type of measurement has an inherent bias towards a normal distribution in that it is essentially an averaging process, and the central limit theorem shows that distributions of means tend to be normally distributed (Fashing & Goertzel, 1981; Sartori, 2006). In other words, the average of averages will necessarily produce a normal distribution even if the variable being measured does not distribute normally.

The tendency of objective tests to produce normal distributions is also a function of item difficulty (Walberg et al., 1984) and test error. Recall that the normal curve was originally referred to either as the "law of frequency of error" or "the normal curve of error" (Hacking, 1990; MacKenzie, 1981). Sartori (2006) observes:

> When the responses to the items of a test or scale are poorly intercorrelated and when a large number of people fill it out, the scores are very likely to be normally distributed. This characteristic of the averaging process is useful in calculating probable errors in random sampling. But when averaging is used in testing or measurement, it may mean that the greater the amount of error, the greater the likelihood of a normal distribution of scores, even if . . . the variable being measured is not normally distributed. All objective tests contain a certain amount of error. . . . Thus, it is not surprising that summated (or averaged) scaling devices tend to give normal distributions. (p. 415)

Crucially, "the problem comes when this effect is interpreted not as the obvious result of an error which is unavoidable, but as a confirmation of a preconceived idea that the variables being measured are *really* normally distributed" (Sartori, 2006, p. 415).

Even given the theoretical bias of objective tests toward normal distributions there is empirical evidence indicating that actual test scores "are seldom normally distributed" (Nunnally, 1978, p. 160). Micceri (1989), for example, examined the distributional characteristics of 440 large-sample achievement and psychometric measures obtained from journal articles, research studies and national, state, and district tests. Major sources of test data included the California Achievement Tests, the Comprehensive Test of Basic Skills, Stanford Reading Tests, Scholastic Aptitude Test (SAT), and the Graduate Record Exam (GRE). In all, Micceri's sample included 46 different test sources and 89 different populations. His analysis indicated that all of the 440 distributions he examined were "significantly non-normal at the alpha .01 significance level" (p. 156) reinforcing Karl Pearson's conclusion that "the normal curve of error possesses no special fitness for describing errors or deviations such as arise either in observing practice or in nature" (Pearson, 1900, p. 174), including the distribution of test scores.

The presumption that social and psychological variables distribute normally "has been shown to be invalid by those methodologists who have taken the trouble to check it out. Its persistence in the folklore and procedures of social institutions is a reflection of institutionalized bias, not scientific rigor" (Fashing & Goertzel, 1981, p. 28). The normal curve is a product of random errors. Human behavior, which is always influenced by social factors, is never random and, therefore, should not be expected to produce normal distributions (Fashing & Goertzel, 1981). Still, among educators and psychometricians, the conundrum of the normal curve has largely been treated as a technical problem, not a conceptual one. Many educational researchers, for example, appear to take comfort in Monte Carlo studies indicating the robustness of parametric statistical tests in the face of non-normal distributions, yet ignore what the normal curve signifies: a theory of human difference that has no empirical basis.

The normal curve as a representation of individuals: The myth of the "average animal"

The myth of the normal curve has given rise to the premise that the mean is a meaningful representation of groups—and individual group members—to which it is applied. In the theoretical case of a perfect normal distribution, observations will cluster about the mean. It is well known that, in the case of phenomena that result in a perfect, bell-shaped curve, 95% of observations will fall within two standard deviations of the mean. Sixty-eight percent fall within one standard deviation of the mean. When the normal curve is applied to human populations, the area demarcated by one standard deviation on either side of the mean is often referred to as the "average range," a statistically constructed space where people are assumed to share essential characteristics by virtue of the simple fact that they do not differ significantly from the norm (i.e., average). Reading achievement tests, for example, construct "average readers" who, presumably, share essential learning traits and require common curricula. These same tests also play a role in defining students who fall outside the average range, students whose profiles differ from average—or normal—and who, it is assumed, share essential qualities that may require special education.

The mean as a representation of average (or normal) within a normal distribution is fundamental to the special education enterprise. The mean constructs categories of exceptionality by identifying traits and abilities that separate children with disabilities from the general population of students (e.g., students with intellectual disabilities are defined as performing significantly below the mean on intelligence tests) providing the primary rationale for special education. The use of means to indicate traits and abilities groups of children with disabilities share (e.g., the average student with learning disabilities) justifies and maintains special education research and practice focused on categories of exceptionality. Research into best instructional practices for students with learning disabilities, for example, presumes that students with learning disabilities share characteristics related to their learning that distinguish them from students who are not learning disabled.

The problem is that the normal curve is a poor representation of human differences. As the evidence we reviewed above indicates, human traits do not tend to cluster about the mean in a bell-shaped distribution. Yet, even in the theoretical case of a perfect normal distribution, the mean provides a misleading portrayal of individual traits and abilities within particular populations. Writing over 70 years ago in the *Journal of Comparative Psychology*, Knight Dunlap (1935) warned of the dangers of reporting data solely in terms of the average animal, "an animal which is entirely mythical" (p. 1). Dunlap observed that in his "list of Great Experiments in Bad Psychology there is one research in which the average value presented as significant is a value which every person in the experiment conspicuously avoided" (p. 2). Put differently, the average for any particular group of people may apply to no one person in the group. In the context of special education research, the reliance on means to represent groups of students with disabilities mischaracterizes individual students. The finding that the average student with learning disabilities, for example, is deficient in some trait compared to non-learning disabled students may not apply to individual students with learning disabilities. Dudley-Marling, Kaufman, and Tarver (1981), for example, reported that learning profiles that were claimed to be characteristic of students with learning disabilities were not always found in individual students with learning disabilities. Additionally, it was found that many non-LD students did present these profiles. Similarly, demonstrating the effectiveness of an instructional strategy with a statistically constructed average student with intellectual disabilities obscures the likelihood that the strategy was ineffective with at least some children. No reading intervention, for example, has been found to be successful with all children, all of the time (Duffy & Hoffman, 1999) even if various interventions have been found to be effective on average.

Overall, the statistically constructed average student with disabilities is a mythical individual who bears little resemblance to individual students with disabilities. Yet, statistical averages have frequently been the basis of generalizations about students with disabilities "even though the average pattern might not correspond to a single individual member of a statistical group" (Danziger, 1990, p. 153). The irony is that special education, which focuses on the needs of individual students, is undergirded by a model of human variation that tends to efface individual differences.

Conclusion

The concept of normality, in which human diversity is characterized by a bell-shaped curve and "given populations are viewed generally around the idea of a statistical norm" (Waterhouse, 2004, p. 72), is "one of the most powerful ideological tools" of modern society (Hacking, 1990, p. 169). Davis (1997) observed that "there is probably no area of contemporary life in which some idea of a norm, mean, or average has not been calculated" (p. 9). The assumption, based on the normal curve, that it is normal — and natural—for some proportion of the population to be well below average has been used to justify persistent social, economic, vocational, and academic inequities that plague contemporary American society. There is no reason to pursue public policies aimed at eliminating poverty, for example, if extremes in income distribution—and competence —are viewed as natural manifestations of the normal curve (e.g., Herrnstein & Murray, 1994). As Fashing and Goertzel (1981) put it,

> the myth of the normal curve has occupied a central place in the theory of inequality. Apologists for inequality in all spheres of social life have used the theory of the normal curve, explicitly and implicitly, in developing moral rationalizations to justify the *status quo*. (p. 15)

In the context of schooling, the assumption that the academic performance of similarly aged students tends to cluster about the mean justifies whole class instruction and one-size-fits-all curricula that efface individual differences among students. Indeed, the inability of some students to profit from routine, whole class instruction is taken as *prima facie* evidence that they fall outside the normal range. Further, taking the normal curve as a model of human variation suggests that this situation is natural. The theory of the normal curve predicts that a fraction of students will necessarily fall at the lower end of the normal distribution. These students are deemed to be exceptional. In this way, the normal curve provides a rationale for special education that situates learning problems in the heads of individual learners and not in the structures of schooling that produced so much failure in the first place (Dudley-Marling, 2004). The theory of the normal curve also underpins an approach to special education research that relies on studies of mean differences to establish categories of exceptionality based on shared characteristics that distinguish students in one category of exceptionality from students in other special education categories and from normally achieving students. Studies of mean differences are also used to identify best practices for students in particular special education categories.

We argued at the beginning of this chapter that special education theory, research, and practice are underpinned by a conceptualization of normality based on the normal curve. However, as this review has illustrated, the normal curve is "normal" only in the case of random errors. There is "no reason to expect sociological variables to be normally distributed. Nor is there any reason to expect psychological variables to be if they are influenced by social factors" (Fashing & Goertzel, 1981, p. 27) as they always are. The normal curve is a poor model of social reality, and, therefore, human diversity cannot be understood with reference to a fictitious average (or normal) person. Nor can individual human differences be relegated to the distant boundaries of a bell-shaped distribution.

Exploding the myth of the normal curve undermines the representation of disability (or difference) as deviation from the mythical "normal." Consequently, we need alternative ways of conceptualizing the meaning of difference that is not based on the normal curve of errors. In the opening of this chapter we quoted Lennard Davis (1997) who issued a clarion call to disability studies theorists "to reverse the hegemony of the normal and to institute alternative ways of thinking about the abnormal" (p. 26). Upsetting the normal curve as a model of human diversity challenges the practice of equating difference with deviance and diversity with exceptional. In the realm of human experience, diversity is not the exception but the rule (Gould, 1997). In other words, it is normal to be different, a conclusion that demands a radically different conceptualization of special education theory, research, and practice.

Interrogating the normal curve as a foundational concept in special education reveals a fundamental anomaly in special education theory, research, and practice. Individualization is the *raison d'être* of special education; yet, special education theory, research, and practice are informed by a model of diversity that obscures individual differences. From the perspective of individual students, the discourse of science, as taken up in special education, obfuscates more than it enlightens (Gallagher, 1998; Gladwell, 2006). Relying on aggregate measures of central tendency, for example, provides a means for special education researchers to cope with diverse and inconsistent behaviors of individuals (Danziger, 1990). However, "the reference to an aggregate seems to be an unnecessary extra step if the goal of the particular study is to understand how development takes place within a given organism or psychological system.... [Further] aggregation of data entails ignoring the holistic nature of the phenomena from which those data were derived" (Surgan, 2001).

If it is normal to be different, "it is only by attending with care to each child that the noble aim of equality of education for all children can be achieved" (Carini & Himley, 2010). "Attending with care to each child" requires approaches to research—case studies, single subject research, classroom ethnography, and teacher research, for example—that illuminate the development of individual students. At a minimum, special education researchers—indeed, all educational researchers—must give more attention to reporting measures of variance in their data. In intervention studies, for example, reporting the proportion of students in treatment groups that actually improve relative to control groups (and the proportion of students in control groups who outperformed students in the treatment groups) should be a routine practice. Similarly, researchers who report effect sizes should also indicate the degree of overlap in the distributions of scores for treatment and control groups. For example, an effect size of .8, which in the world of social science is considered to be "large" (Cohen, 1969), means that 79% of the control group falls below the mean for the experimental or treatment group. It also means, however, that 21% of the control group scored higher than the mean for the treatment group (Coe, 2002). Of course, the meaning of effect sizes is much more difficult to ascertain in the case of significantly non-normal distributions which, as we have argued, are common in human affairs.

Attending to the needs of individual children also demands instruction that responds to the development, background knowledge, and experience of particular children. Curriculum-based instruction, universal design, and response-to-intervention are promising developments in this direction. Equally important is creating classroom structures that enable teachers to provide students with frequent, intensive, explicit, and individualized support and direction based on ongoing, individualized assessment (Dudley-Marling & Paugh, 2004). Readers and Writers Workshops and center-based instruction are examples of classroom organization that provide opportunities for teachers to work with students individually and in small groups and collect the in-depth assessment data needed to provide appropriate instruction for individual students.

The normal curve is a powerful construct that, in the context of schooling, limits the interpretations available for thinking and talking about children (McDermott, Goldman, & Varénne, 2006). Teachers' interpretations of student learning typically involve categorizing each child in relation to a significant social boundary—based on the normal curve—"that separates 'normal' from 'deviant' pupils" (Waterhouse, 2004, p. 72). So challenging the normal curve means confronting the everyday language educators use to interpret students' learning. As a beginning we need to challenge teachers, researchers, and school administrators to focus less on what children cannot do and more on what they are capable of given the right conditions, including challenging curriculum. As McDermott, Goldman, and Varénne (2006) put it, "to counteract the cultural inclination to focus on what is wrong with individual children, we must seek data showing children more skilled than schools have categories or time to notice, describe, diagnose, record, and remediate" (p. 15). We must stop asking what's wrong with children who struggle in school—that is, how they compare to some mythical norm—and ask, instead, what makes them smart (Miller, 1993).

Endnotes

1. Standard scores are also called *z scores* which indicate distance from the mean in standard deviation units.
2. Skewness indicates the extent to which a distribution is asymmetrical. In a right- or positive-skew distribution the tail of the distribution extends to the right. Income among American families is an example of a positive-skew distribution, i.e., most people make less than $100,000 and only a small proportionate make more than $1,000,000. In other words, income distributions are skewed toward lower incomes.

References

Bradley, J.V. (1977). A common situation conducive to bizarre distribution shapes. *The American Statistician*, 31(4), 147-150.

Bradley, J. V. (1968). *Distribution-free statistical tests*. Englewood Cliffs, NJ: Prentice Hall.

Carini, P. F. & Himley, M. (2010). *Jenny's story: Taking the long view of the child, Prospect's philosophy in action*. New York: Teachers College Press.

Coe, R. (2002). *It's the effect size, stupid: What effect size is and why it is important*. Retrieved April 8, 2008 from http://www.leeds.ac.uk/educol/documents/00002182.htm

Cohen, J. (1969) *Statistical power analysis for the behavioral sciences*. New York: Academic Press.

Cronbach, J .L. (1970). *The essentials of psychological testing*. New York: Harper & Row.

Danziger, K. (1990). *Constructing the subject: Historical origins of psychological research*. New York: Cambridge University Press.

Davis, L. J. (Ed.) (1997). *The disability studies reader*. New York: Routledge.

Dudley-Marling, C. (2004). The social construction of learning disabilities. *Journal of Learning Disabilities, 37*, 482–490.

Dudley-Marling, C. & Paugh, P. (2004). *A classroom teacher's guide to struggling readers*. Portsmouth, NH: Heinemann.

Dudley-Marling, C., Kaufman, N. J., & Tarver, S. G. (1981). WISC and WISC-R profiles of learning disabled children. *Learning Disability Quarterly, 4*, 307-319.

Duffy, G. G., & Hoffman, J. V. (1999). In pursuit of an illusion: The search for a perfect method. *The Reading Teacher, 53*, 10–16.

Dunlap, K. (1935). The average animal. *Journal of Comparative Psychology, 19*, 1–3.

Fashing, J. & Goertzel, T. (1981). The myth of the normal curve: A theoretical critique and examination of its role in teaching and research. *Humanity and Society, 5*(1), 14–31.

Gallagher, D. J. (1998). The scientific knowledge base of special education: Do we know what we think we know? *Exceptional Children, 64*(4), 493–502.

Galton, F. (1869). *Hereditary Genius*. London: Macmillan.

Geary, R. C. (1947). Testing for normality. *Biometrika, 34,* 209–242.

Gladwell, M. (Dept. of Social Services, 2006) "Million-Dollar Murray," *The New Yorker,* February 13, 2006, p. 96.

Gould, S. J. (1997). *Full house: The spread of excellence from Plato to Darwin.* New York: Three Rivers.

Graham, J. L. (1939). A paradox in the use of the normal probability curve. *American Journal of Psychology, 52,* 293–296.

Hacking, I. (1990). *The taming of chance.* Cambridge, UK: Cambridge University Press.

Herrnstein, R. J. & Murray, C. (1994). *The bell curve: Intelligence and class structure in American life.* New York: Free Press.

Lagemann, E. (2000). *An elusive science: The troubling history of educational research.* Chicago, IL: University of Chicago Press.

MacKenzie, D. (1981). *Statistics in Britain, 1865–1930: The social construction of scientific knowledge.* New York: Columbia University Press.

McDermott, R., Goldman, S., & Varénne, H. (2006). The cultural work of learning disabilities. *Educational Researcher, 35,* 12–17.

Micceri, T. (1989). The unicorn, the normal curve, and other improbable creatures. *Psychological Bulletin, 105*(1), 156–166.

Miller, L. (1993). *What we call smart: A new narrative for intelligence and learning.* San Diego, CA: Singular.

Nunnally, J. C. (1978). *Psychometric theory.* New York: McGraw-Hill.

Pearson, K. (1900). On the criterion that a given system of deviations from the probable in the case of a correlated system of variables is such that it can be reasonably supposed to have arisen from random sampling. *The London, Edinburgh, and Dublin Philosophical Magazine and Journal of Science, 50,* 155–175.

Porter, T. M. (1986). *The rise of statistical thinking.* Princeton, NJ: Princeton University Press.

Quetelet, M. A. (1842). *A treatise on man and the development of his faculties.* New York: Burt Franklin.

Sartori, R. (2006). The bell curve in psychological research and practice: myth or reality? *Quality and Quantity, 40*(3), 407–418.

Schroeder, C.M. (February, 2003). *There are infinitely many normal distributions: Not all normal distributions are standard normal.* Paper presented at the annual meeting of the Southwest Educational Research Association, San Antonio, TX.

Surgan, S. (2001). Is random rrror useful for developmental psychology? *Forum: Qualitative Sozialforschung / Forum: Qualitative Social Research, 2*(3). Retrieved August 15, 2007, from http://www.qualitative-research.net/fqs-texte/3-01/3-01surgan-e.htm

Thomas, G. & Loxley, A. (2001/2008). *Deconstructing special education and constructing inclusion.* Philadelphia, PA: Open University Press.

Walberg, H. J., Strykowski, B. F., Rovai, E., & Hung, S. S. (1984). Exceptional performance. *Review of Educational Research, 54*(1), 87–112.

Waterhouse, S. (2004). Deviant and non-deviant identities in the classroom: Patrolling the boundaries of the normal social world. *European Journal of Special Needs Education, 19,* 70–84.

Wechsler, D. (1935). *The range of human abilities.* Baltimore, MD: William & Wilkins.

THREE

Educational Researchers and the Making of Normal People

Deborah Gallagher

Every kind of measurement results in a statistical distribution. And statistical distributions are the basis for deciding in most cases what is "normal." (Kauffman & Hallahan, 2005, *Special Education: What It Is and Why We Need It,* p. 18)

So, why should we discuss statistical distributions? Simply put, statistical distributions of achievement or performance are the basis for special education: to understand special education, one must understand statistical distributions. Special education is designed for and is necessary for individuals whose scores on tests or whose performances on other types of measures are at the extremes—much lower or higher than typical. (Kauffman & Hallahan, 2005, *Special Education: What It Is and Why We Need It,* p. 20)

By giving so much attention to measurement we risk the criticism that we are overly concerned about numbers and test scores. We do not mean to imply that the essence of a child's identity can be captured in a single score, or even a set of scores. We do mean to acknowledge, though, that measures, whether they be test scores or observations, are critical to special education because by definition an exceptional learner is one who differs from the norm—the average, the typical. (Kauffman & Hallahan, 2005, *Special Education: What It Is and Why We Need It,* p. 21)

First we make up our claims to truth, then we forget that we made them up, then we forget that we forgot. (Nietzsche, *On the Genealogy of Morals*—trans. Douglas Smith, 1887; repr. London: Oxford University Press, 1997)

In his acclaimed book, *The Taming of Chance*, Hacking (1990) argued that the rise of statistics and attendant reckoning of probability marked a momentous shift not only in how people experience the world but also how they perceive themselves and each other. During the late 19th century, probability offered the possibility of "taming chance," thus supplanting the Age of Reason's philosophical determinism that depicted the world as ruled by the causal laws of nature. And, because humans were likewise ruled by the laws of nature, determinism in the form of human nature offered a predictably safe, albeit somewhat dim, view of people and social interaction. Brought under mathematical control, the concept of chance long associated with "superstition, vulgarity, and unreason" (p. 1) supplanted determinism as the refuge of choice from a random and volatile world.

The relentless compilation of statistical data leading to the taming of chance, Hacking explained, inevitably required the formation of ever-expanding sets of categories into which people could be sorted and classified. Those conforming to the central tendency were "normal" while those who did not were thought "pathological." Deviations from the mean thus unseated the notion of human nature for the more useful creation of "normal people." In turn, creating normal people made it possible to "improve —control—a deviant subpopulation by enumeration and classification" (Hacking, 1990, p. 3).

In this chapter, I first provide a brief historical recounting of the rise of statistical probability, the development of the normal curve, and the creation of "normal people." This historical recounting sets the stage for understanding the expansion of the field of scientific school psychology and the development of corresponding procedures for inquiry that have shaped the contours of contemporary educational research. In the process I elaborate on a set of recurring themes emerging from this recounting and demonstrate that the currently ascendant discourse of scientific educational research (evidence-based practices) bears all the hallmarks of the ideological commitments that fueled their conception.

The Development of Statistics and Probability

The statistical tools central to "scientific" educational research and mental testing have been around for so long that few recall if they ever knew the very illuminating philosophical and ideological substance of their historical origins. Given their largely taken-for-granted status as a set of neutral procedures one might be forgiven for finding it difficult to counter blithe, passionate, or patronizing assertions that educational research employing scientific "experimentation" is, "still the single best methodological route to ferreting out systematic relations between actions and outcomes" (Feuer, Towne, & Shavelson, 2002a, p. 8). From this perspective long dominating the social sciences as well as educational research, what could be more final or more desirable than the appeal to methodological neutrality? All else becomes ideology and exposes educational researchers not only to costly errors and dubious credibility but also to the dreaded abyss of perpetual disputes adjudicated only by the untoward exercise of power.

Although many have decisively effaced the epistemological and ontological claims to theory-free observation (Hanson, 1958; Kuhn, 1962; Nagel, 1986; Taylor, 1971), the spectator theory of knowledge (Dewey, 1929; Rorty, 1979, 1980, 1982), and fact/value distinctions (Putnam, 1981; Rorty, 1979), an unyielding confidence in the neutrality of statistical procedures has served as an apparently advantageous refuge from skeptical critics. Statistical formulae are comprised of numbers, and, it is said, numbers don't lie. And in that they don't lie, they provide a non-human bulwark between all too human researchers with their competing ideological commitments and the results of scientific research.

For this reason among others, a level of historical background is in order. This is so particularly for the Disability Studies in Education community because this history is brimming with evocative insights into the creation of the normal versus abnormal binary, the medical model of disability, and the pathologizing of difference. As I have indicated elsewhere, "to point out that research procedures are human constructions is to state the obvious" (Gallagher, 2006, p. 98). This includes statistical procedures, despite a mask of neutrality that tends to obscure the human element that weaved and massaged them into existence.

Because the history of statistics is as technically detailed as it is historically significant, the goal in this paper is to describe only as much of the necessary technical detail necessary to reveal its social, political, and ethical consequences for educational research. My purpose, in other words, is to provide enough background to establish the major themes that defined the development of statistical reasoning in the rise of the social sciences. In general, providing this historical background both expands on and complements the historical data Dudley-Marling and Gurn offer in their critique of the normal curve in Chapter 2.

It all began with the counting—that, and the "modern notion of the state" (Hacking, 1975, p. 18). Porter (1986), in fact, traced the origin of the word "statistics" to its early practitioners who were called "statists." As he further explained, the best, most efficient way to consolidate state power, central administration, and bureaucratic efficiency was to maintain extensive numerical accounts of the people and resources that represented the wealth and well-being of the state. The practice of keeping such records stretches back to very early times as births, deaths, and marriages were chronicled in church records, but at the beginning of the 19th century this activity became more widespread, extensive, and a formalized function of the state. The periodic census initiated in the more advanced states of Europe and the U.S., in conjunction with the rise of statistical bureaus, resulted in a deluge of numerical information, the extensive range and variety of which eventually induced curiosity about recurring patterns. Especially intriguing were those patterns surrounding voluntary (moral) activities such as marriage, divorce, crime, and suicide.

These patterns, or regularities, suggested that a case could be made for the existence of certain moral and social laws, laws of human nature akin to, as prime example, the Newtonian laws that governed the natural world. In the eyes of Enlightenment thinkers, the possibility of such laws seemed self-evident. To discover these laws using their statistical science offered the prospect of preventing and alleviating the social sores of crime, poverty, madness, and deviancy of all kinds. And so by the close of the 1830s, visions of social improvement and progress generated a strong sense of reformist zeal spurring the development of the social sciences as an organized study aimed at wide-scale social transformation. Much of what had previously been understood as falling under the purview of the church in terms of human imperfections thus became the focus of law, government, and medicine. "In this way," Hacking (1990) remarked, "a medical notion (pathology) was transferred to the body politic on the back of statistics" (p. 64).

But descriptive statistics offered little in the way of utility if a more formal means for isolating the causes of social pathology could not be used in the service of prediction, control, and amelioration. It is here that the calculation of chance, or probability, came into play. The concept of chance had been around a long time—since the 17th century. Games of chance (the rolling of dice and flipping of coins) provided motivation for the initial forays into probability theory (see, Stigler, 1986). Almost immediately, its usefulness became apparent for calculating such things as the appropriate size of legal trial juries and the rates for life insurance and annuities. Nineteenth-century French mathematician Simeon Poisson's law of large numbers was a singular achievement because it demonstrated that statistical information gathered from very large groups of people allowed for a much more precise calculation of probability. More importantly, the ability to predict the frequency of social events using probability calculations over time on large populations made even year-to-year or place-to-place fluctuations appear less arbitrary and, subsequently, more subject to efficient administrative control. But this was not without momentous consequences that were largely unnoticed at the time.

One of those consequences concerns the way probability calculations fundamentally altered people's understanding of themselves. Knowing anything about individuals who committed suicide (in terms of their motives, circumstances, and so on), for example, was no longer necessary or even important. The inevitable effect of this breakthrough was the subordination of the distinctiveness of the individual to the much more useful concept of depersonalized corpus of the masses. The concept of the person as human disappeared or became for the most part irrelevant. We now detect this subordination as residing at the core of schooling. As we will see, the power of this idea was only one of the ways that the rise of statistical thinking brought about an elemental change in the way people thought about the self, each other, and the meaning of relationship one to the other.

Another elaboration that must be made here extends the line of reasoning above regarding the Newtonian mindset, reformist visions, and the erosion of determinism animating the culture of the probability theorists. The cultural and intellectual milieu surrounding the advance of statistical probability procedures not only set the conditions of their conception but made them possible. Absent Newton's metaphor of the mechanistic universe, the thought of ultimately locating the forces that ruled the social world with predictable precision would not have emerged as plausible if it would have occurred at all. A strong case can also be made that it was no accident that efforts to perfect the procedures of statistical probability emerged not only within but because of the particular historical context. What were needed at the outset of industrialism were the means and methods of controlling class conflict (Ross, 1991). Finally, were it not the case that determinism had fallen on hard times given popular objections to its implicit denial of human agency (among other factors), it is more than unlikely that strictly causal laws of determinism would find their replacement in the laws of chance, all without sacrificing the sense of confident certainty (Hacking, 1975).

Creation of the Normal Curve and Normal People

The use of statistics in 19th century found its way into what was to become the new social physics through the person of Adolphe Quetelet, a Belgium astronomer. As an astronomer, Quetelet was well acquainted with the error curve used to calculate the position of planets or other astronomical bodies. By taking multiple measures and averaging them, astronomers could arrive at the most precise (or what was deemed the correct) one. When plotted on an axis, these measures formed a bell curve, then referred to as an error curve (see, Stigler, 1986 for a more comprehensive treatment of error theory). Fascinated by the regularities that turned up in population statistics, Quetelet applied these statistics of error curve logic to arrive at his concept of "the average man" (*l'homme moyen*).

As Stigler (1986) clarified, what Quetelet had actually envisioned was not a single "average man," but average men (and women) representing various groups such that differences among and relationships between these groups could be compared based on anthropometric data. Later his calculations sought to capture particular group tendencies for crime, drunkenness, and the like. In a manner of speaking Quetelet's conception of the average man was a master stroke, both professionally and politically. On the professional front it provided the foundation for his vision of the new social physics. Politically, and not a little ironically, its egalitarian portrayal of the common man went a long way toward advancing its charismatic grip on the popular imagination. "The average man," Stigler wryly observed, "was a fictional being in his creator's eye, but such was his appeal that he underwent a transformation, like Pinocchio or Pygmalion's statue, so that he still lives in the headlines of our daily papers" (p. 170).

The cultural and social consequences of the creation of the average man can hardly be overstated. As Stigler further elaborated, for Quetelet and others caught up in the quest to make the social scientific, the average man was a tool for eliminating the randomness of individual acts and personal distinctiveness, and so allowing unambiguous facts and universal regularities to emerge. In turn, it furnished the indispensable starting point for mathematical rules useful for rational administrative decision-making and created "a vivid and concrete symbol of a society, an embodiment of the target and ultimate benefactor of nineteenth century social reform" (Stigler, 1986, p. 171).

What was average became what was normal (Fendler & Muzaffar, 2008). To be average was to be consistent with what is expected, what is orderly, what is acceptable. Hacking (1990) painted a disconcertingly vivid picture of the profound shift in our thinking about ourselves and others produced by the idea of normal:

> People, behavior, states of affairs, diplomatic relations, molecules: all these may be normal or abnormal. The word [normal] became indispensable because it created a way to be "objective" about human beings. The word is also like a faithful retainer, a voice from the past. It uses a power as old as Aristotle to bridge the fact/value distinction, whispering in your ear that what is normal is also all right. But also…it became a soothsayer, teller of the future, of progress and ends. "Normal" bears the stamp of the nineteenth century and its conception of progress, just as "human nature" is engraved with the hallmark of the Enlightenment. We no longer ask, in all seriousness, what is human nature? Instead we talk about people. We ask, is this behavior normal? Is it normal for an eight-year-old girl to…? Research foundations are awash with funds for finding out what is normal. (Hacking, 1990, pp. 160–161)

As he further pointed out, the concept of normal has had a decidedly coercive effect on people. If to be normal is to be all right, one is prompted, urged almost instinctively to aspire to the normal state, to conform to ideals of what is normal received from experts and internalized in the everyday consciousness. Subsequently, to be abnormal was to be avoided at all costs because, as French philosopher Georges Canguilhem (1991) made clear, the scientific process that established the concept of normal also made pathological and abnormal synonymous.

But the project that Quetelet began was left to others to complete. His interpretation of the error law was quite literal in that whatever human traits either of body or character diverging from the average represented an error. It was Galton's task to fulfill the ideological commitments of his eugenicist visions by reconceptualizing the error curve as a continuous normal distribution (and probable errors into standard deviations) so that desirable—that is, above average—people were not viewed as errors (see, MacKenzie, 1981; Porter, 1986). Among his other contributions, which MacKenzie frankly noted, "arose directly from his eugenic concerns" (p. 59), were the concepts of correlation and regression. These concepts, later elaborated in statistical form by Karl Pearson, made it possible to deal with multiple dependent variables. Correlation and regression, as it turned out, would become indispensable statistical tools for the development of mental testing instruments for predicting school performance.

In larger terms, Galton's (and Pearson's) devising of correlation and regression supported their contention that nature, left to its own devices, would trend toward mediocrity. There would be fewer abnormal people at the undesirable end of the normal curve but also fewer exceptional and desirable people at the right hand side of the curve as well. So, without explicit intervention and control to increase the number of desirably exceptional people far above the mean, there could be no progress. Indeed, humans would become increasingly and inexorably mediocre. Worse yet, if the birth rate of those below average outpaced the rate of those above average, or more explicitly those far above average, it portended a Malthusian social catastrophe in the making.

As noted above, my purpose in discussing this history was to bring specific themes to the forefront, demonstrating how the goals of state administered social control (eugenic ideology particularly aimed at the underclass), elimination or subordination of the individual with push for conformity, the medicalization of human diversity, and a utilitarian cost/benefit mindset at the expense of communitarian cohesion of community were built into the rise of statistics from its very early origins. These themes continue through to the rise of American social sciences in general and to the field of school psychology in particular.

The Rise of Educational Psychology and Scientific Research

As Danziger (1990) established, among the various schools of thought in the emerging field of modern psychology, it was the Galtonian type that gained dominance at the beginning of the 20th century. Galtonian eugenics, and the research methodology and procedures it produced, formed the basis for educational research. The early editions of the *Journal of Educational Psychology* confirm Galton's influence on the field. For example, the March 1911 issue included a eulogy for Galton that opened with the following statement:

The death of Sir Francis Galton, which occurred on January 17, within a few
weeks of his eighty-ninth birthday, has snapped one of the few remaining links
that connect the scientific men of the present generation with the great leaders
of the nineteenth century thought. (No author, 1911, p. 149)

And, as is well known, E. L. Thorndike emerged as the leader in the new field
of educational psychology. In his introduction as the first editor of the *Journal of
Educational Psychology*, he set the stage for the field of educational psychology stating: "The extent to which the intellectual and moral differences found in human
beings are consequences of their original nature and determined by the ancestry
from which they spring, is a matter of fundamental importance for education"
(Thorndike, 1910, p. 9). The distinctly eugenicist overtones of this statement
were not merely inadvertent or the result of unfortunate phraseology. Thorndike
was himself both an ardent and active supporter of the American eugenics movement and was a member of the *Eugenics Section* of *the American Breeders Association*,
the *Eugenics Society of the USA*, the *American Eugenics Society*, and the *Eugenics Research Association*. In 1913, for example, he delivered a classic eugenics address at
Columbia University entitled *Eugenics: With Special Reference to Intellect and Character*
(read full text in Aldrich, Carruth, & Davenport, 1914).

From its inception, the purpose of educational research envisioned by educational psychology brought together the dominant themes of scientific objectivity and the social control of "the dependent, delinquent, and defective classes"
(Ross, 1991, p. 68). This goal in turn raised the necessity for group categorization.
These themes are epitomized in Thorndike's aspirations for his budding field:

> The science of education can and will contribute abundantly to psychology. Not
> only do the laws derived by psychology from simple, specially arranged experi-
> ments help us to interpret and control mental action under the conditions of
> school-room life. School-room life itself is a vast laboratory in which are made
> thousands of experiments of the utmost interest to "pure" psychology. Not
> only does psychology help us to understand the mistakes made by children in
> arithmetic. These mistakes afford most desirable material for studies of the ac-
> tion of the laws of association, analysis and selective thinking. Experts in educa-
> tion studying the responses to school situations *for the sake of practical control* will
> advance knowledge not only of the mind as a learner under school conditions
> but also of the mind for every point of view. (Thorndike, 1910, p. 12, emphasis
> added)

Educational psychologists, like academics in the early 20th century American social sciences as a whole, demonstrated their usefulness by positioning themselves
as neutral brokers—scientific technicians charged with providing administrators

and policy makers with objective, factual knowledge on which to base decisions (Danziger, 1990; Ross, 1991; Smith, 1994).

Three main categories of research emerged from the early days of educational psychology: (1) efficient methods of memorizing; (2) mental testing; and, (3) the classroom experiment with control and experimental groups. If these categories resonate with contemporary demands for evidence-based practices and scientifically based research, that is because the latter are the direct descendants of Galtonian psychology.

Evidence-based Practices: Everything Old Is New Again

In his *2002 Dewitt Wallace-Reader's Digest Distinguished Lecture*, Robert Slavin (2002), a leading advocate of evidence-based, experimental design research in education announced that, "At the dawn of the 21st century, education is finally being dragged, kicking and screaming, into the 20th century." He couldn't have been more accurate or more ironically candid. Slavin, along with other passionate enthusiasts for "scientifically based research" (see for example, Feuer, Towne, & Shavelson, 2002a, 2002b; Shavelson & Towne, 2002), portrayed the randomized clinical trial as the gold standard of rigorous scientific research, with matched-group or quasi-experimental studies running a close second. "Evidence-based policies," stated Slavin (2002), "could finally set education on the path toward the kind of progressive improvement that most successful parts of our economy and society embarked upon a century ago" (p. 20). Indeed, the revolutionary transformation of 19th and early 20th century statistics created by the eugenics movement was absolutely necessary for evidence-based practices to emerge (Smith, 1994).

It should be noted here that randomized clinical trials as well as matched-group designs, rely on parametric statistics to ensure the highest level of statistical precision. In turn, parametric statistical tests such as analysis of variance (ANOVA) and multiple analyses of variance (MANOVA) require continuously distributed variables with a normal distribution. Plainly stated, these statistical procedures depend upon the normal curve. Although non-parametric tests such as the Mann-Whitney or Chi-square can be used, they have far lower statistical power and are said to be less "robust." The point here is that the normal curve, with all of its eugenic ideology intact has been imported into 21st century calls for evidence-based research and practice. And, as was the case with early 20th century pioneers of scientific education, the rationales for the current demand for scientifically based educational research are aimed mainly at poor, minority, and disabled students—the modern day embodiment of the previous century's dependent, delinquent, and defective classes. A notable exception is research on gifted students, but that only serves to strengthen the case being made here.

While evidence-based research technically requires the normal curve, it is also dependent on the powerful public appeal of its quantitative and normative hegemony. Porter (1995) cogently captured this point:

> Grades in school, scores on standardized examinations, and the bottom line on an accounting sheet cannot work effectively unless their validity, or at least reasonableness, is accepted by the people whose accomplishments or worth they purport to measure. When it is, the measures succeed by giving direction to the very activities that are being measured. In this way individuals are made governable; they display what Foucault called governmentality. Numbers create and can be compared to norms, which are among the gentlest and yet most pervasive forms of power in modern democracies. (p. 45)

What Porter is suggesting here can be stated in stronger terms. What if what has been learned (i.e., the concept of normality) was unlearned? If people stopped believing that numbers, statistics, and the normal curve are objective, that they represent a non-subjective, apolitical form of knowledge and understanding of reality, their power to persuade would simply vanish. Put differently, what Smith (1994, p. 60) called the "adulation of the almighty fact," along with the very concept of normal, would be better understood as a faith-based initiative packed with political intent.

That the call for evidence-based practices "validated" by scientifically based research obscures a deliberate political agenda has not entirely escaped notice. Schwandt (2005) made the case that today's calls for evidence-based research and practices are part of a conservative political agenda for promoting privatized education and weakening teachers unions. "Sooner or later," he predicted, "this approach will eliminate all failing public schools; only the fittest will survive" (p. 303). As he also pointed out, the notion that evidence-based practices in education will reform or fix what's wrong with public schools effectively paves over and obscures the very profound differences in social and economic conditions that frame poor and minority children as low achievers, ignores racial and cultural discrimination, and redirects public attention away from the educational inequality of under-resourced schools.

Lincoln and Cannella (2004) recognized the push for evidence-based practices and scientifically based research as a backlash against diverse forms of research. In their critique of government mandates for scientifically based research, or what they termed "methodological conservatism and governmental regimes of truth," they argued that,

> Power is embedded within a regulatory technology that appropriates and excludes, a system of governmental order that creates an illusion that there are no

boundaries, only the laws of universalist science that would be followed for the common good (Foucault, 1991). Justified in the name of caring for the population, a sovereignty is created over what is accepted as research knowledge and how resources are to be managed. (pp. 7–8)

Stating the case in similar terms, Hodkinson (2010) characterized contemporary efforts to sanction research solely on the basis of technical standards as an "ideological smokescreen through which the powerful protect and legitimate their preferred positions."

Through this preferred position, scientific educational researchers make themselves necessary to the state that in return supplies the resources necessary for their research production and reproduction. On another level, as Popkewitz (2004) elucidated, "the new expertise of science fills 'needs,'" while simultaneously "producing that need through the comparisons of one child to another or to a norm" (p. 67). Once some children are placed into categories, as inevitably they must be, resources are needed to conduct research, write books and articles, design and implement interventions and so on (Thomas & Loxley, 2007). Thus is created a symbiotic relationship between the aspiration of the state to engineer "progressive" social control and the seemingly benign endeavors of scientific educational researchers to deliver objective technologies aimed at helpful, therapeutic, and ameliorative interventions.

This intervention is intended, of course, to make the abnormal individuals normal, to assist them in catching up with their peers. Exposing the contradictory nature of this goal, Brantlinger (2004) pointed out that, with the normal curve, there is no such thing as "catching up." Depicting this apparent dilemma as a Catch 22, she confirmed that so long as the normal curve and its constitutive discursive practices prevail, some children will always belong in the abnormal, below average box. This situation subsequently makes ridiculous the very reason for "special" and remedial education and, at the same time, points to the absurdity of *No Child Left Behind*.

Conclusion

What I have tried to demonstrate in this chapter is that the discourse of "science" and the corresponding practices of contemporary educational research (evidence-based practices) are the enduring heirs of the "taming of chance," the development of the normal curve, statistical probability, and the subsequent invention of "normal" people. Importantly, the invention of "normal" people involved an ironic twist because the research methodology and its products (e.g., mental testing instruments) which purported to assess individual differences "actually eliminated individuals by reducing them to the abstraction of a collection of points in a set of aggregates (Danziger, 1990, p. 108). Once the "individual" is assigned to a category (or aggregate), he or she does not belong to other categories, most specifically the category understood to be "normal." He or she must therefore be dealt with accordingly, which almost inevitably involves segregation and exclusion.

This historical analysis of the development of "scientific" educational research brings us to a crucial point concerning inclusive education—shifting the conversation toward belonging and away from inclusion is difficult, if not impossible, so long as the discourse and corresponding practices of "scientific" (evidence-based) research remain dominant. As Thomas and Loxley (2007) cogently noted,

> When children are excluded from the mainstream it is because someone feels that they will not fit. To examine why people don't fit, and to help organizations to enable them to fit, we have to understand them as people and to understand the people in the organizations that accept or reject them. The reductionist thrust of special education research has not in general led us to do this, and this has meant that special education has followed a particular route—one that has sought to analyze and fix instead of seeking to include. (p. 43)

So it is that once an individual disappears into an aggregate or category, genuine belonging becomes nearly impossible and all that remains is the prospect of "including" students who will undoubtedly be viewed as, for want of any other term, artificial transplants whose ersatz presence in the general education classroom will inevitably be subject to abiding doubts about their assimilative adequacy.

References

Aldrich, M. A., Carruth, W. H., & Davenport, C. B. (1914). *Eugenics: Twelve university lectures.* New York: Dodd, Mead.

Brantlinger, E. (2004). Confounding the needs and confronting the norms: An extension of Reid and Valle's Essay. *Journal of Learning Disabilities, 37*(6), 490–499.

Canguilhem, G. (1991). *The normal and the pathological* (C. R. Fawcett & R. S. Cohen, trans.). New York: Zone.

Danziger, K. (1990). *Constructing the subject: Historical origins of psychological research.* Cambridge, UK: Cambridge University Press.

Dewey, J. (1929). *The quest for certainty: A study of the relation of knowledge and action.* New York: Minton, Balch.

Fendler, L., & Muzaffar, I. (2008). The history of the bell curve: Sorting and the idea of normal. *Educational Theory, 58*(1), 63–82.

Feuer, M. J., Towne, L, & Shavelson, R. J. (2002a). Scientific culture and educational research. *Educational Researcher, 31*(8), 4–14.

Feuer, M. J., Towne, L, & Shavelson, R. J. (2002b). Reply. *Educational Researcher, 31*(8), 28–29.

Foucault, M. (1991). Governmentality. In G. Burchell, C. Gordon, & P. Miller (Eds.), *The Foucault effect: Studies in governmentality* (pp. 87-104). Chicago: University of Chicago Press.

Gallagher, D. J. (2006). If not absolute objectivity, then what? A reply to Kauffman and Sasso. *Exceptionality, 14*(2), 91–107

Hacking, I. (1975). *The emergence of probability: A philosophical study of early ideas about probability, induction, and statistical inference.* Cambridge, UK: Cambridge University Press.

Hacking, I. (1990). *The taming of chance.* Cambridge, UK: Cambridge University Press.

Hanson, N. (1958). *Patterns of discovery.* Cambridge, UK: Cambridge University Press.

Hodkinson, P. M. (2010). The politics of legitimating research. *The Sage companion to research in education.* London: Sage.

Kuhn, T. (1962). *The structure of scientific revolutions.* Chicago, IL: University of Chicago Press.

Lincoln, Y. S., & Cannella, G. S. (2004). Dangerous discourses: Methodological conservatism and governmental regimes of truth. *Qualitative Inquiry, 10*(1), 5–14.

MacKenzie, D. A. (1981). *Statistics in Britain,1865–1930: The social construction of scientific knowledge.* Edinburgh, Scotland: Edinburgh University Press.

Nagel, T. (1986). *The view from nowhere.* New York: Oxford University Press.

No author. (1911). *Journal of Educational Psychology, 2*(3), 149–150.

Popkewitz, T. S. (2004). Is the National Research Council Committee's report on scientific research in education scientific? On trusting the manifesto. *Qualitative Inquiry, 10*(1), 62–78.

Porter, T. M. (1986). *The rise of statistical thinking: 1820–1900.* Princeton, NJ: Princeton University Press.

Porter, T. M. (1995). *Trust in numbers: The pursuit of objectivity in science and public life.* Princeton, NJ: Princeton University Press.

Putnam, H. (1981). *Reason, truth, and history.* Cambridge, UK: Cambridge University Press.

Rorty, R. (1979). *Philosophy and the mirror of nature.* Princeton, NJ: Princeton University Press.

Rorty, R. (1980). Pragmatism, relativism, and irrationalism. *Proceedings and addresses of the American Philosophical Association, 53,* 719–738.

Rorty, R. (1982). *Consequences of pragmatism.* Minneapolis, MN: University of Minnesota Press.

Ross, D. (1991). *The origins of American social science.* Cambridge, UK: Cambridge University Press.

Schwandt, T. A. (2005). A diagnostic reading of scientifically based research for education, *Educational Theory, 55*(3), 285–305.

Shavelson, R. J., & Towne, L. (Eds.). (2002). *Scientific research in education.* Washington, DC: National Academy Press.

Slavin, R. E. (2002). Evidence-based education policies: Transforming educational practice and research. *Educational Researcher, 31*(7), 15–21.

Smith, M. C. (1994*). Social science in the crucible: The American debate over objectivity and purpose, 1918–1941.* Durham, NC: Duke University Press.

Stigler, S. M. (1986). *The history of statistics: The measurement of uncertainty before 1900.* Cambridge, MA: Belknap.

Stigler, S. M. (1999). *Statistics on the table: The history of statistical concepts and methods.* Cambridge, MA: Harvard University Press.

Taylor, C. (1971). Interpretation and the sciences of man. *Review of Metaphysics, 25,* 3–51.

Thomas, G., & Loxley, A. (2007) [2d ed.]. *Deconstructing special education and constructing inclusion.* Berkshire, UK: Open University Press.

Thorndike, E. L. (1910). The contribution of psychology to education. *Journal of Educational Psychology, 1*(1), 5–12.

FOUR

Decentralizations and Redistributions: A Complex Reading of Normality

Brent Davis & Dennis Sumara

Not-Normal Distributions

What's the magnitude of an average earthquake? The wealth of an average person? The "size" of an average war? The population of an average community? The connectivity of an average Internet hub? The impact of an average idea? On the surface, it might seem as though there are reasonable and accurate answers to at least some of these questions. But, in fact, none actually makes sense. On the matter of earthquakes, for instance, it turns out that minor tremors are so frequent and numerous that if they were to be pooled and averaged with more major events, a normal or representative quake would be imperceptible to unaided senses. Similarly, the statistic obtained by dividing all of the world's capital by its human population is utterly meaningless—indeed, worse than meaningless, many have argued. Such a datum conceals the obscene wealth of a few and the intense poverty of so many. The same reasoning can be used to critique and discard constructs such as average disputes, average cities, average hubs, and average ideas.

Statisticians realized the impossibility of some of these constructs early on, recommending alternatives to the mean as a "measure of central tendency" for phenomena that have a skewed-from-normal distribution. For example, at first glance, it would seem that the notion of median—the middle point when all of a set's data are sequenced according to magnitude—would be useful to character-ize average wars and communities. Or perhaps the mode—the most frequently occurring datum in a set—would be useful in making sense of average wealth or average ideas. But it turns out that these types of averages do not work any better in the situations presented, and the reason for their inadequacy is instructive. Not all phenomena obey a normal distribution or something resembling a normal or skewed-normal distribution. Some objects and events are spread out in the world in entirely different ways.

Normal-like distributions have a certain commonsensical appeal. Whether the source of or merely a response to a collective assumption, the familiar bell-shaped curve captures the intuitively compelling notion that, for most measurable phenomena, data points cluster around a central average and taper off rapidly and predictably on either side of that value. And so, for example, the average height of an adult woman in a specific geographic region might be 1.7 m. Most adult women would be within a few centimeters of that mean; a few would be slightly further from the average, and a very small number would be still further. But no one would be 0.3 m or 21 m tall. The curve tells us that probabilities fall toward zero as deviance from the norm grows more extreme.

The sensibleness of such examples is one of the reasons that many research-ers across domains have tended to assume that virtually all variable phenomena must obey a normal distribution. However, earthquakes and wealth—along with market fluctuations, skirmishes and wars, moon craters, fads, power outages, eco-logical disasters, heart rhythms, forest fires, avalanches, city sizes, internet hubs, epidemics, election results, and learning events—are not normally distributed (Buchanan, 2000). Rather, they follow power law distributions. As illustrated in Figure 4.1, with such phenomena, there is a very high likelihood of a minor event, as in the case of an earthquake, and a very much lower frequency of a really mas-sive happening or event. Among phenomena that obey power law distributions, there is no such thing as a typical or normal specimen or fragment.

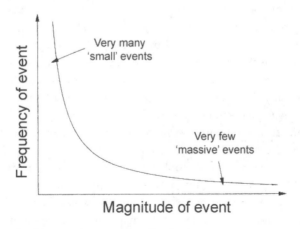

Figure 4.1: A stylized image of a power law distribution.

Of course, as interesting as it might be to highlight the existence of phenomena that are distributed in this other-than-normal way, it is quite another matter to make the leap to education-related phenomena. After all, isn't intelligence like height—which, if not normally distributed, is very close to being so? Or learning (conceptual development) akin to growth (biological development)—which, similarly, seems to abide by some fairly robust and predictable norms? Surely these and related concerns of educators are properly interpreted in terms of means, averages, and norms. However, as we will show below, this is not the case.

Complex phenomena

It would be unfair to say that educationists have been totally oblivious to power law distributions. Deeply inscribed in educational orthodoxy, for example, is the assumption that there is no such thing as a normal question. Benjamin Bloom's (1956) "hierarchy of question types" is a well-known example. The shape that Bloom used to illustrate the distribution of different sorts of questions in a learning context—a pyramid—is loosely suggestive of a power law distribution. That is, there tend to be many lower-level, knowledge-seeking questions and far fewer, higher-level evaluation sorts of questions.

However, rather than being taken up as a description of a dynamic knowledge-producing community, this insight has most often been used to justify a mechanistic approach to teacher questioning, commencing with an obligatory barrage of lower level queries (e.g., knowledge- and comprehension-seeking) and culminating in a synthesis question or two. This pattern might well have gone in a less instrumental direction had educational researchers of the 1950s been acquainted with, first, power law distributions and, second, some of the qualities of the dynamic phenomena that lie behind such distributions. Indeed, such knowledge might have actually prompted them to construe the necessity and inevitability of pyramid-like distributions of questions as one piece of (necessary, but not sufficient) evidence that classroom communities are instances of complex unities.

One of the major shifts in educational thinking over the last several decades has been a rejection of machine-based metaphors and an embrace of more organic notions. This is especially obvious around the topic of learning. Through much of the 20th century, learning was framed in cause–effect terms, which, in turn, supported mechanistic approaches to teaching and curriculum. But that framework began to change in the 1970s and 1980s with a shift toward more holistic, contingent, and exploratory conceptions of learning although this shift has not always been apparent in federal, state, and provincial educational policies.

This movement coincided with the emergence of a broad, transdisciplinary movement that is now known as "complexity thinking" (or "complexity theory" or "complexity science"—see Davis and Sumara (2006) for a more fulsome account of the movement and its many titles) which began with a rejection of the centuries-old assumption that any event can be described in terms of mechanical interactions. Historically, the overarching belief, which rose to prominence in the 1600s, was that the universe is a grand "clockwork" and, hence, everything can be understood by breaking it down into its component parts. This attitude underpinned the rise of analytic science, with its quest for universal laws, fundamental particles, and basic truths. Complexity theorists agree that machines such as clocks and refrigerators, as well as physical systems such as billiard ball collisions and chemical reactions, are indeed the predictable sums of their parts. With a thorough knowledge of the motions of the pieces, one can predict the behavior of the whole.

However, while this analytic attitude has been proven effective in the scientific and technological innovations of the industrial age, the approach has been almost useless in efforts to understand and predict phenomena that include large-scale economies, ecosystems, brains, and events such as those introduced in this chapter's opening paragraph. The reason for the breakdown was not immediately clear, but once it was articulated, it contributed to an intellectual convulsion across disciplines. In brief, certain systems are not made up of inert particles, cogs, switches, or microchips, but are themselves collectives of dynamic systems. For example, societies emerge from, but cannot be reduced to individual citizens. Each human citizen arises in, but is something more than, the interactions of a cluster of bodily organs. Those organs, in turn, comprise and surpass collectives of living cells.

These are complex systems. They can never be reduced to their parts because they are always caught up with other systems in a continuing dance of change. Compared to complicated (i.e., mechanical) systems, complex unities are more spontaneous, unpredictable, irreducible, contextual, and vibrantly sufficient—in brief, they are adaptive. Because complex phenomena transform themselves, tools like Newtonian mechanics and statistical regression are of little use in understanding them.

Of course, there are some phenomena that are difficult to identify as either complicated or complex. In particular, some recent technological developments, especially in robotics, render the distinction a fuzzy one. Nevertheless, the separation of complex phenomena (e.g., learning and spontaneously adaptive systems) from complicated phenomena (e.g., most mechanical systems) is useful when making sense of how to deal with each. Table 4.1 summarizes some of the key differences between complicated and complex systems. (To re-emphasize, these distinctions are not absolute, and they are getting hazier as technologies advance.)

Complicated (mechanical)	Complex (learning)
Physics (Newton)	Biology (Darwin)
Machine Metaphors	Ecosystem Metaphors
Linear Imagery	Cyclical Imagery
Input/Output Flows	Feedback Loops
Efficiency-Oriented	Sufficiency-Oriented
Progress-Oriented	Development-Minded
Reducible	Incompressible

Table 4.1: A Capsule Comparison of Complicated and Complex Phenomena

One might say that every complex phenomenon is an embodied history—an interwoven and ever-changing coherence of frozen accidents that build on sequences of frozen accidents (Buchanan, 2000). Yet, there is no unified or universally accepted definition of a complex system, simply because efforts in this direction tend to be hinged to the phenomenon that is of most interest to the person offering the definition. For example, biologists tend to talk about complexity in terms of living systems, physicists in terms of non-linear dynamic systems, economists in terms of micro- and macro-economies, and so on. Extending this tendency, our own definition reflects our positioning as teachers and educational researchers: complex systems are systems that learn (cf., Davis, Sumara, & Luce-Kapler, 2008). Of course such a definition begs the question, what's a learner?

Comparing Learning Phenomena

We structure our response(s) to the question in three ways. In this section, we begin by offering an example, and then reviewing qualities that are common to all learning/complex systems. In the subsequent section, we develop the notion of comparative dynamics (offered as a contrast to comparative statics) as a means both to make sense of complex phenomena and to appreciate the relevance of complexity thinking to education.

For our example, we look to zebra mussels—tiny, but prolific mollusks that were introduced into the Great Lakes in North America sometime in the late 1970s or early 1980s. No one is certain how it happened, but it likely occurred when a cargo ship purged its ballast tanks after delivering a shipment from Europe. Having no natural enemies, the mussels thrived, quickly spreading through all of the Great Lakes. As their population grew, ominous predictions were made about certain, irreversible environmental disaster. The mussels, it was asserted, would almost certainly upset a fragile and delicate balance.

In fact, none of those dire predictions came to pass although there have been some major consequences. Perhaps the most publicized result is the several billion dollar price tag required to clear mollusks from underwater grates and valves. A lesser-known consequence is that the mussels have actually helped to clarify the turgid waters of the Great Lakes, straining out large amounts of suspended matter as they pump water through their systems. So why was there no ecological disaster?

The ecosystem did not collapse simply because the web of life in the Great Lakes does not exist in a delicate balance. Far from it. As with most ecosystems, it is not static and optimized but vibrantly sufficient. That is, it is a dynamic, diversified, robust, ever-evolving, and constantly learning system. And zebra mussels have now been incorporated (i.e., literally, embodied) by/into that system. Put differently, the relational web, the specific qualities, and the response patterns of the lake ecosystem have changed. The system has learned in a manner that is dynamically similar to the ways that humans, immune systems, societies, species, and other complex unities learn. In fact, the Great Lakes ecosystem is likely even more robust now than it was prior to the introduction of the zebra mussels.

The argument that we are developing is that this sort of learning system is somehow like other, more intimately familiar learning systems such as individual learners, social networks, or bodies of knowledge—and this assertion is intended as more than an analogy or metaphor. To develop this point, we make use of the most common strategy for deciding if a phenomenon is complex, namely, to look for common characteristics. Phenomena such as the Great Lakes ecosystem, an economy, and a brain share some important qualities. For example, they all seem to have stable boundaries and identities, even though they are constantly exchanging matter and information with other systems as they adapt on the fly. One might say that complex unities are stable patterns in the stream of matter or activity, and these stabilities give rise to the appearance of stable identities and fixed boundaries.

Complex unities maintain their coherences without the help of a supervisor, overseer, director, or master organizer. They are self-organizing and self-maintaining, as illustrated in the example of the Great Lakes "learning" to accommodate zebra mussels. In this sense, learning is a constant restructuring of internal relations in order to maintain sufficient coherence.

On this topic, exactly what is learned (i.e., exactly how internal relations are restructured) is determined by the system, not by the event that triggers the learning. This is a point that bears repeating since it has profound educational implications. In somewhat different terms, the learning system is structure determined—it determines what will be learned, not the event or experience that prompts learning to happen. Much in contrast to complicated (mechanical) systems that can be caused to respond in specific ways by external forces, the way that a complex (learning) system adapts to a new situation is rooted in its biological-and-experiential structure—its embodied history. For instance, if you nudge a brick, you can control the outcome by adjusting the force appropriately. However, if you nudge a person, her or his structure will determine the response.

These qualities of self-organization, self-maintenance, and structure determinism reflect the fact that complex unities operate far-from-equilibrium. This realization actually comes as a challenge to some popular theories of living and learning systems, which assume that dynamic systems seek states of equilibrium—reflecting an assumption inherited from the 18th and 19th centuries that individuals and societies maintain steady, unchanging, equilibrated states. In fact, complicated (mechanical) systems do maintain steady, unchanging, equilibrated states —and the notion of "normal distribution" is rooted in studies of such systems (Ball, 2004). But complex (learning) systems do not. For complex systems, equilibrium is death, whereas operating far-from-equilibrium forces them to explore their spaces of possibility—to tinker with new patterns of acting, to modify internal relations, and so on. Such explorations help them evolve new structures and new ways of working.

Returning to the first point in this section, "far-from-equilibrium" does not mean "unstable." Complex unities are stable patterns in the streams of matter or activities, but that does not mean they are balanced or unchanging. As demonstrated in the Great Lakes example, to maintain stability in the flux of existence, a complex unity must be capable of flexible response to emergent circumstances. Had the Great Lakes system been in a state of equilibrium when zebra mussels were introduced—as many assumed it to be—the result certainly would have been disastrous. Fortunately, it was already operating far-from-equilibrium, just as all living humans (and non-humans) are at this moment.

But what is to be gained by likening a brain to complex learning systems like the Great Lakes—or an anthill? And how might such conceptual moves be taken up by educational researchers seeking to better understand the intricacies of learning systems?

Comparative dynamics

A second definition of complexity research, in addition to the "study of learning systems" description offered above, is captured in the neologism comparative dynamics. We use the phrase here in contrast to the much more familiar comparative statistics. The latter is derived from the Latin status, "manner of standing, position, condition." With such cognates as state and statute, statistic carries with it a sense of fixity or immobility—and such connotations are reflected in the portraits of phenomena that arise through much of statistics-based research. We are presented with frozen moments of market shifts, demographic changes, and standardized performances. These portraits are necessarily in the past tense, yet, ironically, ahistorical. A glimpse of an evolution might be gleaned by viewing sequence of these frozen moments, but, in and of themselves, they contain no past and project no future.

By contrast, dynamics derives from the Greek *dynamikos*, "powerful, active, or energetic." Originally referring to a force that produces motion, dynamic is now more commonly used with reference to motion itself. In contrast to a statistical study, then, a dynamical study embraces and traces the motions and evolutions of a form. A study of dynamics is thus necessarily attentive to context, history, and possibility, all oriented by the knowledge that a dynamically adaptive system embodies its history.

When the word comparative is added, the phrases comparative statistics and comparative dynamics point to even greater differences in research emphasis. Comparative statistics focuses on the relationships among phenomena that exist in the same temporal space—in the same frozen moment, as it were. Questions revolve around associations between, for example, oil prices and stock market indices, DDT level and eagle population, and teacher knowledge and student performance. Comparative dynamics is more concerned with the similarities in the profiles of different adaptive phenomena, finding its contrast space among, for example, brain activity, anthill life cycles, stock market trends, lake ecosystem changes, and planetary temperature shifts. Something interesting happens when dynamical traces of such activities, considered on suitable scales, are laid side-by-side: the same sorts of undulating, jagged patterns present themselves. (Consider, for example, the similar traces presented by EEGs and stock market reports.)

Phrased somewhat differently, complex systems are dynamically self-similar. This realization, which is at the core of comparative dynamics, is reflected in popular discourse in the prevalence of notions of bodies: a body of knowledge, a social corpus, the body politic, embodied knowing, and so on. For the most part, these bodies are treated as vibrant and evolving forms, ones with sufficiently stable patterns and coherent identities but with somewhat porous boundaries and the capacities to adapt. Further, many of these bodies seem to be nested in one another. Culture, for example, comprises different social groupings, which in turn comprise individuals.

In fact, this manner of description can be extended in both the micro- and macro-directions, as illustrated in the Figure 4.2. Each layer or body can be simultaneously seen as a whole, a part of a whole, or a complex compilation of wholes. In other words, there is a sort of scale independence. Each layer/body can be described in terms of the co-activities of relatively autonomous agents, and this co-activity is what gives rise to the next level of organization. Of course, these nested bodies don't much resemble one another in terms of their superficial physical appearances. But they do have some profound similarities, both dynamically and structurally.

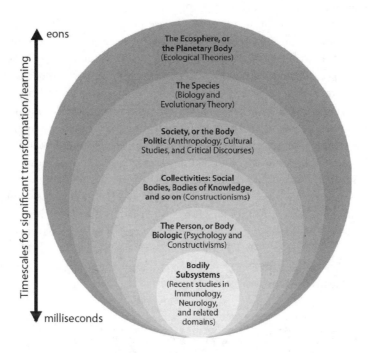

Figure 4.2: Some nested complex (learning) systems.

In terms of system dynamics, the ongoing developments of each of these knowing bodies can be described in terms of evolutionary processes. At every level, knowing is seen as a complex process of co-evolution—that is, of agents (whether species, societies, social groups, persons, cells, or ideas) adapting to and affecting one another and their dynamic circumstances. Put differently, an implication of this conception of knowing bodies is that phenomena such as personal cognition, collective knowledge, and social interaction are tightly interrelated.

Structurally, all of the systems included in the nested circles in Figure 4.2 are examples of decentralized networks. A decentralized network consists of clusters that combine into grander clusters, and this sort of structure is manifest in all living systems and ecosystems. At the moment, this is perhaps most readily illustrated by the ever-evolving structure of the Internet. Very early on in its evolution, it became impossible to draw an exhaustive map of the Internet's connectivity. Part of the difficulty was tied to the pace of its development, but the subtler and more troublesome problem had to do with the layers and levels of connectivity that just "happened." In brief, the Internet quickly became both too vast and too deeply embedded for its structure to be traced. An Internet search for an Internet map would provide several thousand images, affording a sense of not just its particular structure and evolution but the sorts of structures and evolutions that are common to decentralized networked systems.

It appears that decentralized networks are not just useful for describing the relations within physical systems. They can also be used to make sense of the structures of associations in systems of ideas—for example, to describe the structures of association among concepts, metaphors, and other connections that constitute a collective body of knowledge or describe an individual's mind. Memory, language, culture—these and other enacted bodies of knowing are readily interpreted as instances of decentralized networks. In brief, it appears that whenever people interact, establish personal connections, and extend conceptual links, the inevitable result is some manner of power law distribution—of popularity, of impact, of importance, and so on. By way of quick illustration, the word cloud presented in Figure 4.3 was recently generated by pooling the responses of 360 pre-service teachers to the question, "What is teaching, for you, now?" The result is power law distributed: a few of the 118 terms were massively popular in the group, most were suggested only once or twice. There was no typical interpretation (although, on the level of the community, there was an interesting and nuanced collective interpretation).

Figure 4.3: A word cloud used to illustrate a power law distribution of a cluster of interpretations.

The necessary presence of decentralized networks within complex learning phenomena actually helps to explain the ubiquity of power law distributions. To give a brief illustration, Calvin (1996) describes brain structure as follows:

[The] factor of a hundred keeps recurring: a hundred neurons to a minicolumn, roughly a hundred minicolumns to a macrocolumn, a hundred times a hundred macrocolumns to a cortical area …, and there are just over a hundred Brodman Areas when you total those in both cerebral hemispheres. (p. 120)

In effect, this is a description of a power law distribution. With each level jump (e.g., from individual neurons to minicolumns) the number of "agents" decreases by a factor of 100 or so, generating an image very much like the graph in Figure 4.1.

We have, then, an emerging portrait of systems affecting systems as they come together in a bottom-up way into grander systems that, in turn, contribute to contexts and generate governing structures that enable and constrain in top-down ways—albeit systems at different levels of organization operate at very different paces. In other words, in complexity terms, the statistics-based tendency to focus on comparison of forms and phenomena that occur in the same temporal frame is regarded as tragically limited within a complexity frame. We end with a brief discussion of some of the more pressing issues.

Abnormal? or abnormable?

Complexity research is oriented by the realization that understanding is not the same thing as predicting. Returning to the phenomena mentioned in the opening section of this chapter, for example, geophysicists have a reasonably thorough understanding of earthquakes—why they happen, where they happen, and so on —but have very little predictive power. The same is true of researchers who study market activity, social trends, intelligence, and learning.

The difficulty with precise prediction is linked to a paradoxical aspect of such complex phenomena. While they can be explained in general terms, a particular event can only be explained *post facto*, and such an explanation is at best partial and principally descriptive. Examples of these inadequate, but frequent, efforts to interpret are provided in the news virtually every day, as commentators offer reductive reasons for changes in stock market values, crime rates, and other quantifiable cultural phenomena. In point of fact, the reasons that are offered—which generally comprise other similar phenomena, such as employment statistics, consumer confidence, oil prices, house values, bank rates, and so on—really do matter. The problem is that shifts that are dependent on these sorts of constructs are too often portrayed as determined by such constructs.

Complexity thinkers go to great lengths to avoid not just such linear-causal readings but linear-causal and linear-correlational thinking entirely—marking an important shift from the manner of thinking that underpins the pervasive and oft-times inappropriate use of the normal distribution. Stewart (1989) critiqued these tendencies, highlighting that much of measurement- and statistics-based research in recent centuries has been constrained by computability. In brief, non-linear calculations can quickly become intractable, and so early on (as far back as Newton, at least), researchers began to substitute linear approximations for non-linear phenomena, including growth and interdependencies of living forms. It was a practice that was supported by the belief that naturally occurring phenomena are necessarily normally distributed, from which researchers reasoned that relationships among them must be reasonably close to linear. Stewart explained:

> [This] habit became so ingrained that many equations were linearized while they were being set up, so that the science textbooks did not even include the full non-linear versions. Consequently most scientists and engineers came to believe that virtually all natural phenomena could be described by linear equations. As the world was a clockwork for the 18th century, it was a linear world for the 19th and most of the 20th century. (p. 83)

Again, while a linear, clockwork universe is deeply inscribed in the academic psyche, the assumption of normality is even more profoundly embedded. Both are being interrupted now by studies of learning and living systems—at least for some scholars. Over the past three decades, the nested and scale independent forms of fractal geometry, for example, have been steadily replacing lines in characterizations of complex events and forms. And for the past decade, as noted above, power law (and other) distributions have been eroding the ubiquitous application of normal distributions. Implicit in these shifts is a recasting of mathematics as a source of possible models rather than a source of actual explanations. In other words, power law distributions (among other scale free distributions) are not intended as a correction of, replacement for, or addition to normal and normal-like distributions. Rather, power law distributions are part of a shifting mind-set, one that rejects notions of stable, centralized attractors, or, in more popular parlance, norms. This is not to say that stable traits do not emerge; the point is merely that stabilities are themselves contingent, temporary, complex forms.

It is thus that one finds among complexity thinkers some very different attitudes toward diversity than were represented among previous generations. Quetelet, Gauss, and other authors of the normal family of distributions regarded the norm (i.e., arithmetic mean) as "correct" and "true" (cf., Ball, 2004), from which it followed that variation was necessarily deviation. Among complexity researchers, there is more a counternormative sensibility, whereby diversity is understood to be inevitable and necessary. Indeed, diversity is seen as the source of a system's flexible responsiveness—its intelligence, as it were.

Such a shift has immense implications for educational thought and for modern schooling. Long organized around assumptions of norms and predictability, complexity thinking can clearly be aligned with current post-structuralist, queer, and other critiques of normative and normalist accounts of ability, achievement, and identity, for example. Pulling the camera back only slightly, complexity thinking also helps to interrupt the habit of identifying the individual as the unit of analysis, suggesting that whenever a complex phenomenon is named, one must look across levels of organization. Ability, achievement, and identity (among so many other concerns of educators) are not merely psychological issues. For complexivitists, they are neurophysiological, social, cultural, and ecological matters as well. In brief, they and the phenomena they comprise are anything but normal—which is to say that their distributions are not abnormal but *not normable*.

References

Ball, P. (2004). *Critical mass: How one thing leads to another*. New York: Farrar, Straus and Giroux.

Bloom, B.S. (1956). *Taxonomy of educational objectives, Handbook I: The cognitive domain*. New York: David MacKay.

Buchanan, M. (2000). *Ubiquity: the science of history … or why the world is simpler than we think*. London: Phoenix.

Calvin, W.H. (1996). *How brains think: Evolving intelligence, then and now*. New York: Basic.

Davis, B., & Sumara, D. (2006). *Complexity and education: Inquiries into learning, teaching, and research*. Mahwah, NJ: Lawrence Erlbaum.

Davis, B., Sumara, D., & Luce-Kapler, R. (2008). *Engaging minds: Changing teaching in complex times* [2d ed.]. New York: Routledge.

Stewart, I. (1989). *Does god play dice?* Cambridge, MA: Blackwell.

FIVE

Situating Labeling within an Ideological Framework

Donaldo Macedo & Teresa Sordé Martí

As we ponder the challenge to understand the ideology inherent in the social construction of labels, particularly the educational labeling designed to typecast students suffering from various forms of "disabilities," we are reminded of a story told by an immigrant student, Arthur Lomba, from Cape Verde. Coming to the United States in the 1950s as a non-English-speaking student, Lomba worked hard to master English academic discourse to successfully navigate the curricular demands in a new language. One day, he was handed an identification form with four little boxes that required him to identify himself as (1) white, (2) black, (3) American Indian, or (4) Hispanic. At that time there was not an option to mark "other." Since Arthur did not see himself correctly reflected in any of the categories provided on the form, he added a fifth box, which he labeled "human" and dutifully marked with an "X." When he gave the form back, the teacher was perplexed and immediately requested that he identify himself racially. When Arthur said he did not know which box to mark, she insisted that he ask his parents and bring in his passport the next day.

It was incomprehensible to Arthur's teacher that he was not socialized to identify himself purely in terms of racial categories. In fact, Arthur's choice of "human," which should have triggered the teacher to question the racism inherent in the identification form, was subordinated to her need to follow bureaucratic rules—rules inculcated into the psyche as the norm and, as defined by John B. Thompson (1990), "expressed in symbolic forms by means of the strategy of naturalization" (p. 66). According to Thompson (1990), naturalization, a process through which reality is turned into common sense, is a "state of affairs that is a social and historical creation [that] may be treated as a natural event or as the inevitable outcome of natural characteristics" (p. 66). Arthur's teacher had so absorbed this world view that she could not see beyond the "rules" requiring students to identify themselves by race. She had become incapable of seeing that when a person is labeled solely on the basis of "physiological characteristics and the differences between the [races]," it reinforces the reproduction of a racist structure that is, in essence, dehumanizing. By being complicit in the truncation of the necessarily dialectical relationship between "normal" and "abnormal," one consciously or unconsciously engages in a social construct that ignores the adverse consequences of labels. As a result, we rarely question, for instance, when a medical model labels someone as "mentally retarded or mentally ill; that label is a signal to the public to consider that person a deviant who, according to social norms, should be segregated . . . [a process that conditions] nondisabled people to define people so labeled as hopelessly ill and of no potential" (Shapiro, 1994, p. 162). Consequently, once someone like Arthur's teacher adopts such a posture unconditionally, they are almost always unable to imagine people in society with disabilities as able to thrive "when they leave institutions and are placed in 'normal' settings—homes, schools, and jobs alongside other, normally abled people" (Shapiro, 1994, p. 162). By the same token, Arthur's teacher was unable to imagine his humanity outside racial categorizations that, by design, dehumanize.

The effects of segregation in the United States have had adverse educational consequences that have led to overrepresentation of the racial category "other" in special education, where "about 60% to 80% of the pupils taught by these teachers are children from low status backgrounds" (Dunn, 1968, p. 6). In thirty years time, figures for minority overrepresentation in special education do not differ so much. According to data provided by Losen and Orfield (2002), "Black children constitute 17% of the total school enrollment and 33% of those labeled mentally retarded." So, a black child is 2.88 more times likely than a white child to be labeled mentally retarded and 1.92 times more likely to be diagnosed as emotionally disturbed. This reflects a process whereby special education has become, on the one hand, a dumping ground for students who do not fit the "norm" and, on the other hand, a form of exclusion that, in our view, is racist to the highest degree.

Racism is, clearly, not confined to the United States but is an insidious global phenomenon. Similar realities to the U.S. picture for black and other minority children are found in Europe. For instance, in Slovakia, Roma students are fourteen times more likely to be in special education than the share of Roma reported in standard schools (Friedman, Kriglerova, Kubánová, Slosiarik, & Surdu, 2009). The reported data vary from study to study, as no major official efforts are recorded to collect reliable data to show racial disparities in most European countries. The lack of or scarce data segregated by race or SES is a clear symptom of a denied reality in the Old Continent. Obviously, it does not mean that discrimination and racism do not occur, as the undeniable reality is out there. This chapter analyzes the overrepresentation of subordinated groups in special education in the European Union and how subordinated cultural and linguistic students are excluded from an equal education—an exclusion that robs them of the opportunity to access equality in society. However, before turning our attention to the overrepresentation of subordinated groups in special education in the European Union, we first examine how science is perniciously used to legitimize racist practices inherent in the labeling process and how, according to Lilia Bartolomé and Felicity Crawford (in this volume), "students who were perceived to be troublesome or different (e.g., those who were deaf, blind, physically or mentally ill, racially and culturally different) were soon diagnosed based on a scientific test or theory and sent in increasing numbers to specialized institutions where services were restrictive, isolated, and minimal" (Crawford & Bartolomé, this volume).

Scientism as Ideology on Steroids

A true measure of society's egalitarian and democratic practices can be easily determined by examining how "individuals in dominant positions [including institutions of power] typically pursue a strategy of distinction, in the sense that they seek to distinguish themselves from individuals or groups who occupy positions subordinate to them" (Thompson, 1990, p. 158). Hence, ideological distinctions have, at least, two fundamental functions: (1) to establish a norm that, in turn, is naturalized as common sense and against which other individuals or groups are measured—a process that also functions to prevent any "challenge or diverge[nce] from existing social norms; rather, it reaffirms these norms and censures any actions or attitudes that deviate from them. . . and by virtue of this 'pseudo-realism' they normalize the status quo and curtail critical reflection on the social and political order"; and (2) to typecast so as to devalue individuals or groups who do not measure up to the pre-established norm, giving rise to pernicious stereotypes, stereotypes designed to valorize characteristics of those who have the power to profile others and to denigrate those who are profiled by virtue of their class position, gender, race, ethnicity, or disabilities, among other classifications (Thompson, 1990, p. 158).

Once the norm becomes commonly accepted, it is difficult to move beyond the folk theory that shapes and sustains it. Thus, with respect to disabilities, dominant ideological strategies make it difficult to raise such questions as: What is normal? Against what, for whom, and against whom? These questions are often deemed ideological in nature and, therefore, unfit for scientific research. The attempts of educators and social scientists to adopt "hard science" modes of analysis in social science research have given rise to a form of "scientism" rather than science. By scientism we mean the mechanization of the intellectual work cultivated by specialists, which often leads to fragmentation of knowledge:

> A fair amount of things that have to be done in physics or in biology is mechanical work of the mind which can be done by anyone, or almost anyone. . . to divide science into small sections, to enclose oneself in one of these, and leave out all consideration of the rest. (Ortega y Gasset, 1932, p. 111)

These "scientific" educators have often contributed to a further fragmentation of knowledge because of their reductionistic view of the act of knowing. They repeatedly refuse to admit to themselves and to others that their claims of objectivity are, in fact, ideological acts. Objectivity always contains within it a dimension of subjectivity; thus it is dialectical.

While many educators, particularly those who embrace a positivistic mode of inquiry, would outrightly deny the role of ideology in their work, they nonetheless ideologically attempt to prevent the development of any counter discourse within their institution—a counter discourse that could problematize the very notion of "norm." As Paulo Freire pointed out, if these educators were to claim a scientific posture, for instance, "[they] might try to 'hide' in what [they] regard as the neutrality of scientific pursuits, indifferent to how [their] findings are used, even uninterested in considering for whom or for what interests [they] are working"(Freire, 1985, p. 103). Since most educators do not conduct research in the "hard sciences," they uncritically attempt to adopt the "neutrality" posture in their work, leaving out the necessary built-in self-criticism, skepticism, and rigor of hard sciences. In fact, science cannot evolve without a healthy dose of self-criticism, skepticism, and contestation. Yet, a discourse of critique and contestation is often viewed as contaminating "objectivity" in social sciences and education.

Freire also argued that these educators "might treat [the] society under study as though [they] are not participants in it. In [their] celebrated impartiality, [they] might approach this real world as if [they] were wearing 'gloves and masks' in order not to contaminate or be contaminated by it" (Freire, 1985, p. 103). These metaphorical "gloves and masks" represent a form of ideological fog that enables educators to comfortably fragment bodies of knowledge as a means of reducing the intellectual task to pure technicism so as to more easily disarticulate a particular form of knowledge from other bodies of knowledge, thus preventing a more critical reading of the world. Our concern over this technicist approach to the education of students with disabilities via a reductionistic specialization inspired us to develop this chapter where we hope to highlight fundamental knowledge that all teachers working with physically and cognitively challenged students should have or, at least, be exposed to but that are seldom taught in teacher preparation. Freire (1998) contends that "teaching requires a recognition that education is ideological," "always involves ethics," "requires a capacity to be critical," "requires the recognition of our conditioning," "requires humility," and "requires critical reflection," among other foundational beliefs. We believe that teachers who rigorously undergo a course of study that exposes them to the above-mentioned broader knowledge would never allow themselves to fall prey to discriminatory educational practices such as those that reduced Arthur Lomba's teacher to an unreflective functionary who, in turn, reproduced the very racist structure that had deskilled and cheated her educationally.

We believe that broader, more diverse fundamental knowledge is absolutely necessary for the development of a critical reading of the world that implies, according to Freire (1987), "a dynamic comprehension between the least coherent sensibility of the world and a more coherent understanding of the word" (p. 132). This means, for example, that special education teachers in the United States, who have contributed greatly to the technical advancement in the field, should have the ability to understand and appreciate why millions of children who, by virtue of their race, ethnicity, gender, and class, are wrongly referred to their classrooms and further segregated from mainstream education.

Such understanding would invariably necessitate that special education teachers make linkages between their self-contained, technical, special-needs methods and the social and political realities that generate unacceptably high educational failure rates among certain groups of students. The making of such linkages would necessarily require courses on the nature of ideology, ethics, and education—courses that are, by and large, missing from the curriculum of schools of education. While prospective teachers are almost always required, particularly in advanced graduate studies, to take multiple courses in statistics and quantitative research methodologies, no such requirements exist for a course on the nature of ideology. This very selection process that prioritizes certain bodies of knowledge while discouraging or suffocating other discourses is linked to something beyond education—ideology. Thus, the curriculum selection and organization that favor disarticulated technical training over courses in critical theory, which would enable students to make linkages with other bodies of knowledge and thereby gain a more comprehensive understanding of reality, point to the very ideology that attempts to deny its existence through false claims of neutrality. The insidious nature of ideology is its ability to make itself invisible.

Given the anti-intellectual posture of many schools of education, a posture that is manifested either through censorship of certain bodies of knowledge or through the disarticulation between theories of the discipline and empirically driven and self-contained studies, it becomes obvious why these pseudoscientists do not challenge the territorialization of university intellectual activity or in any way risk undermining the status and core beliefs of their fields. The difference, for scientists, is that this blindness or reluctance often contradicts the intellectual imperatives of the very theories they espouse. Indeed, only a theorized discipline can be an effective site for general social critique; that is, a discipline actively engaged in self-criticism, a discipline that is a locus for struggle, a discipline that renews and revises its awareness of its history, a discipline that inquires into its differential relations with other academic fields, and a discipline that examines its place in the social formation of reality (Nelson, 1997).

As these theoretical requirements make abundantly clear, the decision of most teacher-preparation programs is to not expose students to the other fundamental bodies of knowledge that inform their field of study while giving them the necessary critical tools to link these bodies of knowledge in order to more fully comprehend, for example, the ideology of school segregation. These theoretical requirements expose the almost illusory and schizophrenic educational practice in which, as expressed by Carry Nelson (1997), "the object of interpretation and the content of the interpretive discourse are considered appropriate subjects for discussion and scrutiny, but the interests of the interpreter and the discipline and society he or she serves are not" (p. 19).

The disarticulation between the interpretive discourse and the interests of the interpreter is often hidden in the false call for an objectivity that denies the dialectical relationship between subjectivity and objectivity. In effect, this has resulted in an epistemological stance in which scientism and methodological refinement are celebrated while "theory and knowledge are subordinated to the imperatives of efficiency and technical mastery, and history is reduced to a minor footnote in the priorities of 'empirical' scientific inquiry" (Giroux, 1983, p. 87). Perhaps it is this devaluation of history that enables professors at many prestigious schools of education to tell international doctoral candidates "not to cite too many historical sources. In the United States any research that is more than five years old is considered dated." The blind celebration of empiricism has created a culture in which pseudoscientists, particularly in schools of education, who engage in a form of "naive empiricism," believe, according to Michael Schudson (1978), "that facts are not human statements about the world but aspects of the world itself" (p. 6). Schudson (1978) goes on to say:

> This view was insensitive to the ways in which the "world" is something people construct by the active play of their minds and by their acceptance of conventional—not necessarily "true" ways of seeing and talking. Philosophy, the history of science, psychoanalysis, and the social sciences have taken great pains to demonstrate that human beings are cultural animals who know and see and hear the world through socially constructed filters. (p. 6)

What these professors do not realize is that there is a large body of critical literature that interrogates the very nature of what they consider research. Critical writers such as Donna Haraway (1988), Linda Brodkey (1996), Roger Fowler (1979), and Greg Myers, among others, have demonstrated the erroneous claim of "scientific" objectivity that permeates all forms of empirical work in social sciences. According to Brodkey (1996), "scientific objectivity has too often and for too long been used as an excuse to ignore a social and, hence, political practice in which women and people of color, among others, are dismissed as legitimate subjects of research" (p. 10). The blind belief in objectivity not only provides pseudoscientists with a safe haven from which they can attempt to prevent the emergence of counterdiscourses that interrogate "the hegemony of positivism and empiricism," but it is also a practice that generates a form of folk theory concerning objectivity believed only by non-scientists (Brodkey, 1996, p. 8). In other words, as Linda Brodkey (1996) so eloquently puts it, "any and all knowledge, including that arrived at empirically, is necessarily partial, that is, both an incomplete and an interested account of whatever is envisioned" (p. 8). In fact, what these pseudoscientists consider research, that is, work based on quantitative evaluation results, can never escape the social construction that generated these models of analysis in which the theoretical concepts are always shaped by the pragmatics of the society that devised them in the first place (Fowler, 1979). That is, if the results are presented as facts originally determined by a particular ideology, these facts cannot in themselves illuminate issues that lie outside of the ideological construction to begin with (Myers, 1986; Kozol, 1996). We caution educators that these evaluation models can provide answers that are correct and nevertheless without truth. A study that concludes that African American students perform way below white mainstream students in reading is correct, but such a conclusion tells us very little about the material conditions in which African American students work in the struggle against racism, educational tracking, and the systematic negation and devaluation of their histories. We propose that the correct conclusion rests in a full understanding of the ideological elements that generate and sustain the cruel reality of racism and economic oppression. Thus an empirical study will produce conclusions without truth if it is disarticulated from its sociocultural reality. For example, an empirical study designed to assess reading achievement of children who live in squalid conditions must factor in the reality faced by these children, as described by Jonathan Kozol (1996):

> Crack-cocaine addiction and the intravenous use of heroin. . .are woven into the texture of existence in Mott Haven. Nearly 4,000 heroin injectors, many of whom are HIV-infected, live here. Virtually every child at St. Ann's knows someone. . .who has died of AIDS. . . . One quarter of the women of Mott Haven who are tested in obstetric wards are positive for HIV. Rates of pediatric

AIDS, therefore, are high…. Depression is common…. Fear and anxiety are common…. Many cannot sleep…. Asthma is the most common illness among children here. Many have to struggle to take in a good deep breath. (p. 4)

An empirical study that neglects to incorporate in its design these cruel realities will never be able to fully explain the reasons behind these children's poor performance. While pseudoscientists will go to great lengths to prevent their research methodologies from being contaminated by the social ugliness described by Kozol in order to safeguard their "objectivity" in, say, their study of underachievement of children who live in ghettos, the residents of these ghettos have little difficulty understanding the root causes of their misery, as described by a resident of Mott Haven named Maria:

> If you weave enough bad things into the fibers of a person's life—sickness and filth, old mattresses and other junk thrown in the streets and ugly ruined things, and ruined people, a prison here, sewage there, drug dealers here, the homeless people over there, then give us the very worst schools anyone could think of, hospitals that keep you waiting for ten hours, police that don't show up when someone's dying . . . you can guess that life will not be very nice and children will not have much sense of being glad of who they are. Sometimes it feels like we have been buried six feet under their perceptions. (Kozol, 1996, p. 39)

What Maria would probably say to researchers is that another doctoral dissertation is not needed to find what is so obvious to the people sentenced to live in this form of human misery. By locking children in oppressive and dehumanizing conditions we encourage academic underachievement. Once this pattern is established, it is easy for researchers like Herrnstein and Murray (1994) to conclude that blacks are intellectually inferior to whites. What Maria's description of the human misery of her neighborhood makes clear is how distorted the results of empirical studies can be when they are disconnected from the sociocultural reality that informs the study to begin with. In addition, such distortion feeds into the development of stereotypes that, on the one hand, blame the victims for their own social misery and, on the other hand, rationalize the genetic inferiority hypotheses that are advanced by such pseudo scholars like Murray and Herrnstein. What empirical studies often neglect to point out is how easily statistics can be manipulated to remove the subjects' human faces through a process that not only dehumanizes but also distorts and falsifies reality.

The inability to link research with larger critical and social issues often prevents educators from engaging in a general critique of the social mission of their own educational enterprise and also from acknowledging their roles in the reproduction of the values of the dominant social order, as exemplified by Arthur's teacher in the opening of this chapter. We now turn our attention to the overrepresentation of subordinated groups in special education in the European Union.

Educational segregation and the politics of inequality in Europe

In order to understand the overrepresentation of subordinated students in special education classes in the context of the European Union, we need to situate our discussion within the generalized xenophobia enveloping these countries, which has led to the promulgation of laws to contain immigration—a process that invariably requires constant demonization and the use of labels to characterize the "other," as Italy's Prime Minister Silvio Berlusconi so callously made evident when he stated: "I don't want Italy to be multiethnic. We are very proud of our traditions" (Rizzo, 2006).

With these words, Berlusconi announced the approval of Italy's "foreignness" law, which can be viewed as another step in the criminalization and persecution of the immigrant populations whose cultures are considered inferior. Unfortunately, Berlusconi's sentiments are echoed by similar pronouncements made by, for example, Jean Marie Le Pen in France, contradicting the discourse that claims the "end of racism." Xenophobia undergirds a concerted effort by the dominant classes in these developed nations to socially construct something dangerously sinister—an echo of white supremacist ideologies that allowed fascism and nazism to flourish. Hence, we argue that, as we enter the 21st century, one of the most pressing challenges facing educators in developed nations is the specter of an "ethnic and cultural war" that constitutes, in our view, a code phrase for racism. Central to the cultural war is the facile call for a common culture and the over-celebration of myths that attempt to inculcate us with beliefs about the supremacy of Western heritage. At the same time, the dominant ideology creates instruments that degrade and devalue other cultural narratives along the lines of race, ethnicity, language, gender, sexual orientation, and disability.

Within the current worldwide economic crisis a space is being created in the public sphere where racist and xenophobic discourses that existed in the past are re-emerging. In the European Union, for example, the Italian government approved measures that remind us of not-so-distant European historical episodes that faced little opposition. The Italian minister of the interior and many mayors called on the citizenry to take justice into their own hands and contribute to the eradication of "all Roma settlements that exist in Italy" (Povoledo, 2008).

From the very beginning of the measurable increase of immigration, so-called illegal immigrants in Italy have been victims of a process of criminalization that has resulted in the promulgation of the "foreignness law," which requires medical doctors and landlords to turn in undocumented immigrants. The most controversial aspect of the law is the prohibition of birth registration for "illegal" babies in the official registry, creating an invisible population without any rights or social protection. The logic is flawed but compelling: Do not register the babies of immigrant families and help the government to combat crime.

Italy is not the only country in the European Union where we find examples of growing racism. Demonstrations with racist slogans are spreading throughout Europe. In Greece, five immigrants were injured after being attacked by a far-right group carrying posters saying, "Stranger equals crime" or "We are foreigners in our own country." In Hungary, seven Roma were killed and community leaders reported that at least thirty Molotov cocktails were thrown at Romaní families (Mirga, 2009). Creating scapegoats by labeling weaker society members as undesirable is not new, but, in times of crisis, the process increases exponentially. As the current economic crisis in Europe worsens, causing rising unemployment levels, conservative sectors have coalesced to promote this vitriolic discourse. In education, discourses that blame immigrant students and cultural minorities are also not new. Despite numerous investigations that show that any legal measure that segregates has detrimental effects on the segregated students, this type of intervention is currently enacted with impunity throughout Europe.

In this section we analyze two examples of these measures: first, the overrepresentation of Roma pupils in special education schools in Central and Eastern European countries and, second, the problems that arise with measures aimed at addressing diversity but end up reproducing existing inequalities between cultural groups. We conclude with a call for a pedagogy of imagination that involves inclusion rather than exclusion, a pedagogy that embraces the involvement of the entire community and requires the inclusion of all groups. It is a pedagogy that enables people to overcome racist and xenophobic discourse from below by imagining alternate possibilities. This chapter is a call to teachers to combat racism and xenophobia that dehumanizes those that are categorized as disabled or as racially and ethnically "other."

Let's turn first to overrepresentation of Roma pupils in special education schools. In Slovakia, according to the Roma Education Fund recent survey, Romaní students make up to 60% of all the primary and secondary students attending any kind of special educational facilities (Friedman et al., 2009). Other studies already showed that in the Czech Republic in 1997 Roma children were fifteen times more likely to be referred to special education classes than non-Roma children (Tritt, 1992). In Hungary in 2003, 98% of students in special education schools were Roma, while Roma account for less than 7% of the total population (Cahn, 1999). More recent statistics indicate little progress reversing this trend.

Human rights organizations have denounced this form of discrimination that inevitably leads to an education that is of significantly lower quality than that received by mainstream (i.e., "normal," non-Roma) students. These children are thus condemned to second-class citizenship. In most cases, there are no established procedures for transferring students into the mainstream education system once labeled and assigned to a special education school. Hence the assignment usually means forever. In the Czech Republic and Slovakia, after completing their substandard education in these second-class schools, students in special education are only eligible to attend vocational schools, branding these institutions "schools of brooms and mops" (Danova, 2001).

One of the main practices denounced as a violation of these children's human rights is the procedure followed to assign them to such schools. From design to implementation, each step is more superstitious than scientific. The intelligence test used to diagnose students, for example, represents a significant barrier for Roma children who have not mastered the dominant language. Furthermore, it has been demonstrated that these tests do not take into account Romaní culture, thus conflating cultural understanding and learning disabilities. In some cases, Roma children are assigned to special education without even taking the test and without the consent of their families, a clear violation of parental rights to access the necessary information in order to make appropriate decisions regarding the education of their children. While we acknowledge that many of these children need extra supports, their parents are encouraged only to send their children to separate schooling with other Roma children. The European Committee on Romaní Emancipation (ECRE) argues that Romaní parents often agree to transfer their children to these schools under pressure from experts. These parents' silence is usually construed as a lack of parental interest, but as ECRE notes, Romaní families, like parents all over the world, want the best future for their children.

Some families in the Czech Republic and Croatia, with the assistance of nongovernmental associations, have taken their cases to the European Court of Human Rights in Strasbourg to determine whether discrimination was involved in the decision to send Roma children to special education schools. A school case has been prosecuted in the same court against the Czech education system of segregation of Roma children in special education. From Croatia, fifteen students reported being pushed into classes with only Romaní boys and girls. The educational consequences of this forced separation are extremely damaging. Based on a system of educational tracking, students labeled as under-prepared receive a watered-down curriculum, a process that invariably leads to stigmatization of these students.

There are examples of parents who have mobilized against psychologists' decisions to send their children to special education schools and whose children are now successfully integrated into mainstream schools. At the organizational level, Roma leaders have proposed alternatives to avoid this type of discrimination; for example, the creation of pre-schools based on the official language of the country, allowing Roma children to develop dominant language mastery before entering the regular educational system. This policy would at least help differentiate linguistic from cognitive problems before making decisions about which school a student must attend. Other organizations have proposed the transformation of special education schools into mainstream schools or, at the very least, that teachers in mainstream schools be equipped with the necessary knowledge and skills to address the specific needs of the majority of Roma students. Although the European Parliament (2009) passed a resolution condemning any measure that involved segregating immigrant or minority students, segregation continues to be part of the everyday life of many students of immigrant background in Spain as well as many other European countries. In Catalonia, Spain, four centers have been created exclusively for immigrant students. One of them is in Vic, a town where the far-right party holds enough votes to have representatives in the local government and has already carried out a plan to manipulate the assignment of immigrant students to avoid a higher proportion of them in any particular school. Such manipulation usually results in denying students' access to teachers with the necessary skills to address immigrant students' specific linguistic and cultural needs.

Students from ethnic minorities have been most affected by measures that, under the principle of diversity, have segregated and discriminated against them, preventing them from participation in mainstream classrooms (Aubert, Flecha, Garcia, Flecha, & Racionero, 2008). These measures do not refer openly to any particular ethnic or cultural stance, but are, instead, justified with explanations that focus on pedagogical and psychological barriers to learning, often alluding subtly to beliefs that these students have a lower level of knowledge, have not mastered the host country language, or lack "appropriate" schooling habits. Without explicitly stating that these measures are aimed at children of cultural minorities and immigrants, these educational spaces have been filled exclusively by them as a form of cultural quarantine that immunizes mainstream students from contamination by those whose language and culture fall outside the boundaries of "normal" Europeans.

Generally, when there is a focus on diversity, the education program deflects attention from the root causes for the perceived "gaps" or "deficiencies." Instead of factoring in cultural, linguistic, economic, and racial discrimination that students face in schools and in society, educators rely on a deficit orientation that locates the problem with the student, his language, or his culture and legitimizes discriminatory educational practices—practices based on the rationalization that these students need fixing, an educational ideology that is intractably linked to the deficit theories of the past. These measures are framed as a means of offering more to those who have less, to compensate for social inequalities, but they represent a form of false generosity that legitimizes educational exclusion and the maintenance of inequality.

These diversity measures have taken many different forms, but they share two general characteristics: (1) the physical exclusion of subordinate boys or girls from mainstream classrooms and, therefore, (2) a *de facto* separation from the group-class reference along the lines of gender, ethnicity and culture that, in turn, calls for the downward adaptation of curriculum, which leads to the decline of objectives and learning content. Curriculum has been designed specifically for these anti-pedagogical spaces, giving priority to the social aspects of learning rather than instrumental knowledge and skills that are essential in today's information society. In this way, although theoretically designed to meet the needs of a diverse student population and to compensate for their "deficiencies," their education has been turned into a conundrum that leaves them behind, where educational inequalities have increased rather than decreased. If these students require accelerated learning to achieve appropriate levels for their ages and progress, these anti-pedagogical contexts tend to ignore opportunities for learning and teaching by adapting to the status quo. In this way, instead of increasing learning they have, in reality, reinforced school failure.

Despite good intentions, many of these approaches to dealing with diversity assume that certain cultures and social classes have deficits that prevent them from normal progress in the education system. This rationale ignores the skills, abilities, and qualities that students bring to the classroom. The *a priori* labeling as "disadvantaged" is taken as an immutable fact that, in turn, determines the students' futures instead of helping them grow beyond the barriers often imposed on them or increasing their opportunities for learning that, in our view, is the duty and responsibility of any educational system.

Segregation has resulted from negative assumptions with respect to Roma and immigrant students. These students have been prevented from improving their academic performance, thereby limiting their professional and academic aspirations (among many other personal costs). We know, for example, that the classrooms where curriculum is adapted downward (a form of dumbing down) are referred to disparagingly by mainstream students as the "zoo class," among other epithets, or that the lower-level groups, divided along "ability" lines, are labeled "the idiot group." For these reasons and more, in these anti-pedagogical spheres where the linguistic, cultural, and cognitive needs of students are largely unmet, the result is reduced opportunities that do not motivate Romaní and other minority students to stay in school—a process that can be called "coerced" expulsion.

These segregationist practices destroy students' expectations, aspirations, and opportunities. Once these students are coerced into leaving schools and are greeted with joblessness and hopelessness, they frequently fulfill dominant society's expectations as "dangerous" and "criminals" when they engage in petty crimes as a survival mechanism. As criminals, they are often sentenced to long stints in jails, costing society enormously more than it would have cost to provide them access to quality education in the first place.

The stated objective of segregated special education schools and classrooms, ensuring that students will eventually join mainstream classrooms, is almost never achieved. There are many factors that prevent it, beginning with the disparaging labels applied to these students that lead to low expectations by teachers, families, and society and the replacement of the standard curriculum with a dumbed-down track that educators cynically call "the happiness curriculum." This process prevents them from partaking in a future where they are treated with the dignity and respect they deserve. A fourteen-year-old Roma girl shared her feelings regarding her new placement in a low-level group: "Let's see if I learn more in this class because I am one of them illiterate. I know things, but not as much as my class." She was then asked the reason why there were so many students separated from mainstream classes. She replied: "Because they are being really bad, talk a lot. . .and they are stupid" (Sordé Martí, 2006).

Instead of preparing the subordinate students to return to the mainstream classroom, what happens in practice is that learning is decreased gradually, a process of deskilling students that, in turn, generates negative attitudes toward school marked by low educational motivation, absenteeism, misbehavior, and, ultimately, dropping out—a convenient euphemism for "pushed" out (Fine, 1991). It is all part of the vicious circle of school failure and exclusion that affects students whose cultural, ethnic, and linguistic backgrounds have been labeled "undesirable," "deficient," and in need of fixing. To the extent that diversity continues to be an undeniable reality of the mainstream classroom, negatively labeled students are replaced by the constant in and out flow of minority students occurring with ever-increasing immigration.

The measures meant to contribute to overcoming failure in the long term, end up doing just the opposite. In reality, the deficit orientation that guides and shapes the education of Roma and immigrant students in the European Union reinforces existing inequalities. Research has amply demonstrated that any measure that involves educational segregation is ineffective in overcoming the so-called school failure of groups that have been traditionally excluded. School segregation creates dual educational systems through the siphoning of students into special education schools or the separation of subordinate students into different classrooms within the same school. These methods reinforce the rise of racism in many European countries. For those students who are labeled so as to be separated, school is not a space of social transformation that prepares them for a better future. There is a consensus that tracking students means unequal access to education that could provide personal development and social improvement as students have an opportunity to interact with people of different cultures and social classes and promote multicultural exchange. In such settings, higher levels of learning are more likely to be realized. Families, and especially women who are actively interested in the education of their children need to unite their efforts to imagine and support schools that dare to open their doors to equal and high-quality learning regardless of students' language, culture, race, disability, gender, or ethnicity.

Conclusion

In order to imagine education that dares to stop discriminatory practices that devalue, demonize, and dehumanize students solely based on their non-white and non-mainstream backgrounds, educators need to not only develop political clarity but also to acquire critical tools that will enable them to effectively challenge a dominant ideology that does not democratically educate all students. They must develop pedagogies that go beyond privileging a select class of elites and functionaries and guarantee the achievements of the few at the expense of the dreams, desires, and aspirations of the majority. In addition to a language of critique that would unveil the perniciousness of discriminatory education practices, educators must have the courage and ethical integrity to denounce any and all attempts that actively dehumanize the very subordinate students from whom they make their living as teachers or community workers. To do otherwise is to willfully embrace a form of illiteracy and poverty pimping. Educators need to stand up and say that no human being is illegal, alien, or abnormal. Legality does not always translate into morality. While slavery was legal, it was never moral for one human being to own another.

We want to reiterate the importance of a bottom-up dialogue for equality that is infused with a pedagogy of hope that, in turn, is informed by tolerance, respect, and solidarity; a pedagogy that rejects the social construction of images that dehumanize the "other," that points out that in our construction of the other we become intimately tied to that other, that teaches us that by dehumanizing the other we become dehumanized ourselves. In short, we need a pedagogy of hope that guides us toward the critical road of substantive democracy, toward reclaiming our dignity and our humanity. A pedagogy of hope will point us toward a world that is more harmonious and more humane, less discriminatory, less dehumanizing, and more just. It will reject policies of hatred, bigotry, and division while celebrating diversity within unity. In other words, a pedagogy of hope points to the "path through which men and women can become conscious about their presence in the world. The way they act and think when they develop all their capacities, taking into consideration their needs, but also the needs and aspirations of others" (Freire, 1985, p. 11).

The creation of otherness not only fosters ignorance on the part of those in power but also fails to provide the dominant group with the necessary tools to empathize with the demonized "other." The dominant group loses its humanity in its inability to feel badly about discriminating against other human beings. The dominant group's ability to demonize and its inability to empathize with the other point to the inherent demon in those who dehumanize.

While we dehumanize foreigners and so-called illegals, we need to be reminded of our own dehumanization when we knowingly and sometimes unknowingly engage in the process of "othering," in which the only purpose served is dehumanization. Instead of dehumanizing foreigners and "illegals," we should accept Carlos Fuentes' (1999) challenge to imagine the children of "illegals" as "the young teachers of their own and others; they are the new businesspeople rapidly growing and diversifying U.S. services and production; they are the new doctors and lawyers and architects and biologists and politicians; they are the new singers and actors and dancers and stage directors and painters and musicians enriching U.S. culture with contrast, diversity, and generosity" (p. 15).

In order to imagine the human possibility envisioned by Carlos Fuentes requires both humanity and humility—a humility that guides and shapes the act of reading the word while giving the necessary coherence to reading the world. Through this process we can courageously, angrily, and aggressively denounce any and all forms of inequality and discrimination shaped by racism and initiate a pedagogy of hope that takes seriously a new reading of the world. We will then understand that, according to St. Augustine, "hope has two beautiful daughters and their names are Anger and Courage. Anger at the way things are and Courage to see that they do not remain as they are."

References

Aubert, A., Flecha, A., Garcia, C., Flecha, R., & Racionero, S. (2008). *Aprendizaje en la sociedad de la información*. Barcelona: Hipatia Editorial.

Brodkey, L. (1996). *Writing permitted in designated areas only*. Minneapolis, MN: Minnesota University Press.

Cahn, C. (1999). *A special remedy: Roma and schools for the mentally handicapped in the Czech Republic*. Budapest: European Roma Rights Center.

Danova, S. (2001). *Desegregation of "Romani schools:" A condition for an equal start for Roma*. Report published by the European Roma Rights Center and the Open Society Institute's Roma Participation Program.Sofia, Bulgaria.

Dunn, L.M. (1968). Special education for the mildly retarded—is much of it justifiable? *Exceptional Children, 35*(1), 5–22.

European Parliament. (2009). *European Parliament resolution of 2 April 2009 on educating the children of migrants*.

Fine, M. (1991). *Framing dropouts: Notes on the politics of an urban public high school*. Albany, NY: State University of New York Press.

Follain, J. (2008, May 11). Italy needed fascism, says the new duce. *The Sunday Times*.

Fowler, R. (1979). *Language and control*. London: Routledge and Kegan Paul.

Freire, P. (1985). *The politics of education: Culture, power, and liberation.* Westport, CT: Bergin & Garvey.

Freire, P. (1998). *Pedagogy of freedom.* Lanham, MD: Rowman & Littlefield.

Freire, P. & Macedo, D. (1987). *Literacy: Reading the word and the world.* South Hadley, MA: Bergin & Garvey.

Friedman, E., Kriglerova, E. G., Kubánová, M., Slosiarik, M. & Surdu, M. (2009). *School as ghetto: Systemic overrepresentation of Roma in special education in Slovakia.* Roma Education Fund.

Fuentes, C. (1999). *Americanos: Latino life in the United States.* (Olmos, E.J, Ybarra, L., & Monterrey, M., Eds.). Boston, MA: Little, Brown.

Giroux, H. (1983). *Theory and resistance: A pedagogy for the opposition.* South Hadley, MA: Bergin & Garvey.

Haraway, D. (1988). Situated knowledges: The science question in feminism and the privilege of partial perspective. *Feminist Studies* 14, 575–599.

Helsinki Watch Report, Human Rights Watch. (1992). *Struggling for ethnic identity. Czechoslovakia's endangered Gypsies.* New York, Washington, Los Angeles and London: Human Rights Watch.

Herrnstein, R.J., & Murray, C. (1994). *The bell curve: Intelligence and class structure in American life.* New York: The Free Press.

Kozol, J. (1996). *Amazing grace: The lives and the conscience of a nation.* New York: Harper Perennial.

Losen, D. J. & Orfield, G. (2002). *Racial inequality in special education.* Cambridge, MA: Harvard Education Press.

Mirga, A. (2009). *Hard times and hardening attitudes: The economic downturn and the rise of violence against Roma.* Office for Democratic Institutions and Human Rights.

Myers, G. (1986). Reality, consensus, and reform in the rhetoric of composition teaching. *College English, 48*(2),154–173.

Nelson, C. (1997). *Manifesto of a tenured radical.* New York: New York University Press.

Ortega y Gasset, J, (1932). *The revolt of the masses.* New York: Norton.

Povoledo, E. (2008, July 3). Italy assailed over plan to fingerprint gypsies. *International Herald Tribune,* the Global Edition of the *New York Times.*

Rizzo, A. (2006, March 3). Berlusconi: Italy must not become "multiethnic, multicultural country." *North County Times.*

Schudson, M. (1978). *Discovering the news: A social history of American newspapers.* New York: Basic.

Shapiro, J.P. (1994). *No pity: People with disabilities forging a new civil rights movement.* New York: Three Rivers Press.

Sordé Martí, T. (2006). *Les reivindicacions educatives de la dona gitana.* Cabrera de Mar, Spain: Edicions Galerada.

Thompson, J.B. (1990). *Ideology and modern culture.* Stanford, CA: Stanford University Press.

Tritt, R.: 1992, *Struggling for Ethnic Identity: Czechoslovakia's Endangered Gypsies.* Helsinki Watch. New York: Human Rights Watch.

Six

Evolutionary Anxiety, Monstrosity, and the Birth of Normality

Steven A. Gelb

The publication in 1886 of Robert Louis Stevenson's gothic tale *The Strange Case of Dr. Jekyll and Mr. Hyde* created a sensation in England (Dury, 2004). Readers shuddered over the transformation of the good, respectable physician Dr. Jekyll into his terrifyingly murderous alter ego, Mr. Hyde, a repulsive, animal-like insinuation of a human being. Hyde's mere appearance inspired revulsion in all who saw him. He was "deformed" (p. 12), "apelike" (p. 73), "troglodytic" (p. 18), "like a rat," and compared to "a dwarf" (p. 44). His terrible character matched his appearance. For sheer enjoyment Hyde trampled a young girl and beat a man to death with a cane. A character observed about Hyde that "there was something abnormal and misbegotten in the very essence of the creature" (p. 54).

Mr. Hyde is more than a mere literary creation. He is a prototype of abnormality as the category was developed just before the 20th century. The anxiety that resulted from Darwin's connection of humanity and animals catalyzed the late 19th century project to distinguish normality from abnormality. Longstanding myths about human-animal monsters mixed together with evolutionary theory resulted in western society's projection of its most detested and disassociated attributes into the category of abnormality. In this chapter I argue that in spite of its scientific imprimatur, the normality/abnormality dichotomy was infused with irrationalism at its conception. But before turning to this history I discuss the problematic pre-suppositions of the normality/abnormality binary.

The Construction of Abnormality

A widely accepted view "in the field of biology and related disciplines—physiology, biochemistry, psychology—and in the applied fields of medicine, psychiatry, and social relations appears to be that humanity can be divided into two groups: (1) the vast majority possess attributes which are within the normal range; (2) a small minority possess attributes far enough out of line so that they should be considered deviates" (Williams, 1956/1982, p. 22). The assumption that the abnormal are qualitatively different from the normal, that is, distinct in kind rather than degree, is implicit in the fear of abnormality.

This assumption is untenable because the normal/abnormal dichotomy is based upon a distinction rooted in psychometrics rather than in nature. The abnormal individual is, presumably, one whose score on a measure of an attribute is rare (i.e., beyond the boundaries of normal) in comparison to the scores of others in a particular population, either considerably lower or higher than the group average. Too much of some things (e.g., activity level) or too little of others (e.g., intelligence) is deemed to be bad. However, the judgment about what constitutes "too much" or "too little" of given attributes and where to mark the cutoff between normality and abnormality is entirely arbitrary, and, hence open to contestation. Williams (1956/1982) observed that, "the most commonly accepted line of demarcation between normal and abnormal in biological work is the 95% level. That is, all values lying outside those possessed by 95% of the population may be regarded as deviant values, and any individual who possesses such deviant values may be regarded as a deviate" (p. 23). Yet this seemingly clear and objective criterion applied in the field of intellectual disabilities has generated a hundred-year controversy over the definition of "mild" mental retardation that is still unresolved.

Before Darwin, Europeans had assumed the existence of a vast gulf separating animals and humans. Animals were "brutes"—unreasoning, savage, cruel, and carnal. The devil was known as "The Beast" and evil spirits and demons were portrayed through images of animal features on human forms. To the extent that people were civilized, their intelligence, rationality and benevolence marked them as separate from animals. The road to spiritual growth required "animal man" to be transformed into "spiritual man." "Man stood to animal as did heaven to earth, soul to body, culture to nature. There was a total qualitative difference between man and brutes" (Thomas, 1983, p. 35).

Europeans projected onto animals those aspects of their own violent and sexual natures that they feared the most. In reality, it was humans, not animals, who waged war endlessly against each other and engaged in sex throughout the year (Thomas, 1983). Yet when Europeans sought to teach desirable qualities to their children they warned them against behaving like animals, and when they wished to malign a person or a group, linking them to animals was the highest form of insult. Spaniards described indigenous peoples of the West Indies as "talking animals" (Jahoda, 1999, p. 18). In Frankfurt, Germany, the town council tormented the residents of the Jewish ghetto by maintaining a wall mural of an enormous pig being tended to by observant Jews (Elon, 1996). A German scholar wrote that native Americans were

> unquestionably the most depraved among all human, or human-like creatures of the whole earth, and they are not only much weaker than the Negroes, but also much more inflexible, harder, and lacking in feelings. Despite the fact that this communication contains only a few traits of the terrible portrait of the bodily and moral nature of the Americans, one will nonetheless feel, and be astonished, that the inhabitants of a whole continent are so closely related to dumb animals. (Jahoda, 1999, quoted pp. 21–22)

In *The Origin* Darwin did not discuss human evolution; however, others quickly extrapolated his argument about the speciation of animals to humans. By the time Darwin turned his attention to human origins in *The Descent of Man* (1871), German scientist Carl Vogt (1864) had already argued that "savage" races and persons with developmental disabilities were lower in the evolutionary scale than modern Europeans and could be adventitiously studied for clues to humanity's ancestral past. In the light of evolution human difference became a repository for disassociated projections that had been previously directed at animals.

Human/Animal Monsters in European History

A definition of the word "monster," according to the *Oxford English Dictionary*, is "an imaginary animal having a form either partly brute and partly human, or compounded of elements from two or more animal forms." Between the 15th and 18th centuries, Europe produced a vast corpus of writings on monstrosity, a great deal of it focused on human-animal hybrids. Todd (1995) noted that, "the sheer volume of this literature of monsters was immense," spanning everything from popular ballads and broadsides to recondite treatises." At times, reports of monster sightings became so commonplace that they seemed to surface from an "apparently inexhaustible supply of human-animal hybrids (Daston and Park, 2001, p. 173). Pender (2000) observed that England, early in the 17th century, "seemed a fecund mix of monsters" (p. 97). During the European Enlightenment belief in mermaids and mermen was common. Remarkably, belief that some humans had tails lasted until the middle of the 19th century (Jahoda, 1999).

Thirteenth-century Europeans divided the world up into three concentric circles: the innermost "us"; the second, non-Christian "barbarians"; and, the third, "disorder, fears and fantasies" (Zook, 2004). The last was home to three-faced people, men with horses' hooves rather than feet, and dogs' heads. These "monster races" lived at the edge of the earth, in unknown lands, and were naked, cannibalistic, hairy, and sexually perverted. They were outward projections of medieval Europeans' anxieties about sex, religion and aggression. What was new in the 15th century and later was that sightings were no longer confined to the margins of the world familiar to Europeans but were reported in the heart of Europe itself (Daston & Park, 2001).

Reactions to monsters were subsumed within three emotional categories labeled by Daston and Park (2001) as "horror, pleasure, and repugnance" (p. 176). Horror was associated with the belief that a "monster" was a warning from God that foretold an imminent disaster. Pleasure (through fascination) was experienced when rarities were viewed as marvels or wonders of nature and exhibited for amusement. Finally, repugnance emerged in response to the scientific recasting of difference (i.e., "abnormality") as evolutionary error or waste. Although these reactions co-existed with one another, repugnance increasingly predominated as the influence of science grew in the modern era. The confluence of statistical reasoning and evolutionary theory in the late 19th century was the capstone of this process.

The Monster as Religious Portent

The word "monster" is derived from the Latin *monstrare* meaning "to show" and, for a time, the appearance of a monster might be taken as a sign from the heavens sent to show God's wrath. A "culture of monsters" (Daston & Park, 2001, p. 180) developed in the late 15th century in response to tension associated with political and religious developments (especially in Italy and Germany), and the widespread belief that humanity was living through a time of great wickedness (Davidson, 1991). A 16th century professor of medicine who had built a reputation upon his catalogue of "completely wild" races on distant shores wrote that it was no longer "necessary to go to the New World to find beings of this sort; most of them and others still more hideous can still be found here and there among us, now that the rules of justice are trampled underfoot, all humanity flouted, and all religion torn to bits" (quoted in Daston & Park, p. 175).

The most celebrated and historically influential monsters of this genre were the "pope-ass" and "monk-calf," subjects of a bitterly anti-Catholic 1523 German pamphlet by Martin Luther and Phillip Melancthon. The "pope-ass" and "monk-calf" were drawn as part-Catholic cleric, part-animal hybrids and their discovery, according to the authors, foretold great catastrophes (Davidson, 1991).

Melancthon argued that the pope-ass, with its head of a donkey atop a sensuous female human body signified that the Pope was not the true head of the

Christian faith. Other portents that he drew from the creature's body included that

> Its left foot was like a griffon's, because the [Catholic] canons grabbed all the wealth of Europe for the Pope. The female belly and breast symbolized the Papacy's belly, "that is, cardinals, bishops, priests, monks, students and such like whorish people and pigs, because their whole life consists of nothing but gobbling food, of drinking and of sex." The monster's skin was like that of a fish: this symbolised the princes who clung to the papal order; the old man's head on the monster's buttocks signaled the decline of papal power. (Rublack, 2005, p. 1)

Luther claimed that the disfigured monk-calf's prominent ears showed God's displeasure over the practice of confession and his desire for Catholic clerics, monks and nuns, to abandon their convents. Together the monsters signified the approach of terrible famines, wars, possibly even the imminent destruction of the world (Davidson, 1991).

Monsters as Marvels

Such wailing and gnashing of teeth were absent when monsters were viewed as rare and unusual marvels that provoked a sense of wonder. Today, the appreciation of marvels is manifested in the intense fascination that attends exhibits of Egyptian mummies, moon rocks, and plasticized human bodies. In European history monstrous marvels were long collected and displayed by royalty and the nobility in cabinets of curiosity, but they were also displayed publicly in markets, fairs, taverns, parlors, and even churches (Pender, 2000).

Exhibits of "monsters" could be profitable and parents often exhibited atypical children for a fee. Some even argued that monsters were God's blessing on poor families (Daston & Park, 2001). Others sought to create monsters by unnatural means. A 17th century man confessed to an act of bestiality claiming that he was poor and hoping to sire a monster to make a living. In England, parents of "prodigies" made handsome sums selling the rights for display of their dead children (Pender, 2000).

Others created monsters through ruses. Dessicated "mermaids" and "mermen" stitched together from parts of animals were exhibited for profit between the 17th and 19th centuries. In London, in 1822, between 300 and 400 people a day paid to see a "mummified fishlike body standing erect on a curve just above the tail, with a wizened simian head and quasi-human hands, arms, shoulders, and shriveled breasts" (Altick, 1978, p. 302). This creation, assembled from parts of a monkey and a salmon, was later displayed in the U.S. by P.T. Barnum as "the Fee Jee Mermaid" (Altick, 1978, p. 303).

Fairs in England commonly displayed people who, it was claimed, had "degenerated into animals" (Todd, 1995, p. 147). Examples included the "Northumberland monster," a man who resembled a horse; a boy whose skin was covered with "fish scales," another with "bristles like a hedge-hog" (Todd, 1995, p. 147); and a boy deemed "the Lobster Boy" (Wilson, 1993, p. 95). There was also a "most strange and wonderful creature" from the East Indies, labeled the "Man Teger (sic)" (Altick, 1978, p. 38) and other hybrids called "The Frog Man," "The Camel Girl," "The Leopard Child," and "Jo-Jo, the Dog-Faced Boy" (Thomson, 1997, p. 69).

John Merrick, the supposed "Elephant Man" of the 19th century, was described by his physician as "the loathing insinuation of a man being changed into an animal" (Davidson, 1991, p. 53). A longstanding European legend told of a stylishly dressed woman with the head of a pig who ate from a silver trough. She was immortalized in an 1815 portrait that was widely viewed (Wilson, 1993). A 1628 report described "the birth of a monster with a human face, the head and the rest of the body covered with an armour fashioned from scales" (Wilson, 1993, p. 57). A purported "man-pig" was born in Brussels in 1564 "having a man's face, arms, and hands…and having the hind legs and hindquarters of a swine and the genitals of a sow" (Davidson, 1991, p. 51).

A notorious fraud occurred in England in 1726, when a young woman named Mary Toft convinced eminent physicians and much of the populace that she had given birth, over a month's time, to seventeen rabbits. In fact, she and her husband had concocted a hoax in order to enrich themselves. She placed in her vagina parts of small dead rabbits that had been purchased for that purpose, then "delivered" them to astounded physicians while convulsing in (false!) labor. Toft's initial attending physician preserved the rabbit pieces and kept scientific notes that he sent to leading medical authorities in London, in hopes of receiving an invitation to present the case to the Royal Society.

Others, including Nathanael St. Andre, "Surgeon and Anatomist to the Royal Household" of King George I, also became interested and involved with Mary Toft. After examining the woman and witnessing her performance, St. Andre became her staunchest scientific supporter. New developments in the case were publicized in newspapers, and King George I sent a second observer, Cyriacus Ahlers, "Surgeon to his Majesty's German Household" to write a report. When Ahlers concluded, in contrast to St. Andre, that the affair was a hoax, a physician of even higher authority, Sir Richard Manningham, was called in to adjudicate between the conflicting scientific verdicts. Mary Toft was then brought to London, isolated and watched night and day by the eminent physicians—as well as many curious members of the nobility—to await more rabbit births. This was more than she had bargained for and under the pressure of observation and interrogation she finally confessed that the whole affair had been a hoax.

The Toft affair illustrates the strength and resilience of the belief in animal-human monsters in 18th century England. Even after the month-long affair was revealed as a hoax, it remained a popular subject of discussion and controversy for five more months. Todd (1995) noted that "everyone for whom any record exists appears to have entertained the possibility that Mary Toft's claims were true" (p. 44). In 1750, twenty-four years after the fact, an author stepped forward to insist that Toft really had given birth to rabbits and her confession was false (Todd, 1995).

Toft's claim was believable to people in her time for two reasons. The first was that it fit into the longstanding myth of animal-human monsters, and the second was that her explanation for the cause of the monstrous births fit with prevailing scientific theory. She had claimed that she was startled by rabbits in a field while pregnant and then continued to think about them for months as her pregnancy advanced. This was taken as confirmatory evidence for the widely believed theory of imagination which held that a pregnant woman's attention and thought were potent prenatal influences on the developing fetus (Talbot, 1898).

Many other women made claims similar to Mary Toft's. One stated, for example, that her child was born in the form of a lobster because while pregnant she had become fixated upon a large lobster at the market which her husband later retrieved and brought home at her urging (Wilson, 1993). Another said she gave birth to a boy with the face of a frog because she had held a frog in her hand for a long time as a cure for an ailment. The power of imagination was thought to even affect animal pregnancies. A farmer's wife complained that her cow gave birth to a calf born with a large hat after the cow saw a woman pass by the farm in the very same hat at the moment of conception (Wilson, 1993). The theory of the imagination was one of many postulated causes of monsters. In 1573, Ambroise Pare, author of a medical text that was popular in both France and England (Pender, 2000), listed thirteen causes of monsters that combined religious, magical, and pre-scientific elements:

> The first is the glory of God. The second is his anger. The third, too great a quantity of semen. The fourth, too small a quantity. The fifth, the imagination. The sixth, the tightness or smallness of the womb. The seventh, the indecorous position of the mother, as when, being pregnant, she sits too long with her thighs crossed or squeezed against her belly. The eighth, because of a fall or blow directed against the belly of the pregnant mother. The ninth, because of hereditary or accidental illness. The tenth, because of the decay, or corruption of the seminal fluid. The eleventh, because of the mixing or mingling of the semen. The twelfth, because of trickeries of malignant tavern rogues. The thirteenth, because of Demons or Devils. (cited in Wilson, 1993, p. 68)

Pare's first cause, "the Glory of God," sent forth monsters as benign marvels or wonders whose existence was evidence of the Creator's wisdom and ingenuity, while the second, "his anger," brought forth monsters that evoked horror because they foretold punishment through calamity. The ninth cause, "hereditary or accidental illness" foreshadowed science's appropriation of monstrosity in the 19th century.

Monsters as Medical Anomalies and the Birth of Normality

As learned societies developed in both England and France in the 17th century, explanations of the causes and meaning of difference moved away from folklore and religion toward more natural, scientific-sounding explanations. England's Royal Society began publishing *Philosophical Transactions* in 1665 and included within its early pages several empirical accounts purporting to prove Pare's fifth cause of monstrosity: the imagination of pregnant women. Similarly, a 1667 report described a woman who saw an ape on a stage which purportedly caused her to give birth to an ape of her own (Wilson, 1993).

The ascendant scientific view, however, and the one that would be adopted by evolutionists toward persons with disabilities, was to see difference as a deviation, a mistake, or an error from a normative plan. Although this explanation is now associated with the scientific, medical model, it had been expressed much earlier in religious contexts. Writing in Florence, Italy, in 1560, Benedetto Varchi argued against the then widely accepted view that monsters could be appreciated as evidence of nature's creativity. They were, he wrote, violations of nature's laws of regularity and uniformity that had been decreed by God. The proper reaction to them should be neither admiration nor fear but revulsion (Daston & Park, 2001).

In the 18th century, French scientist Etienne Geoffrey Saint-Hilaire offered a similar argument while refuting the idea of monstrosity through divine inspiration (Wilson, 1993). Thomson (1997) pointed to Saint-Hilaire's invention of the term "teratology"—the science of studying monsters—as an important milestone on the way to a medical model of normality. From this point forward, monsters were to be considered affronts to the ordered structure of nature. Writing on monsters took on a more somber tone that included exasperation with those who persisted in portraying them as marvels. Fontonelle maintained that, "philosophers are quite persuaded that nature does not play, that she always inviolably follows the same rules, and that all her works are, so to speak, equally serious" (quoted in Daston & Park, 2001, p. 205). Monsters could now be valued only for their ability to shed light on the universal, inflexible regularities—or norms—from which they deviated.

Darwin and other evolutionists added a new chapter to this corpus when they accepted and published secondary reports that suggested atypical persons were animal-human hybrids. In this they not only confirmed the legend of such monsters but also, through their use of the new language of evolutionary theory, provided it with an impressive scientific imprimatur.

The idea that evolution might just as well be regressive as progressive haunted Europeans in the late 19th century. Darwin and other evolutionists argued that human civilization was a recent and fragile development and that persons who were not fully evolved still lived in advanced societies. Evolutionary regression, or degeneration as it was more commonly referred to, produced beings who were developmentally arrested at a prior, lower stage of evolution: in these the human form served to conceal hereditary vices, marks of an atavistic beast within (Bowler, 1989; Talbot, 1898).

A fictional literature based upon this scientific perspective brought these anxieties to a wider reading audience. In addition to Stevenson's *Dr. Jekyll and Mr. Hyde*, degenerate humans with brute tendencies were the subjects of Bram Stroker's *Dracula,* Jack London's *Sea Wolf,* H. G. Wells' *Time Machine* and *Island of Dr. Moreau,* and William Butler Yeats' (1956) poem the "The Second Coming" in which a "rough beast" with a "lion body and head of a man," whose "hour come round at last" (p. 185) waits to be born.

Darwin's theory of evolution unintentionally appropriated Europe's long fascination with human-animal hybrids within the framework of its new biological paradigm. The failure of fossil evidence to provide a "missing link" between humans and animals led evolutionists to claim that persons with intellectual disabilities—whom they claimed were characterized by "low foreheads, small brains...projecting tusk-like teeth, suppressed noses, and other marks of arrested development"—could be studied instead (Lesley, 1868, p. 120). Vogt (1864), whose work was approvingly cited by Darwin, wrote that "microcephali and born idiots present as perfect a series from man to the ape as may be wished for" (pp. 194–195). In the second edition of *The Descent* Darwin (1874) himself wrote that "idiots"

often ascend stairs on all fours; are curiously fond of climbing up furniture or trees...resemble the lower animals in some other respects; thus several cases are recorded of their carefully smelling every mouthful of food before eating it. One idiot is described as often using his mouth in aid of his hands while hunting for lice. They are often filthy in their habits, and have no sense of decency; and several cases have been published of their bodies being remarkably hairy. (pp. 40–41)

The claim by Saint-Hilaire and others that human-animal monsters were "errors" for whom the proper reaction was revulsion, was reformulated in the languages of normality and evolution and, over time, applied to people with disabilities. If, as Darwin maintained, intelligence was the mark of fitness for human beings, then those deemed to have less of it were not only to be considered errors but also evolutionary waste (Gelb, 2008).

Human-animal composites, now scientifically labeled "idiots" rather than monsters, continued to turn up in Europe. The eminent British physician, Henry Maudsley (1873) claimed to have discovered an "animal type of brain in idiocy" (p. 47). He described one person with intellectual disability as having the face of an ape, another the face, neck and rudimentary wings of a goose, and a third having a strong resemblance to a bull.

Some classificatory systems of persons with intellectual disability were explicitly based upon similarity to animals. Greisenger created the category of "theroid idiots" (theroid: "suggestive of an animal; beastlike") to label persons he believed resembled beasts (Barr, 1904). In an influential turn-of-the-century textbook, Barr (1904) described "bestial temperament" as one of the identifying characteristics of "low grade moral imbeciles" (p. 81). He further claimed that persons with intellectual disabilities had exaggerated sexual desires due to the dominance of the "mere animal over the psychic forces" (p. 90). Another level in his classificatory scheme consisted of individuals who were "a kind of grotesque travesty of humanity...indeed it is only through imitation—a certain apishness—that they are brought to render in an automatic, rather than intelligent service in the humblest offices of household or nursery" (pp. 127–128). Finally, there were those he called "brother to the ox," useful only for brute, mindless work (Barr, 1904, p. 128).

Following the line of reasoning about monsters pioneered by Saint-Hilaire in the 18th century, Barr (1904) held persons with intellectual disabilities at a scientific distance: "idiocy is not a disease, it is a defect" (p. 130). His case descriptions display revulsion. About one man he wrote: "He has a frightful temper, is bestial and brutal to small children. These characteristics are indicated in his appearance; like that of a bull; and his degenerate mouth" (p. 77).

Frequently, references to the animal-like nature of persons with intellectual disabilities were less explicit, coded within the language of evolutionary theory's shadow, degeneracy theory. So-called "stigmata of degeneration" that supposedly revealed animal traits included asymmetry of the head or face, large and protruding (prognathous) jaws, long arms, open protruding mouths, suppressed noses, coarse skin, and unusually large or small ears (Pick, 1989). References to these stigmata are ubiquitous in clinical reports of the late 19th and early 20th centuries. A representative description stated: "Her face is very asymmetrical, she has defective enunciation, degenerate ears, and a prognathous jaw" (Barr & Maloney, 1920, p. 110).

Attitudes toward the deaf and deaf education were similarly affected by evolutionary theory and illustrate how a specific difference—the use of signs for communication rather than speech—became reframed as an abnormal mark of bestiality. Between 1817 and 1860, sign language had been an important tool of deaf education. Post-Darwin, in the 1860s, a campaign was launched to eliminate sign language and teach deaf children only through speech and lip reading. The new oralist generation of educators viewed sign language as a subhuman characteristic lower in the evolutionary scale than speech, a "tool of savagery" used by pre-human ape-like ancestors (Baynton, 1993, p. 100). Sign language, they reasoned, had lost out to oral language in the struggle for existence between modes of communication. Deaf persons who used sign language were like monkeys, or as one educator wrote in 1867, "creatures human in shape, but only half-human in attributes" (Baynton, 1993, p. 105). By 1900, 40% of deaf students received solely oral education and by the end of World War I, the figure was 80% (Branson & Miller, 2002).

The criminal anthropology of Cesare Lombroso, which combined evolution and degeneracy theory with the European animal-human myth, influenced scientists to seek and locate stigmata of degeneration in criminals, who, they then presumed, were intellectually disabled. Lombroso's insight came to him during a post-mortem analysis of a criminal that uncovered a skull depression similar to a structure found in rodents. He described the degenerate criminal, now understood as the ancestral beast lurking within the human breast, as possessed by "an irresistible craving for evil for its own sake, the desire not only to extinguish life in the victim, but to mutilate the corpse, tear its flesh, and drink its blood" (Lombroso, 1911/1972, pp. xiv–xv). In this way evil, as well as monstrosity, became associated with "abnormality."

In 1914 psychologist Henry Goddard testified with other expert witnesses for the defense in the trial of teenager Jean Gianini who had confessed to a murder. The defense wished to save him from the electric chair by proving that he was feeble-minded, that he felt and thought like an animal and, therefore, was not responsible for the crime. The defense attorney claimed that Jean was "a degenerate" whose head had a "napex" where the "bump of self-esteem should have been located" (Gelb, 1997a, p. 127). Other "stigmata of degeneracy" included distended fingers, abnormal toes, small hands, shambling gait, and a highly arched and narrow palate. The boy's motivation was said to be sub-human. He had hit his victim from behind, it was argued because that is what animal instinct directed him to do (Gelb, 1991).

Everyone Is Abnormal: Toward a Science of Individuality

To this point I have argued that abnormality is a highly loaded term that was deeply inflected with irrationality at its origin. In this concluding section I aim to show that an educational science based on the proposition that all learners are abnormal is a more valid description of reality than the view that they may be categorized as normal and abnormal. This dichotomy is not only loaded down with historical baggage but is also scientifically untenable.

The assumption that people who are labeled abnormal share common attributes that qualitatively distinguish them from people who are normal is a typological fallacy generated by a psychology focused on groups rather than individuals. The operative premise here has been that individual scores are less important than the average around which they are distributed. In constructing normality, an average individual, whose existence is entirely mythical (Dunlap, 1935/1982) is taken to be more real than the individual scores from which the average is computed. This assumption underlies the common practice of reporting statistically significant but meaningfully small differences between group means while ignoring the variation within groups. It explains also the long, fruitless quest in the field of intellectual disabilities to define and reliably distinguish between persons with "normal" and "abnormal" intelligence levels.

Francis Galton, the statistical pioneer who has been described as the person most responsible for promoting the use of the normal curve for purposes of classification (Diamond, 1980), was a firm believer in typology. He argued that "differences, say in stature, between men of the same race might theoretically be treated as if they were Errors made by Nature in her attempt to mould individual men of the same race according to the same ideal pattern" (Galton, 1962, p. 28). Galton acted out this belief by placing photographic exposures of Jewish people on top of one another in an attempt to identify the ideal type from which he (sadly) believed each individual deviated (Gilman, 1981).

However, if many human traits are uncorrelated, the presumption of the normal/abnormal typology collapses completely. Williams (1956/1982) computed the possibility of an individual being measured normal on mathematically uncorrelated traits if normality is defined as scoring within the values of 95% of the distribution. On the first score, by definition, 95% of the sample would be normal. With two measures the percentage drops to 90% and by the tenth measurement to 60%. If one hundred measurements were carried out only six-tenths of one percent of the sample would still be identified as normal. Williams (1956/1982) concluded

that the existence in every human being of a vast array of attributes which are potentially measurable (whether by present methods or not), and probably often uncorrelated mathematically, makes quite tenable the hypothesis that *practically every human being is a deviate in some respects.*...If this hypothesis is valid newborn children cannot validly be considered as belonging in either one of two groups, normal and abnormal. Substantially all of them are in a sense "abnormal." (p. 24, emphasis in the original)

Moreover, Williams tested the hypothesis by drawing and analyzing blood, urine, and saliva from twenty healthy "normal" men at weekly intervals for five or six weeks and then examining the pattern of results (a procedure seldom undertaken) as well as each individual result in comparison to (statistically) normal values. Many individual values were found to be above or below what was considered normal, but more significantly, the pattern of results for every single person was unique.

Typological thinking has been superseded in biology by "population thinking," which accepts the uniqueness of each individual. From this perspective, there is no underlying type from which individuals vary. Individual differences are not errors or deviations but the catalysts of species change and development (Mayr, 1976). The American psychologists who institutionalized the normal curve for categorizing people—James McKean Cattell, Lewis Terman, and Edward Thorndike—were strongly influenced by evolutionary theory, which they mistakenly assimilated to typological assumptions that the theory, properly understood, actually demolished. As Greenwood (1984) explained:

In view of evolutionary biology's emphasis on the continuous production of variability and the complex non-directional dialogue between the variability produced and the variety of environmental pressures to which these variants are subjected, it is clear that the claims of any of these [typological] theories to be evolutionary or to represent the findings of modern science are false. (p. 101)

Near the beginning of the 20th century belief in the normality/abnormality dichotomy led to the establishment of special classes for "mentally defective children" (Channing, 1900, p. 40), those who it was thought differed from the normal "type." This construction of difference drew down upon them the anxiety associated with evolutionary theory and its appropriation of hybrid animal/human monsters. The period known as "the myth of the menace of the feeble-minded" was followed by that in which educators, physicians and psychologists blamed many of society's ills upon persons with intellectual disabilities, understood, like, Jean Gianini, to be more like animals than humans (Trent, 1994). One hundred years later it is easier to identify the irrational associations and the scientific inadequacy of the practice of labeling children as abnormal for the purpose of teaching them. Educational policy and practice should now move beyond the age of monsters and anxiety toward full appreciation of the magnificent range of human diversity.

References

Altick, R. D. (1978). *The shows of London.* Cambridge, MA: Belknap.

Barr, M. W. (1904). *Mental defectives: Their history, treatment and training.* Philadelphia, PA: P. Blakiston's.

Barr, M. W., & Maloney, E. F. (1920). *Types of mental defectives.* Philadelphia, PA: P. Blakiston's.

Baynton, D. C. (1993). "Savages and deaf-mutes": Evolutionary theory and the campaign against sign language in the nineteenth century. In J. V. Van Cleve (Ed.), *Deaf history unveiled: Interpretations from the new scholarship* (pp. 92–112). Washington, DC: Gallaudet University Press.

Bowler, P. J. (1989). Holding your head up: Degeneration and orthogenesis in theories of human evolution. In J. R. Moore (Ed.), *History, humanity and evolution: Essays for John Greene* (pp. 329–353). Cambridge, UK: University of Cambridge Press.

Branson, J., & Miller, D. (2002). *Damned for their difference: The cultural construction of deaf people as disabled.* Washington, DC: Gallaudet University Press.

Channing, W. (1900). Special classes for mentally defective school children. *Journal of Psycho-Asthenics, 5,* 40–46.

Daston, L., & Park, K. (2001). *Wonders and the order of nature, 1150–1750.* New York: Zone.

Davidson, A. I. (1991). The horror of monsters. In J. J. Sheehan & M. Sosna (Eds.), *The boundaries of humanity: Humans, animals and machines* (pp. 36–67). Berkeley, CA: University of California.

Davis, L. (2006). Constructing normalcy: The bell curve, the novel, and the invention of the disabled body in the nineteenth century. In L. Davis (Ed.) [2d ed.], *The disability studies reader* (pp. 3–16). New York: Routledge.

Diamond, S. (1980). Francis Galton and American psychology. In R. W. Rieber and K. Salzinger (Eds.), *Psychology: Theoretical and historical perspectives* (pp. 43–55). New York: Academic.

Dunlap, K. (1935/1982). The average animal. In J. Hirsch and T. R. McGuire (Eds.), *Behavior genetic analysis* (pp. 29–31). Stroudsburg, PA: Hutchinson Ross.

Dury, R. (2004) (Ed.). Robert Louis Stevenson, *The strange case of Dr. Jekyll and Mr. Hyde.* Edinburgh, Scotland: Edinburgh University Press.

Elon, A. (1996). *Founder: A portrait of the first Rothschild and his time.* New York: Penguin.

Galton, F. (1962). *Hereditary genius: An inquiry into its laws and consequences.* New York: World.

Gelb, S. A. (1991). "Destitute of moral sense": Scientific testimony in the 1914 trial of a teenage teacher-murderer. Paper presented at the meeting of the History of Science Society, Seattle, WA.

Gelb, S. A. (1997a). The problem of typological thinking in mental retardation. *Mental Retardation, 35,* 448–457.

Gelb, S. A. (1997b). Sentence in sorrow: The role of asylum in the Jean Gianini murder defence. *Health & Place, 3,* 123–129.

Gelb, S. A. (2008). Darwin's use of intellectual disability in *The Descent of Man*. *Disability Studies Quarterly, 28*. Retrieved from http://www.dsq-sds.org/article/view/96/96, 27 August 2009.

Gilman, S. (1991). *The Jew's body*. New York: Routledge.

Greenwood, D. J. (1984). *The taming of evolution: The persistence of nonevolutionary views in the study of humans.*

Jahoda, G. (1999). *Images of savages: Ancient roots of modern prejudice in western culture*. New York: Routledge.

Lesley, J. P. (1868). *Man's origin and destiny*. Philadelphia, PA: Lippincott.

Lombroso, C. (1911/1972). Introduction. In Gina Lombroso-Ferrero, *Criminal man according to the classification of Cesare Lombroso* (reprint edition). Montclair, NJ: Patterson Smith.

Maudsley, H. (1873). *Body and mind* [2d ed.]. London: Macmillan.

Mayr, E. (1976). *Evolution and the diversity of life*. Cambridge, MA: Belknap.

Pender, S. (2000). In the bodyshop: Human exhibition in early modern England. In H. Deutsch and F. Nussbaum (Eds.), *Defects: Engendering the modern body* (pp. 96–126). Ann Arbor, MI: University of Michigan Press.

Pick, D. (1989). *Faces of degeneration: A European disorder c. 1848–1918*. Cambridge, UK: Cambridge University Press.

Rublack, U. (2005). *Reformation Europe*. New York: Cambridge University Press.

Talbot, E. S. (1898). *Degeneracy: Its causes, signs, and results*. London: Blackwood Scott.

Thomas, K. (1983). *Man and the natural world*. New York: Pantheon.

Thomson, R. G. (1997). *Extraordinary bodies: Figuring physical disability in American culture and literature*. New York: Columbia University Press.

Todd, D. (1995). *Imagining monsters: Miscreations of the self in eighteenth-century England*. Chicago: University of Chicago Press.

Trent, J. W. (1994). *Inventing the feeble mind: A history of mental retardation in the United States*. Berkeley, CA: University of California.

Vogt, C. (1864). *Lectures on Man: His place in creation, and in the history of the earth*. London: Longman, Green, Longman, and Roberts, Paternoster Row.

Williams, R. J. (1956/1982) Biochemical variation: Its significance in biology and medicine. In J. Hirsch and T. R. McGuire (Eds.), *Behavior-genetic analysis* (pp. 22–28). Stroudsburg, PA: Hutchinson Ross.

Wilson, D. (1993). *Signs and portents: Monstrous births from the Middle Ages to the Enlightenment*. London: Routledge.

Yeats, W. B. (1956). *The collected poems of W. B. Yeats*. New York: Macmillan.

Zook, P. (2004). Review of a lecture about medieval European perceptions of foreigners, heretics and monsters (Review of Debra Higgs Strickland Lecture at Hood College, February 29, 2000). Retrieved May 11, 2004, from http://novaonline.nvcc.edu/eli/eng251/monsters.htm.

SEVEN

"Requires Medication to Progress Academically": The Discursive Pathways of ADHD

Rebecca Rogers & Michael Mancini

Introduction

Evan Treader (pseudonym) is eleven years old and in fourth grade. He shows excitement about reading and writing. He proudly shows certificates that name him as "student of the week" and student with the "biggest smile." June, his mother, hangs his near perfect spelling tests on the refrigerator. The following statement is found on Evan's individualized education program (IEP): "Evan is a healthy boy. He does have fine motor difficulties and takes medication for attention deficit hyperactivity disorder (ADHD). He requires medication to progress academically." This statement foreshadows only one of the contradictions embedded in labeling Evan with ADHD. That is, this statement contradicts research indicating that, while stimulant medication such as Methylphenidate (i.e., Ritalin) can be effective in reducing the symptoms of ADHD, there is a lack of strong evidence that it improves academic performance in the moderate or long term, particularly with children who have been diagnosed with a co-occurring learning disability (LD) such as Evan (Carlson & Bunner, 1993; Conners, 2002; Snider, Frankenberger, & Aspenson, 2000).

During a visit to his house for data collection, Evan and I read a book together called *Stars in the Darkness*, a story about a young boy who comes up with a plan with his mother to save his brother from gang life and organize his neighbors to stand in peace. In response to the book, Evan shares the first time he saw a shooting, at six years old.

Like when I reached my house I saw lights….Like you just could hear, "Pow, Pow, Pow." I was running mad fast. I was out of breath.

He has witnessed several shootings since then. The obituaries of relatives and friends hang from their bedroom walls with scotch tape. He and his family attend funerals and court trials. Police, gangs and shootings are a regular part of their talk during play and over homework. When I ask him to tell me about his community he says, "I'm from a place where a lot of stuff goes on."

At the age of eleven years, he can rattle off the names of the gangs in Albany as if he were naming the teachers at his school: OGK. Bloods. Crips. Uptown. Downtown.

When I ask Eva, his four-year old sister, to make a prediction in the story she says, "they probably jumped him and cut him." They both tell me the details of fighting, but like his older sisters, when I ask him, "Why are people fighting?" he cannot tell me.

Evan is reading below grade level, as indicated in school reports and in my assessment of his reading. But there are inadequacies in what the school knows about the context of his life. He has a sophisticated sense of spatial literacy, knowing how to get around the city streets, both walking and in the car. He can negotiate four or five buttons on the remote control of his video game. He independently multi-tasks in this digital environment, and yet his IEP reads, "he has fine motor difficulties" and "needs one-on-one support in completing all tasks."

Evan was held back in first grade, given a disability classification of "speech and language impairment" and provided with an individualized education plan (IEP) for the following year that indicated he would receive special education services within the classroom setting. His classroom teacher recommended to June that she take him to a medical doctor to get evaluated for ADHD. Wanting to make sure Evan succeeded in school, June brought Evan to the health clinic. The same day he was given the label of ADHD and the associated 20 milligrams of Ritalin.

This was in 2005, fourteen years after ADHD was officially listed in the US education policy, the Individual with Disabilities Education Act under the category of "Other Health Impaired (OHI)." This change marked a significant shift in how ADHD was represented in educational policy and practice. The broadness of the language in the policy, coupled by the broad diagnostic criteria for ADHD, opened a window not just for services, but also the inclusion of psychotropic drugs in treating young children (Diller, 1998; Fitzgerald, 2008; Mayes & Erkulwater, 2008). The U.S. Drug Enforcement Agency estimates that the use of stimulant medications to treat ADHD has increased 600% from 1990 to 2000. Since 1990, when the Department of Education included ADHD as a disability under OHI, ADHD has also become the most commonly diagnosed psychiatric disorder of children in the US (DEA, 2000).

Given this backdrop, in this chapter we draw on the tradition of critical discourse studies to describe and interpret how normality is discursively constructed and reproduced across texts and contexts and over time.

The Over-labeling Phenomenon: Perspectives from Critical Discourse Studies

Both ADHD and LD, routine psychiatric labels used in US educational institutions, have been critiqued as being socially and politically constructed (Coles, 1987; Conrad, 2005; Danforth & Kim, 2008; Danforth & Navarro, 2001; Mehan, 1996; Sleeter, 1986; Reid, Maag, & Vassa, 1993). The American Psychiatric Association's *Diagnostic and Statistical Manual of Mental Disorders*, now in its fourth revised edition (DSM-IV-TR), has been described as the psychiatric profession's "bible" for determining what constitutes normality (Kutchins & Kirk, 1997). Lacking any evidence regarding the etiology of psychiatric disorders, the DSM has been critiqued for using an inherently subjective, quasi-scientific, and non-transparent process for determining what behaviors and symptoms constitute "abnormality," thereby ostensibly defining what should be considered "normal" behavior in a range of life domains (Wakefield, 2005). In addition, the DSM-IV, and the psychiatric profession as a whole, has been publicly critiqued recently for being influenced by pharmaceutical industry money and lobbying (Carey, 2006; Carey & Gardiner, 2008). One of the most contentious areas has been the over-diagnosis of children with psychiatric disabilities (i.e., ADHD) and their subsequent over-medication in education systems.

Teacher reports are used as a primary source of information when making a diagnosis of ADHD. Research has indicated that teachers are prone to over-identify children, particularly boys, with ADHD (Glass & Wegar, 2000; Nolan, Gadow, & Sprafkin, 2001). For instance, Nolan et al. (2001), found that when teachers used a DSM-IV referenced symptom inventory to screen 3,006 children, they identified almost 16% as having ADHD (over three times the national prevalence rate). More striking was the finding that screening prevalence rates for African American students were 39.5% (as much as 10 times the national average). The over-identification of disruptive behaviors as mental diseases using subjective measures, and the use of powerful stimulant medication such as Ritalin with toxic side effects as the primary means of treatment, may have implications for the long-term health and psychological integrity of many children—particularly children of color (Breggin, 1995).

Educational and medical labels, as social categories, gain legitimacy through discourse practices (Fairclough, 1995; Foucault, 1972; Wodak, 2001). Discourse practices are used to reference the mutually constitutive nature of discourses and social practices in the construction, reproduction and distribution of social categories, such as learning disabled and ADHD. Mandated by IDEA, schools move through common discursive pathways in classifying, labeling and sorting so-called deviant behaviors, whether learning disabilities, attention deficit hyperactivity disorder or behavioral disturbances such as oppositional defiant disorder (ODD). This has also been documented in the medical (Cordella, 2004), mental health (Floersch, Townsend, Longhofer, et al., 2009; Mancini & Rogers, 2007; Hall & White, 2005; Hall, Kirsi, Parton, & Tarja, 2003); and education literature (Mehan, 1996; Rogers, 2003). As discourse practices gain credibility they become naturalized and seen as "the ways things are" (Foucault, 1972).

Research Methods

Participants and research context

The Treaders are an African American family living in Sherman Hollows, an inner city neighborhood in upstate New York. The Treaders receive housing, income, and food assistance. June Treader, Evan's mother, dropped out of school at the end of ninth grade. She returned to adult education classes to work on her GED but never completed the program. She works as a housekeeper at a hotel and walks to and from work every day. Lester, Evan's father, has a GED and is trained as a plumber. He is a former member of the US Army. The family has an extended social network living in the neighborhood.

Evan Treader is the focal case study participant in this chapter. In 2000, when the original study ended, Evan was two years old. In 2009, Evan was eleven years old. Evan attended pre-school and has four sisters (ages three to twenty-one). Evan enjoys playing basketball, riding his bike, reading books and baseball cards, and playing video games. He is often in charge of watching his younger sister.

Evan attends a public elementary school, walking distance from his home. The school is one of the twelve elementary schools in an urban district that serves close to 9000 K-12 students. Eighty five percent of students at his school are eligible for free or discounted lunches. Ninety five percent of the students are children of color (African American, American Indian or Hispanic). The average student-teacher ratio is 12:1.

Teachers describe Evan as "functioning below grade level" and "shy but works well with adults." In first grade, Evan worked for twelve weeks with a Reading Recovery teacher and according to her reports, Evan "made slow, but good progress over twelve weeks. His reading level increased 3 Reading Recovery levels. He can independently write 35 words, up from 15 words. His confidence level has grown as well, and he now boasts of Reading Recovery level 4 books 'they're too easy!'" The teacher discontinued working with Evan because his teachers thought he was receiving sufficient supplemental services, and he was transitioning into a summer school program.

Between first and fourth grade, the teacher comments on his report cards repeatedly indicate that Evan is "below grade levels in all areas" and "he tries really hard to follow the classroom rules" and "at home please work on the basic sight words." Assessments of Evan's reading indicate that in fourth grade he is reading at the beginning of a second grade level. At school he receives speech and language therapy, remedial reading, occupational therapy and class-within-a class support from a special education teacher. At the end of fourth grade he was re-evaluated by a psychologist and placed in a self-contained special education classroom for his fifth grade year.

Data collection and analysis

The data for this chapter represent one piece of a longitudinal ethnographic study examining the literate lives and educational trajectories of the Treaders. The original study lasted from 1996 to 2001 (Rogers, 2003). From 2007 to 2009, I (Rebecca) returned to conduct a follow-up study with the Treaders. During this restudy, I was both a participant and observer during the study, spending four days at a time, four to six hours a day with the family every several months. I participated in the events of their daily lives —hanging around the house, going to the hospital to visit sick relatives, providing rides to the store and to social service agencies. I also served as a literacy teacher—carrying out reading and writing workshops in their home. I conducted interviews, collected documents and recorded observations in fieldnotes at home and in the community.

Specifically, for this chapter, we draw on fieldnotes, interviews with Evan and his mother and documents collected (e.g., report cards, IEPs, newspaper articles, notices of school meetings) and policy (the diagnostic criteria for ADHD from the DSM-IV and IDEA). Our analysis began with cruces or points of inconsistencies and contradictions that exist within or across texts and contexts. As I captured various data points about Evan's diagnosis of ADHD, I asked him and his mother to help me understand conflicting information.

After data collection ended we analyzed these texts more closely, drawing on orders of discourse (Foucault, 1972). Orders of discourse are the levels of discursive practices (textual, institutional frames and sociopolitical and historical contexts) that work together to create meaning (and order) in the social world.

We looked across three levels of discourse practice. First, is the textual level. This level includes the artifacts of Evan's history of participation in school and home (e.g., report cards, IEP, observations). Next, are the institutional frames that give order to the texts, making them into "regimes of practice" that circulate and are reproduced or challenged (e.g., testing, labels of ADHD and LD, special education services). The third level is the sociopolitical and historical contexts of the discursive practices (e.g., reauthorization of IDEA to include ADHD as OHI). At each of these levels, we moved through the stages of analyzing the linguistic composition of the text (e.g., coherence, syntax, lexical items) but our representation of the linkages between the discourse practices in this chapter stays closer to the level of orders of discourse than a textually oriented discourse analysis.

Defining (and Critiquing) Normality

Attention deficit hyperactivity disorder (ADHD)

To understand how the ADHD label arose in Evan's life, we need to understand the policy backdrop for the diagnosis and treatment of ADHD. According to the aforementioned DSM-IV-TR, ADHD is defined as a "persistent pattern of inattention and/or hyperactivity–impulsivity that is more frequently displayed and is more severe than is typically observed in individuals at comparable level of development." Furthermore, symptoms of inattention and hyperactivity must have been present before the age of seven, "some impairment" from symptoms must be present in at least two settings (e.g., school and home), and there must be "clear evidence of interference with developmentally appropriate social, academic, or occupational functioning. The disturbance must also not be better explained by another mental disorder (i.e., depression, schizophrenia, pervasive developmental disorder)" (APA, 2000).

Table 7.1 lists the symptoms needed in order to meet the inattentive and/or hyperactive criteria for ADHD. In order to receive an ADHD diagnosis, a person must exhibit six (or more) of either of the inattention and/or hyperactive symptoms for at least six months to a degree that is maladaptive and inconsistent with developmental level (APA, 2000). The most common treatment for ADHD is the use of the stimulant medication such as Methylphenidate (Ritalin) or mixed amphetamine (Adderall). While generally considered safe in low to moderate doses and effective for moderate to severe ADHD, stimulant medications have side effects that include disturbances in sleep and appetite as well as restlessness and anxiety. There is also evidence that stimulant medication for ADHD is misused and abused by adolescents and young adults since the effect of these medications is similar to cocaine and/or methamphetamine (Prudhomme-White, Becker-Blease & Grace-Bishop, 2006).

The individual with disabilities education act

The Individual with Disabilities Education Act (IDEA) is a U.S. federal law that requires public schools to provide all eligible children with disabilities a "free appropriate public education (FAPE) in the least restrictive environment appropriate to their individual needs." The law also requires public school systems to develop "Individualized Education Programs" (IEPs) that provide special education and other programs unique to each child. Children diagnosed with attention deficit hyperactivity disorder can receive IDEA services under the "Other health impairment" category defined as,

> [H]aving limited strength, vitality or alertness, including a heightened alertness to environmental stimuli, that results in limited alertness with respect to the educational environment, that:
>
> (i) Is due to chronic or acute health problems such as asthma, attention deficit disorder or attention deficit hyperactivity disorder, diabetes, epilepsy, a heart condition, hemophilia, lead poisoning, leukemia, nephritis, rheumatic fever, and sickle cell anemia; and
>
> (ii) Adversely affects a child's educational performance. (Authority: 20 U.S.C. 1401(3)(A) and (B); 1401(26)

Either A or B. 6 or more of the following symptoms have been present for at least 6 months to a point that is disruptive and inappropriate for developmental level. There must be clear evidence of impairment in social, school or work functioning.

A. Inattention	B. Hyperactivity
• Often does not give close attention to details or makes careless mistakes in school work • Often has trouble keeping attention on tasks or play activities • Often does not seem to listen when spoken to directly • Often avoids things that include mental activity for a long period of time • Often does not follow instructions • Is often easily distracted • Is often forgetful in daily activities	• Often fidgets with hands, feet or squirms in chair • Often gets up from seat • Often runs about or climbs when and where it is not appropriate • Often has trouble playing quietly • Is often "on the go" • Often talks excessively

Table 7.1: Diagnostic Criteria for ADHD from DSM-IV

The terms "attention deficit disorder or attention deficit hyperactivity disorder" were added to the official list of conditions that could make a child eligible for services under the "other health impairment" (OHI) category of IDEA in 1991. The diagnosis of ADHD was attached to existing "Other Health Impairments" in IDEA, naturalizing this new classification in an already established legislative history. Thus, at the same time establishing the disorder as a full-fledged, concrete disability and opening a pipeline of potential patients and pharmaceutical customers. This category was added under strong lobbying of ADHD advocacy groups (i.e., CHADD) heavily funded by the pharmaceutical industry (Diller, 1998). The results have not disappointed. Since 1991, there has been an explosion in the diagnosis of ADHD in children (Diller, 1998). Methyelphenidate has been the fourth most prescribed drug in the U.S. since 2003 (Prudhomme-White, Becker-Blease, & Grace-Bishop, 2006; Safer & Zito, 1996). It should be noted that the law does not require children diagnosed with ADHD to take medication for those disorders in order to receive special education services.

Evan's Case: The Acquisition of a Child by ADHD

In 2005, when Evan was in first grade, following the classroom teacher's recommendation, June brought Evan to the health clinic to get evaluated for ADHD. June reported that during this thirty-minute exam, the doctor asked her a series of questions about Evan's behavior at home and at school. Relying on June's reports, rather than on first-hand observations, the doctor labeled Evan as ADHD by the end of the exam and wrote a script for 20 milligrams of Ritalin to be taken twice a day. At first, Evan was given the Ritalin at home but after he did not take it several times, the school nurse was asked to administer the drug to Evan, twice a day (Interviews, 6/05).

Currently, there is not a conclusive test to determine if a person actually has the syndrome ADHD. No information regarding the etiology of the disorder exists. There are no medical tests that can conclusively confirm a diagnosis of ADHD. The professional is directed to come to a determination based on extraordinarily subjective criteria that can increase the chances of misdiagnosis either through a misinterpretation of behavior or bias. When looking at the criteria for diagnosis of ADHD, it is important to note the vague and ambiguous language (see Table 7.1). For instance, the qualifier "often" is open to the interpretation of the diagnostician. Further, the DSM-IV criteria indicate that "*some* impairment from the symptoms is present in two or more settings (e.g., at school/work, at home)" and that "*some* symptoms that cause impairment were present before age 7 years." Meanwhile, "symptoms" of the inattention and hyperactivity are often common behaviors of young people. Exactly at what point does being "on the go" or "disliking school" stop being commonly exhibited behaviors of children and start being evidence of a functional brain disorder? The APA provides guidelines that the "symptoms" must be "maladaptive and inconsistent with developmental level," but what exactly does that mean? While there are a number of standardized tests that measure the presence of ADHD such as the SNAP-IV (Swanson, Nolan, & Pelham, 1982) and the Vanderbilt ADHD diagnostic (Wolraich, Lambert, Doffing, et al., 2003) with demonstrated reliability and validity, it is unclear that professionals providing ADHD diagnoses actually use these instruments regularly.

In January 2008, June reported that Evan stopped taking medication because she did not have the money to pay for it. She explained, "The school nurse knows that he don't have his meds 'cause he don't have insurance." June reported that Evan no longer qualified for health insurance with social services. At three hundred dollars a refill, she cannot afford to pay for it. She also stated, "The school didn't call me to tell me he was acting up or nothing" (interview, January 2008). In other words, there was no evidence that his behavior was inappropriate while he was not taking his medication.

The fact that June consented to this medical (and associated educational label) but sometimes cannot afford the medicine is a conundrum because on the one hand she is agreeing to the label that the school recommended, but she is responsible for the "cure" (e.g., Ritalin). Because he does not receive the medication, he (and his mother) are seen as non-compliant and risk further stigmatization from the school. In either case, whether he takes the medication or not, the school is never critiqued nor held responsible for his learning. Rather, his learning difficulties are seen as a symptom of an underlying disability that can be treated with medication.

In December 2008, both June and Evan tell me that he doesn't take Ritalin at home, only in school. June stated, "He doesn't need it at home because at home he is up and running around and in school he can't do that." And my observations concur. I observe him at home playing video games for an hour, uninterrupted. I watch him playing basketball with keen attentiveness. He reads books with his sister, in his seat for twenty minutes (fieldnotes 12/08, 1/09). And yet the diagnosis of ADHD hinges on behaviors that are consistent in two contexts. After five months he was put back on the medication.

In Evan's case, what is problematic is the all too common way in which he is diagnosed as having ADHD and then subsequently medicated. Several problems exist with regard to the process of Evan's diagnosis. First, a pediatrician diagnosed Evan as having ADHD. This doctor is likely to have had little training in diagnosing psychiatric disorders. Second, the pediatrician relies solely on secondhand teacher accounts relayed through Evan's mother and his mother's observations of his behavior at home. At no point are Evan's behaviors actually observed by the diagnosing professional. Third, at no point is Evan given a standardized

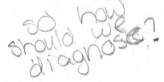

measure or test with proven reliability for the diagnosis of ADHD. Instead, the diagnosing professional relies on a subjective set of questions to the mother and child. Fourth, at no point does the diagnosing professional ask about situations or incidents in which Evan's behavior would be an exception to the ADHD diagnosis. Diagnosis according to the DSM is only focused on the existence of problem behaviors rather than assessing times when Evan exhibits positive or healthy behaviors (Saleebey, 2005). And fifth, repeated measures are not utilized. That is, Evan is diagnosed and placed on medication at once in the same visit. When examining the methods used by the diagnosing clinician, it is unclear whether Evan meets the full criteria for ADHD. In this scenario, the normal curve does not even apply as the distribution relies on the use of reliable and valid measurement over time. The methods used by the diagnosing pediatrician are neither reliable (consistent and stable) nor valid (actually measure ADHD). In this scenario we cannot even determine where Evan's behaviors fall on the normal distribution of behaviors because the methods for measuring those behaviors are unreliable and invalid. In other words, the basic rules of the normal distribution are violated.

As problematic is the lack of alternatives to medication. Can Evan's problems in school be corrected through behavioral strategies such as providing him with engaging and relevant materials, changes in diet, exercise, and sleep patterns? There is no evidence that this is even explored as an option or at least as an adjunctive approach. In fact, Evan's IEP states that he requires medication to progress academically, even though no evidence suggests that stimulant medication enhances academic performance (i.e., learning) (Carlson & Bunner, 1993; Conners, 2002; Snider, Frankenberger, & Aspenson, 2000).

Evan's perspective: "When I take it I be payin' attention."

In interviews in 2007 and 2008, I asked Evan about his diagnosis of ADHD, the medication he is taking and the effects of the medication. Table 7.2 shows comparative data across two years. In 2007, we have a 48-line discussion. A year later, we have a 141-line discussion. In 2007, he doesn't know the name of the medication but does tell me the time he needs to take it and that "I go down to the nurse and take my medication." The next year, he knows much more about the administration of the drug. He independently offers the name "Ritalin," tells me about the delivery mechanism (a capsule in the morning and a tablet in the afternoon), the dosage (30 milligrams). He also shows more independence in taking the drug. Whereas he referred to going to the nurse in the previous year, here he does not mention the nurse. Rather he states, "I take the capsule in the morning and the tablet in the afternoon...."

There are other differences across the two years. In 2007 he cites the reason he is taking Ritalin is because "sometimes I don't be payin' attention." In 2008 he

Interview December 2007	Interview December 2008
48 lines about medication and behaviors	141 lines about medication and behaviors
Doesn't know the name of the medication.	Independently offers "Ritalin" as the name of the medicine.
Administration of drug: I need it at like 12:00. I have one here and one at 12:00. I go down to the nurse and take my medicine."	Administration of drug: "I take the capsule in the morning and the tablet in the afternoon at 12 o'clock." Without prompting offers the time, delivery mechanism (capsule and tablet) and dosage (30 milligram).
Discusses why he is taking the medication: "Sometimes I don't be paying attention."	Discusses why he is taking the medication: B: How did you first get on Ritalin, do you remember? E: We, um, like went to the doctor and I was eating too much sugar. B: And what did the doctor say? E: I need to be on Ritalin. B: What did your E: My, um doctor gave me um like some pills B: Yeah E: Cause I'm hyper. B: Do you think you are hyper? E: (pause) No. B: No, why not? E: Because
How long he has been on Ritalin: "I don't know."	How long he has been on Ritalin: "A long time. Since I was in third grade."
Discusses effects of taking the drug: "When I take it I be payin' attention."	Discusses effects of taking the drug: "I can pay attention and stuff." "I feel calm."
Discusses effects of not taking the drug: "Like in the morning I be, like in the end of the day, my memory is confusing and I don't know what we be doing. Like last time I fell and I bumped my head on my friend's desk."	Discusses effects of not taking the drug: "I feel sad or mad. I feel mad when people mess with me."
"It tastes nasty."	"It tastes weird."

Table 7.2: Evan Talking about Ritalin across Two Years

states, "We, um, like went to the doctor and I was eating too much sugar." "What did the doctor say?" I asked him. Evan responded, "I need to be on Ritalin….My, um, doctor gave me like some pills…cause I'm hyper." Important to note that both years he uses language from the diagnostic criteria of ADHD. However, in 2008, the behavior he cites shifted from attention to hyperactivity. It is important to note that he does see himself as hyperactive.

When I ask him about how long he has been on it, his answer shifts from "I don't know" (2007) to "a long time" (2008). Both years he discusses the effects on him when he is on and off the drug. In 2007 when he is on Ritalin he says, "When I take it I be payin' attention." The next year he states, "I can pay attention and stuff" but also adds, "I feel calm."

He also notices changes in his mood and behavior when he is off the drug. In 2007 he cites changes in his memory at the end of the day "my memory is confusing and I don't know what we be doing." A year later he cites an emotional response when he is not taking the drug, "I feel sad or mad. I feel mad when people mess with me." He places responsibility for his cognition, emotions and actions on the medicine, not within himself.

Later in the interview I ask him if his schoolwork is too easy or too hard. He admits that when the work is too hard, he cannot pay attention. He states, "I like can't pay attention like can't read when there is like a long word." I ask, "Did you ever tell your teacher that?" His responds, "No, she say 'go try it.'" His comment suggests that he may not be reading appropriate level texts throughout the school day, one reason why it is hard for him to stay focused on reading.

Over time, Evan is much more detailed in his responses about ADHD, the language he uses to identify with characteristics of ADHD ("hyper") and the medication. And yet, while adults are responsible for the diagnosis and medication of Evan, the consequences of diagnosis are borne by Evan because he is the one who takes stimulant medication and bears the stigma of a psychiatric label.

June's perspective: "He's not in special ed., he just do special work."

After three years of receiving special education services, the labels and associated routines become so normalized to Evan and his mother they seem to fade away. Evan is receiving inclusive special educations services and the family interprets this as his being in a "regular classroom" and not classified as a special education student. When I ask June about his educational programs, she does not know that he has an IEP and is receiving special education services.

Rebecca: So he's in a special ed. program?
June: Uh uh. [no]
Rebecca : He's not in special ed?

June : No, he's in his regular class.

Rebecca: If he has an IEP, he's in special ed.

June: He's not in special ed., he just do special work.

Rebecca: I think he's in special ed.

June: They didn't say he was in special ed. He just do special work, like he do reading, writing, but he's in the normal class like the other kids.

Rebecca: Yeah he's in the regular class, but he has been in special education since first grade.

June: He's not in it no more.

Rebecca: He's not?

June: That was when he was in first grade. He's in the third grade now.

Rebecca: But they have special ed. services in the classroom, so he's in the regular classroom, but he has an IEP, an individualized education plan. He's still considered to be a special education student to get those services.

June: Yeah. But like I told them, it would probably be better for him 'cause the situation that he's off into. 'Cause he's hyper and they can put him in a little group with one or two so he can learn what he's supposed to learn. Every since then, he been doing real fine though.

Rebecca: So did you have to go to a meeting for him for that? Special ed.?

June: Uh huh.

Rebecca: You did? And what did they tell you at the meeting?

June: Nothing, they just said he doing real good. They did an evaluation of him last year.

June relies on the linguistic markers "regular" and "special education" to understand Evan's placement and progress in school. The school, however, does not routinely use the term special education in official and unofficial reports of his progress. Further, because he receives inclusive special education services, June assumes that Evan is in a "normal class." Her use of the term "normal" suggests that a self-contained class would be "abnormal." Indeed, June has a history of being critical of the school defining her children through disability classifications (Rogers, 2003). However, she readily identifies Evan as "hyper" and agrees that small group instruction works well for him. She does not realize that the diagnosis of ADHD falls under IDEA as OHI and this qualifies Evan for additional special education services.

His report cards during the 2007-2008 academic year (third grade) use equally ambiguous language. The teacher wrote:

> We are concerned with Evan's progress in the integrated setting. Evan was recently evaluated by the school psychologist in order to help determine an appropriate placement for next year.

Under "grade placement for next year" is written "self contained." Here, like elsewhere in the report card the words "special education" are not used. This, combined with the inaccurate assumption recorded on his IEP that, "he requires medication in order to progress academically," makes it difficult for June to understand how to make the best educational decisions for Evan.

Conclusion

This case study demonstrates that normality is a shifting social construction comprised of several competing interests. Disability rights groups and parent advocacy groups certainly seek to end discrimination and ensure that all people with disabilities have a right to an adequate public education. However, at the same time, pharmaceutical companies and mental health professions also want to expand their influence and power (Saleebey, 2005). City, state, and federal politicians, largely funded by business interests, seek to explain the achievement gap as resulting from individual differences, rather than address the complex institutionalized systems that maintain inequality. And schools want some way to compensate for shrinking budgets, overwhelmed teachers, and overcrowded classrooms. To these competing and interrelated interests, children like Evan are social commodities. They are the raw material needed to satisfy the varying needs of these groups. Whether or not Evan actually suffers from a medical condition called ADHD is beside the point. The power, resources and influence that his mere diagnosis provides to these groups is all that matters and is what will keep Evan classified, in perpetuity, as "disordered" (e.g., Conrad & Potter, 2000).

The subjective, deficit-dominated discourse used to classify Evan's behavior is unmoored from any scientific etiology and as a result there is no way to determine whether Evan's behavior is the result of an internal, medical condition or a natural response to his environment (Wakefield, 2005). Despite this, the powerful institutions described above have manufactured an ideology that learning disabilities and attention deficit disorders are chronic medical conditions requiring pharmaceutical intervention and that the process of diagnosing these conditions is scientifically reliable, objective and valid. Through the use of their institutional power, these groups have used these discourses of deficit to create policies, laws and agreements that label, classify, position and treat Evan's disability (Saleebey, 2005). There is evidence that Evan, his teachers and his mother have already begun the slow process of internalizing his diagnosis so that it becomes a part of his overall identity and thereby accepting that mythology that his behaviors, feelings and belief stem, at least in part, from his diagnosis and must be managed by medications. Evan and his mother no longer question the scientific validity of his diagnosis. It is accepted as a fact that Evan will struggle with this condition forever. Evan, thus, becomes a potential lifelong customer to the pharmaceutical industries that played a silent role in his diagnosis (e.g., Conrad & Potter, 2000).

The discourses of disability and deficit place the blame of Evan's poor academic performance squarely on his shoulders by stating that he requires medication to achieve academically. By labeling Evan as abnormal, the environmental contexts in which Evan lives, learns and plays are absolved of any responsibility. Evan's abnormality means that his teachers, school, family, and neighborhood must be normal. The responsibility for change is his alone. Furthermore, the discourse of deficit ignores Evan's ability to negotiate an environment wrought with peril on a daily basis. His strengths in these areas are never taken into account because they are not valued skills.

Evan's case leads us to question the conflation of behaviors, medication, learning trajectories and the ways in which a growing number of families and children are "forced to consume policy" (Woodside-Jiron, 2003, p. 180). Indeed, the ways in which public policies are interpreted in the everyday life of school socializes us into what is thinkable and unthinkable, what is normal and what is abnormal (Scollon, 2008). While we focus on addressing the apparent epidemic of attention and behavioral disturbances of children in schools as solely a medical phenomenon, we fail to address the societal conditions of violence, crime, unemployment, lack of healthcare, poverty and the hopeless, anger and despair that can result.

Author's Note

The author wishes to acknowledge the funding received through the NCTE Research Foundation that supported the research reported on in this chapter.

References

American Psychiatric Association, (2000). *The diagnostic and statistical manual of mental disorders* [4th ed.; text revised]. Washington, DC: American Psychiatric Association Press.

Breggin, P. R. (1995). The hazards of treating "attention-deficit/hyperactivity disorder" with methylphenidate (Ritalin). *Journal of College Student Psychotherapy, 10*(2), 55–72.

Carey, B. (2006, April 20). Study finds a link of drug makers to psychiatrists. *The New York Times*. Retrieved December 19, 2008 from http://www.nytimes.com/2006/04/20/health/20psych.html?scp=3&sq=tufts+drug+firms+&st=nyt.

Carey, B & Gardiner, H. (2008, July 12). Psychiatric group faces scrutiny over drug industry ties. *The New York Times*. Retrieved December 19, 2008 from http://www.nytimes.com/2008/07/12/washington/12psych.html#

Carlson, C. L & Bunner, M. R. (1993). Effects of methylphenidate on the academic performance of children with attention-deficit hyperactivity disorder and learning disabilities. *School Psychology Review, 22*(2), 184–198

Coles, G. (1987). *The learning mystique: A critical look at "learning disabilities."* New York: Pantheon.

Conners, C. K. (2002). Forty years of methylphenidate treatment in attention-deficit/hyperactivity disorder. *Journal of Attention Disorders, 6* (suppl. 1), S17–S30.

Conrad, P. (2005). The shifting engines of medicalization (The Leo G. Reader Award lecture), *Journal of Health and Social Behavior, 46,* 3–14.

Conrad, P. & Potter, D. (2000). From hyperactive children to ADHD adults: observations of the expansion of medical categories. *Social Problems, 47*(4), 559–582.

Cordella M. (2004). "You know doctor, I need to tell you something: A discourse analytical study of patient's voices in the medical consultation." *Australian Review of Applied Linguistics, 27*(2):92–109.

Danforth, S. & Kim, T. (2008). Tracing the metaphors of ADHD: A preliminary analysis with implications for inclusive education. *International Journal of Inclusive Education, 12*(1), 49–64.

Danforth, S. & Navarro, V. (2001). Hyper talk: Sampling the social construction of ADHD in everyday language. *Anthropology and Education Quarterly, 32*(2), 167–190.

Diller, L. H. (1998). *Running on Ritalin: A physician reflects on children, society, and performance in a pill.* New York: Bantam Doubleday.

Drug Enforcement Agency (DEA) (2000). Congressional Testimony. Hearings before the Committee on Education and the Workforce: Subcommittee on Early Childhood, Youth and Families. (Testimony of Terrance Woodworth). Downloaded on 7/6/2009 from: http://www.justice.gov/dea/pubs/cngrtest/ct051600.htm

Fairclough, N. (1995). *Critical discourse analysis: The critical study of language.* New York: Longman.

Fitzgerald, T. (2008). Controlling the black school age male: psychotropic medications and the circumvention of public law 94–142 and Section 504. *Urban Education.* Retrieved December 8, 2008 from http://uex.sagepub.com/cgi/content/abstract/44/2/225.

Floersch, J., Townsend, L., Longhofer, J., et al. (2009). Adolescent experience of psychotropic treatment. *Transcultural Psychiatry, 46*(1), 157–179.

Foucault, M. (1972). *The archeology of knowledge.* London: Tavistock.

Glass, C. S. & Wegar, K. (2000). Teacher perceptions of the incidence and management of attention deficit hyperactivity disorder. *Education, 121*(2), 412–421.

Hall, C. & White, S. (2005). Looking inside professional practice: Discourse, narrative and ethnographic approaches to social work and counseling. *Qualitative Social Work 4,* 379–390.

Hall C., Kirsi, J., Parton, N., & Tarja, P. (eds.). (2003). *Constructing clienthood in social work and human services: Interaction, identities and practices.* London: Jessica Kingsley.

Kutchins, H. & Kirk, S. (1997). *Making us crazy. DSM: The psychiatric bible and the creation of mental disorders.* New York: Free Press.

Mancini, M. & Rogers, R. (2007). Narratives of recovery from serious psychiatric disabilities: A critical discourse analysis. *Critical approaches to discourse analysis across disciplines, 1*(2), 35–50.

Mayes, R. & Erkulwater, J. (2008). Medicating kids: Pediatric mental health policy and the tipping point for ADHD and stimulants. *Journal of Policy History, 20* (3), 309–343.

Mehan. H. (1996). The construction of an LD student: A case study of the politics of representation. In M. Silverstein & G. Urban (Eds.), *Natural Histories of Discourse,* 253–276. Chicago: University of Chicago Press.

Nolan, E. E., Gadow, K. D., & Sprafkin, J. (2001). Teacher reports of DSM-IV ADHD, ODD and CD symptoms in schoolchildren. *Journal of the American Academy of Child and Adolescent Psychiatry, 40*(2), 241–249.

Polanczyk, G., Silva de Lima, M., Horta, B. L., Biederman. J., & Rohde, L. A. (2007). The worldwide prevalence of ADHD: A systematic review and metaregression analysis. *American Journal of Psychiatry, 164*(6), 942–948.

Prudhomme-White, B., Becker-Blease, K.A., & Grace-Bishop, K. (2006). Stimulant medication use, misuse and abuse in an under-graduate and graduate student sample. *Journal of American College Health, 54*(5), 261–268.

Reid, R., Maag, J., & Vasa, S. (1993). Attention deficit hyperactivity disorder as a disability category: A critique. *Exceptional Children, 60*, 198–214.

Rogers, R. (2003). *A critical discourse analysis of family literacy practices: Power in and out of print.* Mahwah, NJ: Lawrence Erlbaum.

Safer, D. J. & Zito, J. M. (1996). Increased methylphenidate usage for attention deficit disorder in the 1990s. *Pediatrics, 98,* 1084–1089.

Saleebey, D. (2005). Balancing act: Assessing the strengths in mental health practice. In S.A. Kirk (Ed). *Mental disorders in the social environment: Critical perspectives* (pp. 23–44). New York: Columbia University Press.

Scollon, R. (2008). *Analyzing public discourse: Discourse analysis in the making of public policy.* New York, New York: Routledge.

Sleeter, C. (1986). Learning disabilities: The social construction of a special education category. *Exceptional Children, 53*, 46–64.

Snider, V. E., Frankenberger, W., & Aspenson, M. R. (2000). The relationship between learning disabilities and attention deficit hyperactivity disorder: A national survey. *Mental Retardation and Learning Disability Bulletin, 28*(1), 18–38.

Swanson, J. M., Nolan, W., & Pelham, W. E. (1982). SNAP rating scale. Educational Resources in Education, ERIC.

Wakefield, J. (2005). Disorders vs. problems in living in DSM: Rethinking social work's relationship with psychiatry. In S. A. Kirk (Ed.), *Mental disorders in the social environment: Critical perspectives*, 83–95. New York: Columbia University Press.

Wodak, R. (2001). The discourse historical approach. In R. Wodak & J. Meyer (Eds.), *Methods of critical discourse analysis*, 63–94. London: Routledge.

Wolraich, M. L., Lambert, W., Doffing, M. A., et al. (2003). Psychometric properties of the Vanderbilt ADHD diagnostic parent rating scale in a referred population. *Journal of Pediatric Psychology, 28*, 559–568.

Woodside-Jiron, H. (2003). Language power and participation: Using critical discourse analysis to make sense of public policy. In R. Rogers (Ed.), *An introduction to critical discourse analysis in education*, 173–205. Mahwah, NJ: Lawrence Erlbaum.

EIGHT

Assessment and the Policing of the Norm

Eileen W. Ball & Beth Harry

The hegemony of the norm in American education is nowhere so evident and so dangerous as in the process for assessing children for placement in special education programs. A three-year ethnographic study (Harry & Klingner, 2006) of the placement process for children in high incidence categories, learning disabilities (LD), cognitive disabilities (CD), and emotional/behavioral disorder (EBD), noted an explicit faith in assessment as the scientific gateway to special education. The vast majority of school personnel in the study referred to a child's special education placement as the appropriate outcome of a relatively infallible testing process based on developmental and achievement norms. A typical expression of this sentiment was, "You meet criteria or you don't meet criteria. The testing stands on its own" (p. 103). The findings of that study largely contradicted this belief, showing that the assessment process was fraught with pre-conceived notions about children and their families, excessive pressure from external forces such as state-wide testing, as well as the opinions of referring teachers, and a pervasive, deep-seated belief that the source of children's difficulties lay within the children. Because of this belief, child-study teams paid little or no attention to the classroom context from which children were referred; rather, they relied on the testing process to identify presumed intrinsic deficits and weed out from general education those children whom the testing proved did not "belong."

In this chapter we take issue with this unquestioned belief as it applies to the two most crucial aspects of cognitive testing—IQ and academic achievement. In the minds of those who believe in the infallibility of IQ and achievement tests, a child who is found wanting in either of these areas crosses over the elusive border between normalcy and disability. Whether the testing process is used to determine eligibility for LD, CD, or EBD placements, it is dependent on deeply flawed assumptions. Our central argument is that standardized testing and the assumption that intelligence and cognitive ability are fixed traits that are "normally distributed" among all populations blind us to the power of context and culture both in children's display of their knowledge and in professionals' interpretations of those displays. Despite the introduction of increased flexibility in determining learning disabilities in the 2004 re-authorization and 2006 amendment of the Individuals with Disabilities Education Act (IDEA 2004), the belief in tests as infallible and just determiners of a child's placement seems to remain intact (Holdnack & Weiss, 2006). In order to limit the scope of our discussion, we focus on cognitive testing, although it is important to note that the belief in standardized norms permeates educational thought so thoroughly that it is also applied even to social behavior—arguably, the most ambiguous and culturally relative area of human life.

Referral for special education services

In response to findings released by the Commission on Excellence in Special Education (U.S. Department of Education, Office of Special Education and Rehabilitative Services, 2002) and to mounting criticism from a number of parents, educators, and administrators, the re-authorization of the Individuals with Disabilities Education Act (2004) now provides states and local education agencies (LEAs) the authority to choose alternative means of assessment rather than the traditional comprehensive individual assessments administered during the 60-day evaluation period for special education placement. The amendment permits states to opt for an alternative intervention process, known as "Response to Intervention" (RTI), a process of assessment designed to ensure that each student has had the opportunity to learn through the delivery of appropriate, adequate, and scientifically proven effective instruction. According to this model, a child is referred for special education evaluation only after failing to make adequate progress despite increasingly specialized tiers of intervention. The great advantage of this approach is the provision of increased opportunities for a child to learn the desired concepts and skills and for teachers to gain a more valid assessment of the child's understanding and performance. Still, a murky area remains: On what criteria will we provide additional supportive services after a child has failed to respond adequately to these increased learning opportunities?

The implementation of the RTI process currently shows great variability. Although state multidisciplinary teams are encouraged to consider multiple tools that are research based, relevant to each child's needs, and designed to inform and improve students' academic achievement (Honigsfeld, 2009), assessment choices and the use of pre-referral interventions vary greatly in and among states and LEAs. In fact, several studies indicate varied foci, concerns, and results across practices (see Schon, Shaftel, & Markham, 2008). Furthermore, in a study of English language learners (ELLs), Klingner, Artiles, and Méndes Barletta (2006) found that once a child is referred to a team, the student still may have a greater than 50% chance of being placed in special education whether or not identified language issues truly impact their academic achievement. These researchers contend that this pattern occurs because teachers believe they have already tried all possible interventions before they referred the student to the team.

The systematic documentation of a student's response to effective interventions holds great promise for a more individualized and meaningful assessment of a child's needs as well as for the provision of appropriate services. Yet, a summary of research on RTI (Hoover, Baca, Wexler-Love, & Saenz, 2008) indicates that even though the majority of states are recommending some use of RTI, only one-third plan to use it as a replacement for the IQ/discrepancy model, and many states cannot confirm if their districts are implementing any consistent and clear interpretation of the model.

As we see it, a large part of the problem is that the field of education has a long history of commitment to a vision of teaching and learning based on the assumption that intelligence and many other human characteristics are distributed along the "normal curve." If policy makers and teachers believe this, then it will be difficult for them to relinquish their reliance on standardized measures for the open-ended hope that authentic assessment and instruction might provide an avenue toward success for the majority of students (Dykeman, 2006). In effect, if more students were to be successful and progress academically, the normal curve, if one exists, would become negatively skewed with relatively few low values and would be "normal" no more.

The (Il) Logic of the Normal Curve

There exists a provocative historical and mathematical argument challenging the belief that intelligence and school achievement are distributed in a manner resembling a bell-shaped or normal curve (see also Dudley-Marling & Gurn and Gallagher, this volume). McDermott (1987) has long asserted that failure is literally built into our system of education:

> Failure is waiting every morning in every classroom in America; before children or their teachers arrive, failure is there...if American English delivers such a rich vocabulary for labeling and disabling children, often despite proof that they can learn just about anything while not in school, why would we trust that same language to deliver useful words..." (p. 363).

Fendler and Muzaffar (2008) have argued convincingly that the bell curve is not a representation of real things in nature. In a careful historical analysis, these authors trace the invention of the famous curve (attributed to Johann Fredrick Carl Gauss) back to coin tossing studies in the 18th century. In these studies the limit of coin tossing, a binomial distribution, demonstrated that with sufficient multiple trials the number of "heads" tossed will fall along a bell-shaped curve distribution. A second route to the inevitable "anointing" of the normal curve was the result of astronomers who systematically graphed multiple measurements of distances to the stars and found that these measurements distributed "normally" (see Dudley-Marling & Gurn and Gallagher, this volume). In both these cases the normal distribution represents probabilities based on an average. From these recorded observations came the construction of the concept of the "The Average Man." Thus, the normal curve was reified in the social sciences, and it came to be applied to the representation of all manner of social and human phenomena. As a result, standardized tests, which purport to measure "average" behaviors, are routinely revised until results conform to a bell curve.

More than three decades ago, the National Association of Elementary School Principals devoted two issues of its journal, *Principal*, to the subject of standardized testing (Houts, 1977). Morrison's essay on the topic described the process this way:

> ...these [IQ] tests have been *selected* after trial for observed conformity with the normal distribution. Items that showed little correlation with the overall expectations, or with results of previous tests of the kind, have been systematically excluded.... For example, the spread of results for young children given the Stanford Binet test in the 1960 edition was too large compared with the results for other ages. Thereupon, the scoring scheme was adjusted... (The designers call this an "adjustment for a typical variability"). (1977, pp. 85–86)

It is our opinion that few educators who believe in the reality of the normal curve and standardized testing are aware of its history and the process that makes it work. This misconstrued concept is so woven into our sense of the world that even arguments against the value of the bell curve fall victim to the continuing assumption that it is based on reality. Fendler and Muzaffar (2008), for example, contend that most critiques argue against the normal curve on the basis of equity arguments, rather than challenging the validity of the concept itself which seems to be taken for granted.

Ignoring context and culture

The inappropriate application of normal curve thinking to human groups is compounded by the complexity of the impact of enculturation and socialization upon various groups. To begin with, there is no such thing as a homogenous human group. While the standardizing process may include a representative percentage of ethnic groups, these may not be representative of those groups; that is, like the dominant white majority, ethnic groups are not monolithic but are complicated by socioeconomic status (SES), geographic location, immigration/acculturation status, language background, and racial heritage. For example, an individual designated "Hispanic/Latino," "Black," or "Asian" may be of any national heritage, any racial mixture, any social class level, any level of acculturation to U.S. culture, and any level of English language acquisition. The vast range of backgrounds among individuals from any of these groups makes it impossible to assume that inclusion of some of their members in a standardization sample represents a meaningful estimate of the skills of that "group."

This is important because the standardizing process cannot in any way address the numerous intangible aspects of human response to discrimination and marginalization and its effects on identity. Several scholars have studied the way these processes affect academic achievement, particularly for African American students, who are known to score, on average, 15 points lower on IQ tests. Specifically, Fordham (1988) and Ogbu (1987) have focused on the pressure African American students may feel to present a "raceless" persona or to engage in "acting white" in order to be successful and the likely resistance they express as a result. Beale-Spencer, Dupree, and Hartmann (1997), however, emphasized that an understanding of the broader ecological context of "resistance" is more helpful than the "acting white" argument, which seems to place most of the burden on individual whim rather than a response to racism. Steele's (1997) research with African American college students, meanwhile, has brought these concerns directly to the question of how black males perform academically under the threat of perceived stereotypes and has persuasively demonstrated the depressing effect stereotyping has on students' scores.

These concerns highlight the inadequacy of the assumption that individuals who fall on the boundaries of the "normal curve" are deficient in development or skills, since the curve's reliance on discrete, measurable categories cannot capture the impact of a range of social, cultural and psychological distinctions within groups. This inadequacy is perhaps most glaring in special education's historical reliance on IQ testing as a means of determining eligibility for services.

Embedded Privilege in IQ Testing

The most widely known standardized measure is the IQ score. The extent of reification of this concept is evident in the common parlance by which people speak of an individual as "having an IQ of...," with no acknowledgment of the fact that this measure is simply a score on a particular test. This belief continues despite decades of work demonstrating the cultural and experiential basis of IQ testing (e.g., Gould, 1996; Houts, 1977; Murdoch, 2007; Shelton, 1996). The report of the National Academy of Sciences' study of disproportionality in special education (Donovan & Cross, 2002) described these tests as "tests of general achievement reflecting broadly culturally rooted ways of thinking and problem solving" (p. 284). Yet these tests continue to be seen by school personnel as the "rock" of special education placement (Harry, Klingner, Sturges, & Moore, 2002).

What does IQ testing look like in practice? Consider the case of Kanita, a seven-year-old African American girl in the Harry and Klingner (2006) ethnographic study referred to earlier. As a first grader attending an elementary school in a historically black, low-income urban neighborhood, Kanita was referred for evaluation because of challenging behavior and then given a range of projective tests as well as the WISC III. The detrimental process by which the projective tests were administered has been described elsewhere (Harry et al., 2002), highlighting the alienating effect the questions about her family had on this child. Here, we focus on the "intelligence testing" from which Kanita emerged with an overall score of 107, with 118 on the "freedom from distractibility" scale. We note first, that Kanita's unfamiliarity with items on the test was evident in several sub-tests. For example, in the "what's missing?" questions, she could not identify what was missing from the piano (black keys), and in the information sub-test her confusion about the names of the seasons (winter, spring, summer, fall) illustrated her inability to recall "spring" after figuring out the other three. Who could be surprised at this, knowing that Kanita has lived her short seven years in Miami, where spring is undoubtedly the most elusive of seasons. We turn our focus, however, to this child's responses on the "Similarities" sub-test of the WISC III, with the intent of highlighting: (a) the discrepancy between the child's and the psychologist's expectations for some of the questions; and, (b) Kanita's quick-wittedness in adjusting her answers once she was given a clue as to the types of answers that were expected. In the following excerpt, the psychologist explained that the child should identify similarities between named items. The dialogue moved along quickly, as follows:

Psychologist (P)	**Kanita**
Red, blue?	*colors*
Milk, water?	*you drink 'em*
Candle, lamp?	*you can see by them*
Shirt, shoe?	*you wear 'em*
Piano, guitar?	*you play 'em*
Wheel, ball?	*play with it*
Play with it?	*bounce*
Apple, banana?	*food*

(P: That's a very good answer!
A 2 point answer!)

Cat, mouse?	*animals*
Elbow, knee?	*body parts*
Telephone, radio?	*you listen to 'em*
(P: gives her a prompt)	*(no answer)*
Anger, joy?	*I dunno*
Family, tribe?	*huh?*
Family, tribe?	*I dunno*
Painting, statue?	*you can paint both of them*
Ice, steam?	*they both melt*

It doesn't require a sophisticated analysis to see what was happening here. The test requires definitions based on shared properties of the items, not on their uses. Kanita starts off well, giving the desired answer for *red and blue*, which required that she identify color as the shared property. From items 2 through 5, she shifts to definitions based on her perception of the items' uses—what she does with them. At the seventh item, food, she spontaneously returns to the desired definition by properties, and the psychologist (breaking with the test protocol) responds with great enthusiasm. Kanita, obviously catching on to the clue, stays with this perspective and "correctly" defines the next two items by their properties—animals, body parts. When presented with a more challenging pair of items—telephone/radio, whose common properties are not so readily evident—she shifts back to functional definitions, fails to respond to the psychologist's prompt, gives up on the next two items, and then returns to her functional definitions for the final two pairs.

According to Piaget's (1971) stage theory of cognitive development, the ability to define items or demonstrate skills in more abstract and decontextualized ways indicates higher levels of cognitive development. While there has been much debate about the cross-cultural accuracy of this belief (Glick, 1975; Mpofu, 2004; Rogoff, 2003; Serpell, 2000), let us, for the moment, accept this criterion for the assigning of points on these test items. Reflecting on Kanita's shifting strategies, it is evident that, first, she knew how to identify the properties of the items, as shown in her initial response. We do not know why she shifted to functional definitions from item 2 onward, but we could speculate that, having no reason to know whether her answer was acceptable, she tried another tactic. Or, she may just have been saying the first thing that occurred to her. What is clear, however, is that the psychologist's reinforcement of a "very good" answer prompted her immediately to display the desired cognitive process. Kanita's behavior here illustrates an excellent example of what Snow (1994) calls "reciprocal interaction" in cognitive processing. According to Snow:

A person working on a task learns to change strategy, which affords use of different abilities in the task performance...the task changes as the abilities and strategies brought to bear on it change. Thus, a person who shifts from verbal analysis to spatial visualization midway through a task has changed the task psychologically. A task that affords such learning has changed the person psychologically....A person who learns to shift strategy in one task may start a new task with the new strategy, but also with the transferable idea that strategy shifting sometimes helps. (pp. 6–7)

The testing process in which Kanita was engaged did not seek or allow such reciprocity, however. Kanita's responses suggest that she was spontaneously engaging in such shifting but became more deliberate in response to the psychologist's reinforcement of a correct answer. What might her score have been like if positive feedback had been offered at Kanita's very first answer?

This vignette tells us as much about the testing process as it does about Kanita—perhaps more. First, how easy it would be to underestimate Kanita's abilities based on this task. Second, Kanita's experience reveals much about the power of a reciprocal process in testing: One could easily view the psychologist's prompt as an example of Vygotskyan (1978) instruction in the zone of proximal development or, as we will discuss later, a form of dynamic assessment originally outlined by Feurstein, Rand, and Hoffman (1979). Third, this example highlights the injustice done to a child by assuming that she should know from the start what kind of answer is required and then penalizing her when she does not conform to the psychologist's expectations. If it took only one reinforcing response to teach Kanita what was expected, how much better might she have done on this test with some simple coaching as to the requirements? And why should she not receive such coaching? Her same age peers with college educated parents would probably have learned through their parents' daily questioning exactly how to respond to such a question. Research by Heath (1986) and others have shown how this type of questioning at home prepares the children of white, middle-income families for such school tasks as contrasted with the more practical, unidirectional discourse style traditionally used by African American parents who have limited formal education.

A discussion by Robinson, Zigler, and Gallagher (2000) shows how easy it is for researchers to conflate discourse styles with intelligence. In an otherwise even handed discussion of differences in children's cognitive domains, Robinson et al. (2000) offer an example of executive control skills in verbal-abstract tasks by a six-year-old who was asked to define a series of words. The child said, "Do you want me to tell you the complicated way or just the simple way?" The child then explained that "complicated" meant "giving examples and more than one meaning." (p. 1417). The authors of the article concluded that, "It requires little stretch of the imagination to point to such self-awareness and management skills as representing the central core of intelligence" (p. 1417). We disagree. It is not in any way self-evident that "intelligence" is at the heart of such skills. Rather, we would argue that this child has either been raised in an environment where such forms of discourse are common at the dinner table and in parent-child interactions or the child has been explicitly schooled in such thinking. Instead of seeing this discourse style as an indicator of intelligence, we contend that it is a matter of experience with a particular style of discourse. If the test privileges the experience of such children, why shouldn't children who have not had that advantage receive instruction in what is expected of them? Even without the embedded instruction in valued discourse styles in a family setting, we suspect that a child like Kanita would probably not take long to learn that she should approach a question by "giving examples and more than one meaning." Further, we doubt that it would take her more than one opportunity to see a piano up close to remember that there are black keys interspersed among the white keys.

These reports call into question the prerogative of privacy held by the makers of tests like the Wechsler (2003). It seems clear that one reason that lay people cannot access these tests is that their release to the general public or to classroom teachers would result in a rapid increase in the test taking abilities of children with heretofore "limited" cognitive abilities. Who knows what Kanita's score could have been? We suspect that the distribution of IQ scores, would be skewed beyond recognition. We are not suggesting that specific items be released to the public; rather, we wish to emphasize the effect of leveling the playing field by placing "higher order" thinking and academic discourse styles at the top of the instructional agenda for all children. Providing all children with the opportunity to master the higher order thinking and discourse styles valued by schools is preferable—and more equitable—to using tests to police the boundaries of the normal curve.

(En)Forcing the Normal Curve in Academic Assessment

The issue of assessment of a child's academic skills would seem, at face value, to present a more objective view of children's abilities than does IQ testing. There is, on the surface at least, much less subjectivity involved in determining whether a child has mastered specific reading, writing, or mathematical skills. Nevertheless, there are several aspects of this assessment that are affected by normal curve thinking.

First, we may assume that academic testing functions more equitably than IQ testing because it is typically criterion or standards based. However, tests designed to indicate success or "normalcy" based on cut-off scores generally derive their score based on standardization using a normal curve (Reschly, 2002). This is also true of standardized criterion-referenced tests used during the special education assessment process. As Fendler and Muzaffar (2008) have pointed out, we actually tend to forget that the criterion was arrived at by comparison to norm-based determinations of what level of skill children should master by a specified age. They state:

> For any criterion-referenced test...items are written and chosen through a process of test development in which results from pilot tests get compared to the results of previously established tests, and new test items are continually modified until the new test results correlate with the old test results....(p. 77)

As these authors emphasize, a shift in perspective leads us to focus on the criterion, forgetting its "socially constructed" (p. 77), normative origin.

Second, we must ask how the norms were derived. Normal curve thinking determines that the highest percentage of scores will fall around a central point, and this concept, though comparable to the "toss of a coin," will both represent the "average" child and become a target for all children. More seriously, if these standards and percentages are dominated by groups that comprise the majority of the U.S. school population (U.S. Census Bureau, 2009), we end up weighting average achievement based on the performance of white and middle-class children. This results in the current situation in which we find at one end of the normal distribution children from families whose educational and income level is considerably higher than the average and, on the other end, children from families with lower educational and income level, many of whom are from non-dominant linguistic, cultural, and racial groups. In this way the presumption of the normal curve perpetuates itself and confirms what has come to be known as the social reproduction function of our educational system as demonstrated by several researchers (e.g., Anyon, 1997; Oakes, 2005).

This circular functioning of testing perpetuates a system of values based on the abstract, decontextualized reasoning that marks intelligence testing (Sternberg & Wagner, 1994). The deleterious result of this is that alternative modes of reasoning, problem-solving and creativity are either ignored or actively devalued. Much cross-cultural research demonstrates the variety of ways in which human beings display what Sternberg (1997) has referred to as "successful intelligence." For example, in a review of research with Brazilian street children, Ceci and Roazzi (1994) report on several studies of these children's abilities in solving arithmetic computations. In one study cited by these authors (Carraher, Carraher, and Schliemann, 1985), children with no more than five years of schooling were able to solve 98% of mental arithmetic problems presented in the context of street vending; however, as testers decreased the level of context, the children correctly answered 74% of the problems presented with an intermediate amount of context, and only 37% of such problems presented in the decontextualized manner typical of a school setting. These studies show the importance of context in assessing students' abilities.

Certainly, this situation would be improved by the provision of appropriate opportunities to learn that which is valued in our educational system and to expand educators' understanding of the different approaches to thinking that will bring more children into the normative range. We believe that this should be one of the main outcomes of the RTI movement. However, normal curve thinking works against school success by continuing to adjust achievement expectations when too many "test takers" are successful, and the cut-off score is then considered too lax. This process has become institutionalized in the high-stakes testing movement, fueled largely by the No Child Left Behind (NCLB) Act.

NCLB and High-Stakes Testing

In a collection of essays entitled *Many Children Left Behind*, Meir and Wood (2004) offered a scathing critique of the way NCLB has been implemented. As Meir pointed out, "suddenly every state in the nation feels obliged to initiate a massive program of standardized tests starting at ever younger ages, upon which all critical decisions will hang…" (p. 67). Perhaps the most ironic, one might say ludicrous, aspect of the law reveals that even those who designed the law were unaware of the way standardized, normal curve tests are developed. Darling-Hammond's (2004) essay in this collection explained:

> Unfortunately, the targets—based on the notion that 100% of students will score at the "proficient" level on state tests by the year 2014—were set without an understanding of what this goal would really mean. First, of course, there is the fundamental problem that it is impossible to attain 100% proficiency levels for students on norm referenced tests (when 50% of students, by definition, must score below the norm and some proportion must, by definition, score below any cut point selected). (p. 9)

Following this point, we would ask whether the educational establishment in the U.S. could stand to have the level of success reach 100% if the belief in a normal distribution so permeates our beliefs about achievement and other human traits? Darling-Hammond (2004) argued that NCLB effectively penalizes schools serving the least privileged students by requiring that they show the greatest achievement gains, despite the presence of needier students, larger numbers of students served by special education, and the absence of adequate funding and other supports. Students at the low end of the achievement spectrum, including those designated as "disabled" are "increasingly likely to be excluded by being counseled out, transferred, expelled, or by dropping out" (p. 20) to reduce the percentage of children whose scores adversely affect the schools' adequate yearly progress (AYP) report.

To compound the difficulties with state standardized testing, few state peer review requirements are actually linked to the standards, and most states report that the requirements for adequate standards and assessment peer review are not clear. Furthermore, few staff working on standardized state testing have the technical expertise in either test development or a basic knowledge of the state standards themselves (Wise, 2006). Perhaps most important is that high-stakes state testing measures only a portion of a student's skill and learning. While the repercussions of these tests have profound effects on the educational paths of many students, the reliance on state tests contradicts the comprehensive system of accountability mandated by IDEA (Pardini, 2004).

Conclusion: Looking to the Future

The concerns that led to the shift in requirements in IDEA (2004) reflect a rising consensus that the IQ/achievement discrepancy model, with its reliance on IQ testing, is not working. In contrast, the RTI model, at least in principle, holds promise as a way forward because it attempts to ensure that children have the quality of instruction that will allow their abilities to become evident, rather than seek to fit each child into a pre-determined "natural" law of distribution. As Bloom (1971) observed:

> The normal curve is not sacred. It describes the outcome of a random process. Since education is a purposeful activity in which we seek to have the students learn what we teach, the achievement distribution should be very different from the normal curve if our instruction is effective. In fact, our educational efforts may be said to be unsuccessful to the extent that student achievement is normally distributed. (p. 49)

The entire field of special education has been premised on exactly the point made by Bloom: That even for children thought to have built-in deficiencies, appropriate, individualized instruction should make a difference. We cannot simultaneously believe in this and in the normal curve. If the goal of education is for all children to experience the excitement and success inherent in quality teaching and learning, then curriculum cannot be designed, nor can student learning be assessed, using practices that guarantee that some students must fail. This denies even the possibility of success to some students, and we can be sure that students with disabilities will be largely in this category. Because we know that all children can learn, it follows that a child's progress can only be accurately assessed if we assess precisely those areas in which (s)he has been actively engaged through effective instructional practices.

The promise of RTI

We must note that the concept at the heart of RTI is not new. Rather, it emerges from and reflects a substantial body of theoretical and empirical study of assessment and pre-referral interventions. Indeed, RTI's premise reflects at its core Vygotsky's (1978) principle of instruction in the zone of proximal development as well as Feurstein's model of dynamic assessment (DA) (Feurstein et al., 1979). The central idea in DA is that the tester is simultaneously instructing the learner, giving feedback designed to prompt the child to master the next step, and taking into account the child's learning process as well as the product. This is what occurred when the psychologist testing Kanita broke the rules and reinforced her correct response. The strength of this approach, we believe, is that it truly seeks to understand how the child learns under conditions of effective instruction. While DA has long been advocated by scholars such as Hilliard (1992), recent work by Fuchs, Fuchs, Compton, Bouton, Caffrey and Hill (2007) and a review by Caffrey, Fuchs, and Fuchs (2008) have compared it to the RTI process, pointing to its potential for greater efficiency and speed in supporting children to demonstrate their understanding of skills and concepts rather than waiting for the longer term instructional period (tier 2) usually recommended in RTI models.

The idea of pre-referral interventions also preceded RTI. For many years prior to the IDEA 2004 amendments, researchers were designing, implementing, and reporting positive results from systematic pre-referral interventions. For example, a line of work by Gravois and Rosenfield (2006) consistently found that instructional consultation teams were effective in decreasing by half the odds of minority students' referral. As Reschly (2002) and Reschly, Tilly and Grimes (1999) observed even before the 2004 reauthorization of IDEA made RTI an official alternative, the static, deficit-based traditional assessment needed to be replaced with a more functional approach that would place emphasis on: "interventions rather than internal child characteristics that have little to do with treatment, (b) rigorous problem-solving procedures…, and (c) early intervention and prevention…rather than waiting until failure is sufficiently severe to meet eligibility discrepancy criteria (p. 132).

It seems that many of these earlier efforts are coming to fruition under the concept of RTI, but exactly what form RTI should take will depend on the outcomes of careful research on its implementation. However, there are a few caveats that we believe must be attended to. First, the process must not be so slow that it ends up being another instance of a "wait to fail" model. Perhaps, as Caffrey et al. (2008) have argued, dynamic assessment might provide a quicker and more process oriented approach to screening out children who really do not need to be placed in a lengthy tier 2 intervention.

Second, cultural responsiveness must be a central part of the rigorous problem-solving that is needed to ensure that RTI is implemented to the benefit of all children (e.g., Klingner & Edwards, 2006). There can be no sense in moving away from rigid IQ/discrepancy formulas simply to replace them with rigidly implemented instructional tiers. Klingner and Edwards contend that those who implement RTI must go beyond believing that delivery of evidence-based instructional practices is adequate and move to an understanding that authentic personal connections between students and teachers are essential to student engagement and learning. An essential part of this is attending to the contextual nature of children's learning by engaging in an ongoing analysis of general education classroom and school-wide cultures as a critical component of all RTI models (Vaughn & Fuchs, 2003). It is clear that this can only be accomplished with intensive, on-going professional development and an RTI model that includes flexibility in type and delivery of instructional interventions.

Finally, we believe that authentic assessment must be the key ingredient to replacing the circular and damaging practice of creating a forced fit between children and educational outcomes. According to Neill (2004), a collaboration between Fair Test and the Massachusetts Coalition for authentic reform in education (CARE) resulted in the establishment of three central assessment principles: classroom-based information collected by teachers through a variety of "appropriate assessments and tools"; "independent, well-prepared" school quality reviews at five-year intervals; and, limited use of standardized tests only for the purpose of noting and investigating marked discrepancies between classroom-based information and test results.

What is to be the role of even "limited" standardized testing? What should happen at the tier 3 or tier 4 stages of the RTI model? What measures should we use to determine whether children who have not been responsive to the first two or three tiers are eligible for special education services? Are special education services the best alternative? Advocates for the continuing role of psychology contend that RTI should not come to be viewed as the sole process for determining a child's eligibility for special education services (Berninger, 2006; Holdnack and Weiss, 2006; Ofiesh, 2006). As these authors point out, IDEA (2004) does not rule out comprehensive assessment. Moreover, it continues to require differential diagnosis of specific disabilities as well as a "full and individual initial evaluation" that uses "a variety of assessment tools and instruments" (p. 879). These authors express grave concern that RTI could become as rigid a method of determining disability as discrepancy formulas, and argue that a psychologist's role can contribute to an "in depth understanding of the entirety of the child's strengths and weaknesses in problem solving" (p. 878). In a similar vein, Berninger (2006) argues for replacing the old model of psychologists as "gatekeepers" with a model that includes their full engagement in a systematic process of early screening and instruction regarding reading problems.

We do not dispute the role of psychologists in the process of understanding and serving children, and we agree with the foregoing authors that their involvement should be geared toward guiding and supporting instruction. However, we propose that special education services and funding, including in-depth understanding of a child's processing, memory, or other learner characteristics, should be available to begin at tier 2 of the RTI process. While many will disagree (e.g., Scruggs & Mastopieri, 2002), we believe that if such services are appropriately intensive and individualized, they should benefit from special education funding and support with the expectation that some children will stop needing these services sooner than others, while a smaller percentage of children may continue to need support throughout their academic careers. As it stands now, what Scruggs and Mastopieri referred to as special education's "sparse special education funds," (p. 165) may well be wasted on inappropriate over-identification, mostly of minority students, which could be reduced by effective RTI/DA implementation even at the earliest levels (first tier). To continue to envision special education as a place to which individuals are assigned by virtue of their placement on the normal curve is to continue to assume an intrinsic deficit orientation that sends us on a "hunt for disability" (Baker, 2002). We recommend, rather, the logic proposed by Reid and Valle (2004), that we "reconceptualize LD in terms of human variation rather than pathology"(p. 473). As McDermott (1987) has persuasively argued, we should not let our practices reinforce the belief that failure is something children do rather than something that is done to them. Let us add to the promise that, with systematic and individually tailored instruction, we can open the doors to effective education for all children.

References

Anyon, J. (1997). *Ghetto schooling: A political economy of urban educational reform.* New York: Teachers College Press.

Baker, B. (2002). The hunt for disability: The new eugenics and the normalization of school children. *Teachers College Record, 104*(4), 663–703.

Beale-Spencer, M., Dupree, D., and Hartmann, T. (1997). A Phenomenological variant of ecological systems theory (PVEST): A self-organization perspective in context. *Development and Psychopathology, 9,* 817–833. Cambridge, UK: Cambridge University Press.

Berninger, V. W. (2006). Research-supported ideas for implementing reauthorized IDEA with intelligent professional psychological services. *Psychology in the Schools, 43*(7), 781–796.

Bloom, B. (1971). Mastery learning. In J.H. Block (Ed.), *Mastery learning: Theory and practice.* New York: Holt, Rinehart & Winston.

Caffrey, E., Fuchs, D., & Fuchs, L. (2008). The predictive validity of dynamic assessment. *Journal of Special Education,* Vol. *41*, No. 4, 254–270.

Carraher, T. N., Carraher, D., & Schliemann, A. D. (1985). Mathematics in the streets and in the schools. *British Journal of Developmental Psychology, 3*, 21–29.

Ceci, S.J. and Roazzi, A. (1994). The effects of context on cognition: Notes from Brazil. In R.J. Sternberg (Ed.), *Mind in context: Interactionist perspectives on human intelligence* (pp. 74–104). Cambridge, UK: Cambridge University Press.

Darling-Hammond, L. (2004). From "separate but equal" to "no child left behind" The collision of new standards and old inequalities. In D. Meir & G. Wood (Eds.), *Many children left behind: How the No Child Left Behind Act is damaging our children and our schools* (pp. 3–32). Boston: Beacon.

Donovan, S. M. & Cross, C. T. (2002). *Minority students in special and gifted education.* Washington, DC: National Academy Press.

Dykeman, B. F. (2006, Winter). Alternative strategies in assessing special education needs. *Education,127*(2), 265–273.

Fendler, L. & Muzaffar, I. (2008). The history of the bell curve: Sorting and the idea of normal. *Educational Theory, 58*(1), 63–82.

Feurstein, R., Rand, Y., & Hoffman, M.B. (1979). *The dynamic assessment of retarded performers: The learning potential assessment device.* Baltimore, MD: University Park Press.

Fordham, S. (1988). Racelessness as a factor in Black students' school success: Pragmatic strategy or pyrrhic victory? *Harvard Educational Review, 58*, 54–84.

Fuchs, D., Fuchs, L. S., Compton, D. L., Bouton, B. Caffrey, E., & Hill, L. (2007, May/June). Dynamic assessment as responsiveness to intervention: A scripted protocol to identify young at-risk readers. *Teaching Exceptional Children, 39*(5), 58–63.

Glick, J. (1975). Cognitive development in cross-cultural perspective. In F. D. Horowitz (Ed.), *Review of Child Development Research 4*, 595–648. Chicago, IL: Chicago University Press.

Gould, S. J. (1996). *The mismeasure of man* (2nd ed.). New York: W.W. Norton.

Gravois,T. A. & Rosenfield, S. A. (2006). Impact of instructional consultation teams on the disproportionate referral and placement of minority students in special education. *Remedial and Special Education, 27*(1), 42–52.

Harry, B. & Klingner, J. K. (2006). *Why are so many minority students in special education? Understanding race and disability in schools.* New York: Teachers College Press.

Harry, B., Klingner, J. K., STurges, K., & Moore, R. (2002). Of rocks and soft places: Using qualitative methods to investigate disproportionality. In D. J. Losen and G. Orfield (Eds.), *Racial inequity in special education.* Cambridge, MA: Harvard University Press.

Heath, S. (1986). *Ways with words: Language, life and work in communities and classrooms.* Cambridge, UK: Cambridge University Press.

Hilliard, A. G. (1992). The pitfalls and promises of special education practice. *Exceptional Children, 59*(2), 168–72.

Holdnack, J.A., and Weiss, L. (2006). IDEA 2004: Anticipated implications for clinical practice – integrating assessment and intervention. *Psychology in the Schools, 43*(8), 871–882.

Honigsfeld, A. (2009). Students' learning styles: Design the best teaching strategies. *Insights on Learning Disabilities, 6*(1), 13–20.

Hoover, J. J., Baca, L., Wexler-Love, E., & Saenz, L. (2008). National implementation of response to intervention (RTI): A research summary. Special Education Leadership and Quality Teacher Initiative, BUENO Center-School of Education, University of Colorado, Boulder. Retrieved from National Association of State Directors of SPecial Education, Incorporated. website: http://www.nasdse.org/Portals/0/Natio nalImplementationofRTI-ResearchSummary.pdf

Houts, P.L. (Ed.). (1977). *The myth of measurability: IQ tests.* New York: Hart.

Klingner, J. K., and Edwards, P. (2006). Cultural considerations with response to intervention models. *Reading Research Quarterly, 41,* 108–117.

Klingner, J. K., Artiles, A. J., & Méndez Barletta, L. (2006). English language learners who struggle with reading: Language acquisition or learning disabilities? *Journal of Learning Disabilities, 39,* 108–128.

McDermott, R. P. (1987). The explanation of minority school failure, again. *Anthropology and Education Quarterly, 18,* 361–364.

Meir, S. & Wood, G. (Eds.). (2004). *Many children left behind: How the No Child Left Behind Act is damaging our children and our schools.* Boston: Beacon.

Mpofu, E. (2004). Being intelligent with Zimbabweans: A historical and contemporary view. In R. J. Sternberg (Ed.), *International handbook of intelligence* (pp. 364–390). Cambridge, UK: Cambridge University Press.

Murdoch, S. (2007). *IQ: A smart history of a failed idea.* Hoboken, NJ: John Wiley.

Neill, M. (2004). Leaving No Child Behind: Overhauling NCLB. In D. Meier, Deborah, & G. Wood (Eds.), *Many Children Left Behind* (pp. 101–119). Boston: Beacon.

Oakes, J. (2005). *Keeping track: How schools structure inequality* (2d ed.). New Haven, CT: Yale University Press.

Ofiesh, N. (2006). Response to intervention and the identification of specific learning disabilities: Why we need comprehensive evaluations as part of the process. *Psychology in the Schools, 43*(8), 2006.

Ogbu, J. U. (1987). Variability in minority school performance: A problem in search of an explanation. *Anthropology and Education Quarterly, 18,* 312–334.

Pardini, P. (2004). Ethics in the superintendency. *The School Administrator, 8,* 10–18.

Piaget, J. (1971). The theory of stages in cognitive development. In D. R. Green, M. P. Ford, & G. P. Flamer (Eds.), *Measurement and Piaget.* New York: McGraw-Hill.

Reid, D. K. & Valle, J. W. (2004). The discursive practice of learning disability: Implications for instruction and parent-school relations. *Journal of Learning Disabilities, 37*(6), 466–481.

Reschly, D. L. (2002). Change dynamics in special education assessment: Historical and contemporary patterns. *Peabody Journal of Education, 77*(2), 117–136.

Reschly, D. L., Tilly, W. D., & Grimes, J. P. (Eds.). (1999). *Special education in transition: Functional assessment and noncategorical programming.* Longmont, CO: Sopris West.

Robinson, N. M., Zigler, E., & Gallagher, J. J. (2000). Two tails of the normal curve: Similarities and differences in the study of mental retardation and giftedness. *American Psychologist, 55*(12), 1413–1424.

Rogoff, B. (2003). *The cultural nature of human development.* Oxford, UK: Oxford University Press.

Schon, J., Shaftel, J., & Markham, P. (2008). Contemporary issues in the assessment of culturally and linguistically diverse learners. *Journal of Applied School Psychology, 24*(2),163-189.

Scruggs, T. & Mastopieri, M. (2002). On babies and bathwater: Addressing the problems of identifying learning disabilities. *Learning Disability Quarterly, 25*(3), 155–168.

Serpell, R. (2000). Intelligence and culture. In R. Sternberg (Ed.), *Handbook of Intelligence* (pp. 549–576). Cambridge: Cambridge University Press.

Shelton, A. (1996). The ape's IQ. In J. L. Kincheloe, S. R. Steinberg, & A. D. Gresson (Eds.), *Measured lies: The bell curve examined* (pp. 91–108). New York: St. Martin's.

Snow, R. E. (1994). Abilities in academic tasks. In R. J. Sternberg & R. K. Wagner (Eds.), *Mind in context: Interactionist perspectives on human intelligence* (pp. 3–37). Cambridge, U.K: Cambridge University Press.

Steele, C. M. (1997). A threat in the air: How stereotypes shape the intellectual identities and performance of women and African-Americans. *American Psychologist, 52*, 613–629.

Sternberg, R. J. (2004). *International handbook of intelligence.* Cambridge, UK: Cambridge University Press.

Sternberg, R., & Wagner, R. (1994). Mind in context: Interactionist perspectives on human intelligence. New York: Cambridge University Press.

Sternberg, R. (1997). The concept of intelligence and its role in lifelong learning and success. *American Psychologist,* 52(10), 1030-1037.

U.S. Census Bureau. (2009). *Current Population Survey.* Retrieved September 13, 2009. http://www.census.gov/cps/

U.S. Department of Education Office of Special Education and Rehabilitative Services. (2002). *A new era: Revitalizing special education for children and their families.* Washington, DC. Retrieved October 6, 2009. http://www.ed.gov/inits/commissionsboards/wh-specialeducation/reports/index.html

U.S. Department of Education. (2004). *Individuals with Disabilities Education Improvement Act.* Final regulations to implement the Individuals with Disabilities Education Improvement Act of 2004 (IDEA).

The U.S. Department of Education (ED) published in the *Federal Register* on August 14, 2006, the final regulations to implement the IDEA 2004 and became effective on October 13, 2006. Policy Guidance (Outside Source)—Index of policy documents on the education of infants, toddlers, children and youth with disabilities PUBLIC LAW March 08, 2006. Retrieved July 1, 2009 from http://www.copyright.gov/legislation//FedRegister/finrule/2006-3/081406a.pdf

Vaughn, S. & Fuchs, L. (2003). Redefining learning disabilities as inadequate response to instruction: The promise and potential problems. *Learning Disabilities Research and Practice, 18*(3), 137–146.

Vygotsky, L. S. (1978). *Mind in society: The development of higher psychological processes.* Cambridge, MA: Harvard University Press.

Wechsler, D. (2003). *Wechsler intelligence scale for children—4th edition (WISC-IV®).* San Antonio, TX: Harcourt.

Wise, L.L. (1994). Encouraging and supporting compliance with standards for educational tests (Fall). Alexandria, VA: Human Resources Research Organization (HumRRO).

NINE

Miner's Canaries and Boiling Frogs: Fiction and Facts about Normalcy in Educational and Reading Assessment

Arlette Ingram Willis

This chapter examines and critiques notions of normality from its taken-for-granted everyday usage to its roots and routes in education with a special focus on reading assessment. Of particular importance are the ideological assumptions that frame educational and reading assessment, especially the long held assumption that human intelligence distributes "normally." Examining these collective histories of assessment helps to explain the tradition of categorizing and tracking student academic progress by race, class, and gender and helps to explain why this tradition remains largely unchallenged in current school reform efforts which continue to rely heavily on norm-referenced reading assessments. *The Dynamic Indicators of Basic Early Literacy Skills* (DIBELS), for example, is having a profound affect on the direction of reading instruction in classrooms across the country (see Goodman, 2006, for useful critique of DIBELS).

There is an old tale that if frogs are placed in very cold or very hot water they will adjust, even to the point of being boiled alive as the heat is gradually turned up. The idea that amphibians naturally adapt to their environment, even if it kills them, seems to make sense. It is so unordinary an idea that it seems normal. But, as it turns out, the tale of the boiling frogs is untrue. Biologists have observed that frogs will jump out of boiling water to save their lives. Yet this story continues to appeal, functioning as an allegory to express the idea that people are often slow to acknowledge and react to changes that profoundly impact their lives.

Another popular story recalls that, in the past, coalminers would carry canaries with them into coalmines because canaries' respiratory systems better detected poisonous gases. Unlike the story of boiling frogs, this story turns out to be true. In the early 1900s, it was not unusual for coalminers to carry canaries into coalmines to detect poisonous gases. The tale of the canary in the coalmine serves as a metaphor cautioning us to be alert to problems in seemingly normal circumstances.

Here's another popular story that also has achieved the level of common sense. Over the last hundred years or so people have come to believe that there is a natural—and normal—distribution of intellect that has been used in education as a heuristic to describe, and defend, notions of individual and group differences. And, much like the coalminer's canary, which signaled problems in apparently normal circumstances, high levels of failure among groups long positioned outside the boundaries of normal signal fundamental problems in the structures of schooling and the assumptions that underpin contemporary models of American education. And one of the most powerful assumptions in contemporary schooling, the myth of the normal, bears much in common with the tale of the boiling frogs. Neither is true. Despite its common sense appeal, the evidence indicates that human behavior does not distribute normally (see Dudley-Marling & Gurn; Gallagher; Gelb, this volume).

In order to develop a counternarrative to the myth of the normal curve, I begin by examining the rise of the myth of normality in American education. When, where, and how, for example, did the notion of normal become an indicator of average, common, median, natural, ordinary, regular, standard, typical, or usual? How and why does the concept of normal so often go unchallenged, especially in education? I begin by presenting a short history of the ideological assumptions that underpin the concept of normal, drawn in part from ideas of naturally occurring, racially/ethnically inherited, intelligence. Next, I discuss the influence of these assumptions on reading research and assessment. Finally, focusing particularly on reading assessment, I discuss how these ideological assumptions remain largely unchallenged in current school reform efforts.

Ideological Assumptions Underpinning Normality: A Short History

The normal curve is underpinned by values, beliefs, and assumptions about relations of power that form the bedrock of traditional education research, assessment, and practice (Karier, 1986; Lagemann, 2000; Popkewitz, 1984). The ideological assumptions that undergird norm-referenced reading assessments, for example, can be traced to scientism, positivism, and racism (Willis, 2008). From this perspective, scientism is understood as a panacea to human life based on facts drawn from the natural world; positivism is understood as an acultural, neutral, and unbiased means of knowledge building through direct observation and experimentation; and, racism is understood as the belief that people of different races have different, and perhaps inferior, intellectual ability (here, inferior to whites).

Each of these ideological assumptions serves as a pillar in the field of educational psychology that emerged synchronistically with the development of educational assessments, especially intelligence testing, in the early 1900s. One of the earliest influences on educational assessment was Sir Francis Galton, a founder of the eugenics movement and perhaps the first person to see the potential of the normal curve as a means of sorting individuals. Galton defined eugenics as "the study of the agencies under social control that improve or impair the racial qualities of future generations either physically or mentally" (Eugenics Archive, 2005). He referenced race by skin color and physical features, intellectual traits, and emotive or affective characteristics, all of which he believed were inherited. Galton's concept of superior germ-plasm (the notion that people of Nordic ancestry had superior traits that were inheritable by their offspring) continues to influence current understandings of educational measurement.

Prior to World War I, psychology as a field of inquiry was not taken seriously as a science of human behavior (Samelson, 1977). However, as the U.S. entered World War I, prominent American psychologists, many committed eugenicists, offered their help in testing U.S. Army recruits. The interpretation, and subsequent publication of the results of the Army testing, indicated that the average mental age of native born (white) men was 13, with foreign born (whites) from Mediterranean and Alpine areas below Nordic whites, and African Americans below both groups of whites. Important to this chapter is the claim that there was a "scientifically" proven link between intelligence, ethnicity, race, and national origin.

The results of the Army tests have been challenged by numerous scholars (Montagu, 1945; Rury, 1988; Spring, 1972; Travers, 1983), but what has lingered is the idea that psychological tests can measure innate intellect, that there is a normal curve of intellectual functioning, that African Americans are intellectually inferior to whites, and that people who live in poverty are intellectually inferior to those who do not. African American scholars (Johnson, 1923; Long, 1923; Bond, 1924) effectively rebutted the racial interpretation of the U.S. Army testing. They argued that the psychologists had ignored contextual factors (history of educational denial, social caste system, cultural differences, and economic circumstances of slavery) in the lives of African Americans and the effects these had on their test performance. Yet, the creators of these tests were dismissive of challenges to the ideological assumptions that underpin their tests, the content of the test/test items, the administration of the test, and the published—and often sensationalized—interpretations of the test results.

The apparent success of Army Alpha and Beta tests at sorting individuals and groups according to putatively "innate" intelligence inspired many psychologists to push forward their research and testing agenda into education (Samelson, 1977). Several educational psychologists involved in the creation of the Army intelligence tests, including Lewis Terman, Edward Thorndike, Guy Whipple, and Robert Yerkes, were particularly influential extending the use of intelligence testing into the schools. Their early tests drew on their work with the Army Alpha and Beta tests and were supported by a grant from the General Education Board of the Rockefeller Foundation. By 1920, the intelligence tests that grew out of this work were administered to 400,000 school children in the U.S. (Terman, 1920). Terman interpreted the results of this mass national testing as an indicator of the intellectual functioning of school children and suggested reforms that included tracking students in classes based on test scores. The zeal that accompanied the use of intelligence tests in education was predicated on the "belief of the psychologists that they were scientifically measuring essentially 'native ability' rather than the results of school training" (Samelson, 1977, p. 279). The experience of early school testing results mirrored the experience with the Army tests; students with limited access to schooling and limited English proficiency did not perform as well on standardized tests as students who had completed more schooling. The continued influence of psychological testing on schooling, especially intelligence, cannot be overemphasized.

The concept of an innate intelligence and the natural distribution of intellect among humans as indicated by the normal curve has achieved a level of "common sense" among educators and psychometricians and has served as a foundation for the field of educational psychology and assessment more generally. The influence of educational psychology has been most deeply felt in the proliferation of "intelligence tests [that] were created as an accurate and efficient sorting mechanisms that reinforce dominant values and contribute to social stability by justifying inequality of outcomes as a natural and objective process" (Richardson & Johanningmeier, 1998, p. 711). But the influence of educational psychology in educational assessment presumes that norm-referenced tests are a fair, equitable, unbiased, and culturally neutral measure of innate intellectual ability based on a natural (i.e., normal) distribution of intelligence. However, as I will demonstrate below, educational assessments are not typically fair, equitable, unbiased, or culturally neutral nor is there anything natural about the normal curve. To make this case, I will focus my attention on formal reading assessments, which have had a profound influence on the structures and practice of American education.

The normal curve, individual differences, and early reading research

James Cattell is an important figure in the history of educational testing, reading research, and reading assessment. A disciple of Galton, Cattell conducted early experiments on mental measures using his fellow graduate students as subjects. These graduate students were all very much alike, English-speaking men of European descent, from middle-upper income families. Cattell used the results of his early experiments as his reference point for normal although, in reality, he would later argue that these men were superior and, therefore, far from normal. Eventually, Cattell found himself working in Galton's anthropometric laboratory (1886–1887) at London's South Kensington Museum. Cattell and Galton shared an interest in individual differences, although Galton's focus was more overtly on heredity and racial differences. Cattell's interest in individual differences and testing also coalesced with Galton's notions of eugenics. And, like Galton, he believed that through a study of heredity, psychologists could trace the development of individual intelligence. Moreover, "Galton provided [Cattell] with a scientific goal—the measurement of the psychological differences between people—that made use of the experimental procedures he had developed at Leipzig" (Sokal, 1987, p. 27). Galton's view of individual differences, especially the role played by the inheritability of the intellect also became part of Cattell's agenda in his contributions to "mental testing" in educational psychology and his lifelong pursuit of proof of the superior intellect and character of white male scientists.

Upon his return to the U.S., Cattell developed several psychological tests to measure individual differences, drawing heavily on his work with Galton. Cattell coined the term "mental tests" and argued about the importance of the use of measurement in human affairs, arguing that, "Psychology cannot attain the certainty and exactness of the physical sciences unless it rests on a foundation of experiment and measurement" (Cattell, 1890, p. 373). Throughout his life he remained committed to defending the notion of the inheritability of intelligence in racial/ethnic terms. In an 1896 article, he wrote,

> What can we learn from the tests of elementary traits regarding the higher intellectual and emotional life?…We must use our measurements to study the development of the individual and of the [white] race, to disentangle the complex factors of heredity and environment. (Cattell & Farrand, 1896, p. 648)

Cattell believed that his experiments in mental testing were indicators of intelligence and were racially and ethnically attributable. He also believed that there was an irrefutable connection between intelligence and race/ethnicity; that is, he maintained that there are biological and genetic arguments for differences in intellect as measured by performance on psychological tests. Given that the subjects in his early experiments were often other white male graduate students, Cattell surmised that their responses indicated their superior intellect. He further sought to normalize their characteristics, white, male, middle-to-upper class, and English-dominant, as the standard. Moreover, he sought to demonstrate, scientifically, the superior intellect of white males by comparing their results with subjects of different races/ethnicities and attributing differences to race and ethnicity as opposed to individual differences.

Cattell recognized the possibilities of psychology and the use of mental testing that would be "based on objective measurements of responses to the environment with special reference to individual and group differences and to the useful application of psychology, thus leading to the development of modern educational, clinical, and industrial psychology" (Cattell, 1928, p. 547). It is important to acknowledge that many of the early reading researchers were educational psychologists who had studied under Cattell or one of his students. The ideological assumptions espoused by Galton and carried out by Cattell and other early educational psychologists, coalesced with their involvement in the World War I testing of U.S. Army recruits, modifications to the tests, and the creation of the National Intelligence Test (1919–1920).

Cattell's reading research drew upon his understanding of the mental and physical processes that produced varying reaction times which, he believed, were connected to intelligence and attributable to race/ethnicity. In addition, he sought to measure and identify racial and gender differences, which confirmed his beliefs about the intellectual and moral superiority of white males. To this end, he used Galton's notion of a naturally occurring normal distribution of intelligence to identify (mostly aggregate) differences among students by race/ethnicity, in the process normalizing whiteness in educational and reading assessments. Over time, what Hurd (2008) has called normative whiteness took hold in education more generally. Hurd defines normative whiteness as "a set of social and institutional practices, identifiable but often unexamined, that serve to advantage or empower some groups of students while disempowering or excluding others, particularly along lines of race, culture, and class" (p. 294). As the public school population in the U.S. has grown ever more racially/ethnically and linguistically diverse, the immorality of a stance of normative whiteness has become increasingly apparent.

The normal curve, individual differences, and school reform

The federal government has had an active role in educational testing since the 1910s, and this role has not diminished as evidenced by the extraordinary reach of the No Child Left Behind (NCLB) legislation. The ever-increasing role of the federal government is, however, dependent upon traditions in educational research and assessment that highlight group differences (race, class, gender, language) and portray them as deficits of normative whiteness. Educational research and assessment have, in turn, been strongly influenced by the fields of psychology and measurement. Richardson and Johanningmeier (1998) put it this way:

> The colonization of schooling by psychology and measurement enabled the translation of the concept of equality of humankind as a natural right that requires equal access to education to the concept of equality of opportunity in a meritocracy where opportunity is qualified, or restricted, by the 'natural stratification of intelligence.' (pp. 711–712)

In this section, I share a brief history of reading research preceding No Child Left Behind Act (2002) to illustrate the role that various studies, reports, and assessments have had on current assessment practices in reading. By tracing studies, reports, and programs that preceded NCLB, I am able to show the influence of reading research and assessment on what's considered normal, in this case a normal reader.

A principal focus of reading research over the last fifty years has been to identify instructional practices that would address the problem of why some children more easily learn to read than others—and why some children seem to struggle with reading throughout their school careers. But the search for a magic bullet to solve reading problems has consistently eluded reading researchers. The celebrated First Grade Studies (Bond & Dykstra, 1967), for example, found no reading program that was successful with all students. Notably, this study systematically dismissed research that included African American and Spanish-speaking children (Willis & Harris, 1997). Over twenty years later, the Committee on the Prevention of Reading Difficulties in Young Children of the National Research Council undertook a study of beginning reading, resulting in the book *Preventing Reading Difficulties in Young Children* (Snow, Burns, & Griffin, 1998). This text offered a limited, selective review of literature of beginning reading. And, once again, issues of race, class, gender, and language were given short shrift.

The report of the National Reading Panel (NRP) (2000), commissioned by Congress to provide a comprehensive review of effective reading instruction, has had a powerful influence on reading instruction in American schools. But, like previous reading reports, issues of race, class, gender, and language were not salient concerns for the NRP although many of the studies included in the NRP report identified subjects by race, class, gender, and dominant/home language. A close review of studies included in the report of the NRP reveals that the subjects were predominately white, male, middle class, and English dominant. So it isn't surprising that recommendations that emerged from the report eschewed issues of race, class, and language dominance.

Take, for example, the ancillary materials of the NRP made available free to universities, schools, and the public which include: a video, *Teaching Children to Read*; a book, *Putting Reading First: The Research Building Blocks for Teaching Children to reading, Kindergarten through Grade 3*; and a flyer, *Putting Reading First: Helping Your Child Learn to Read: A Parent Guide, Preschool through Grade 3*. A careful reading of these materials reveals the ideological assumptions underpinning official interpretations of the report of the National Reading Panel, including what counts as normal and acceptable research (Willis, 2009).

The video, for example, begins with patriotic music augmented by photographs and images superimposed against the background of the American flag. The video then claims that "millions of children can be saved from reading failure," a discourse that is unmistakably crises invoking. There is a preponderance of children of color in the video—many receiving assistance from their white peers—in contrast to the actual number of students of color in the studies reviewed by the NRP. The number of students of color in the video implies that the research studies that informed the video were conducted among children who look like those on the video. Again, this was not the case. More seriously, the style and tone of the video present an unflattering and negative image of students of color as learners.

A particular series of frames succinctly illustrates this point. In this series of frames, there are several males of color whose appearance suggests that they are roughly between nine and fourteen years of age. They appear to be in an urban area, under a viaduct in front of a trash bin as an elevated train moves behind them. These "urban" males of color have book bags on their backs or on the ground beside them and paper bags in their hands. They are dressed casually and appear to be smiling, talking, and enjoying one another's company. The audio that accompanies this frame warns:

> When children fail to learn to read this downward spiraling continues until children avoid reading and develop a sense of failure that affects all other aspects of their lives.

The statement supports commonly voiced claims and fears about the academic progress and social fate of young males of color but cannot realistically be drawn from NRP data. The video's prediction, without supportive data, suggests a deeply rooted racist, class-bound, and alarmist viewpoint: poor brown and black males, because they struggle with reading, will likely fail in school and, therefore, will not be productive citizens once they leave school. The producers of the NRP video claim that their recommendations are based on "scientific" research. The video should have induced outrage because of the lack of "scientifically based" support, but barely a whimper resulted, in large part because viewers perceived the abnormal discourse and images of poor young males of color as normal.

A review of other ancillary materials, the book *Putting Reading First: The Research Building Blocks for Teaching Children to Read, Kindergarten through Grade 3* and the flyer *Putting Reading First: Helping Your Child Learn to Read: A Parent Guide, Preschool through Grade 3*, presumably based on recommendations from the NRP "alphabetic" subgroup, also reveals an overrepresentation of children of color. For instance, in the *Putting Reading First* book there are 31 pages of photos and 23 of these photos include children whom I identified as children of color (the flyer uses some of the same photos). Moreover, an Internet search of *Information on Public Schools and School Districts in the United States National Public School Locator 1999–2000* (http://nces.ed.gov/ccdweb/school/school.asp) for the elementary schools listed on the inside cover of the book (from which the children's photos came) revealed the racial/ethnic, linguistic, and socioeconomic profiles presented in Table 9.2 below. For good measure, each school was contacted via the telephone to confirm the accuracy of these data.

The visual images of the NRP video and other ancillary materials distort and misrepresent the findings of the National Reading Panel with regard to children of color. The visual images suggest that adopting the research findings and recommendations will improve the reading performance of children of color (irrespective of the fact that there is very limited research among children of color). More insidiously, the misleading use of images in these materials reinforces pernicious stereotypes that plague schools and the larger society; specifically, that the lives, language, and culture of children of color are a problem that can be fixed by the scientifically based research of the NRP. Given the rapidly shifting demographics of our nation, as more black and brown, non-English/limited English-speaking children enter school, will the educational and reading assessment traditions of using white, middle-class, English dominant students continue to be the norm(al)?

The National Assessment of Educational Progress

The National Assessment of Educational Progress (NAEP) was established in 1964 with a grant from the Carnegie Corporation; however, the first national assessments were not completed until 1969. As with most federal interventions, there was some controversy. Katzman and Rosen (1970), for example, criticized the NAEP for

1. measuring questionable educational outcomes with questionable techniques;

2. classifying student sub-populations on largely irrelevant dimensions and/or insufficient detail; and

3. neglecting to collect information on school characteristics which would identify policy-performance relationships. (p. 584)

Despite these criticisms, NAEP reports have been produced regularly since 1971 presenting student scores in various subjects, including reading, disaggregated by race, gender, and socioeconomic class based on a presumably representative sample of U.S. school children.

NAEP data on subject matter achievement, which has been published in the form of "National Report Cards" for over 30 years, are frequently referenced in policy discussions. For example, in response to a query about whether American students are performing better (or worse) in reading than in the past, the U.S. Department of Education drew on NAEP data to create the following table of aggregate (mean) test scores for 9-year-olds by age, gender, color, and race/ethnicity from 1971 to 1990 (National Center for Education Statistics, 2006).

	1971	1975	1980	1984	1990
9-year-olds					
Total	208	210	215	211	209
Male	201	204	201	207	204
Female	214	216	220	214	215
Race/ethnicity					
White, non-Hispanic	214	217	221	218	217
Black, non-Hispanic	170	181	189	186	182
Hispanic	(1)	183	190	187	189

Table 9.1: NAEP Average Reading Scale Score, by Sex and Race/Ethnicity. Source: http://nces.ed.gov/fastfacts/display.asp?id=147

The NAEP "Report Cards" have exerted a powerful influence on federal education policy and, importantly, notions of young black and Hispanic students as below average (i.e., not normal) readers. This is nowhere more apparent than in the No Child Left Behind (NCLB) legislation which pledges to raise achievement and to "provide every American boy and girl with a quality education—regardless of ethnicity, income or background" (www.NoChildLeftBehind.gov). The following statement from the No Child Left Behind website illustrates the federal government's commitment to leave no child behind.

> We must test all groups of students so we can measure the achievement gap, define it, and attack it with the full knowledge and support of our communities. The President is committed to eliminating the achievement gap, not hiding it within school or statewide averages. That's why he wants each school to examine achievement every year in third through eighth grades by race, ethnicity, economic background, and disabilities. That way we won't leave any group or child behind. (www.NoChildLeftBehind.gov)

To illustrate the need to address educational outcomes, the NCLB website presents several pages of reading achievement data drawn from the NAEP to document achievement gaps between whites and students of color (African Americans, His-

School	Race/Ethnicity		Class (2000–2001)	Language
Charles Fortes	American Indian Asian African American Hispanic White	3 40 89 318 28	Free Lunch —449 Low Income	50% Bilingual
Pleasant View	American Indian Asian African American Hispanic White	3 48 76 159 134	Free Lunch—362 Middle Income	95% English Speaking
Webster Avenue	American Indian Asian African American Hispanic White	4 23 76 190 142	Free Lunch—391 N/A	78 Spanish Speakers
Emma Whiteknact	American Indian Asian African American Hispanic White	0 10 82 12 259	Free Lunch—201 Low-Middle Income	55% English 45% Portuguese

Table 9.2: *Information on Public Schools and School Districts in the United States National Public School Locator*

panics, and American Indians/Alaskan Natives). The scores of Asians/Pacific Islanders were not included, perhaps because (at the time) they were superior to whites. When viewing the data for fourth graders, the text surrounding the tables indicates the percentage of fourth graders who scored at or above the proficient level in reading as measured on NAEP tests. Under NCLB, school districts are required to report annual yearly progress and identify student progress by aggregate differences of race, gender, and social class. The table below indicates consistent growth for students of color on NAEP reading tests since 1992 although most policy makers have tended to focus on the persistent "gap" in achievement between whites and black and Hispanic students.

9-year-olds	1992	1994	1998	2000	2002	2003	2005	2007
White, non-Hispanic	224	224	226	224	229	229	229	231
Black, non-Hispanic	192	185	193	190	199	198	200	203
Hispanic	197	188	195	190	201	200	203	205
Asian Pacific Islander	216	220	221	225	224	226	229	232
American Indian/ Alaskan Native		221		214	207	202	204	203

Table 9.3: Percentage of Students Assessed in Fourth-grade NAEP Reading, by Race/Ethnicity for Various Years, 1992–2007 (The Nation's Report Card, 2007, p. 11).

What I find particularly interesting about these data, however, are the percentages of students tested (see Table 9.2). As can be seen below, the percentages of students of color assessed are extremely small, raising serious questions about the representativeness of aggregate groups and interpretations of student achievement based on these data.

9-year-olds	1992	1994	1998	2000	2002	2003	2005	2007
White	73	72	66	63	61	60	59	58
Black	17	17	15	17	17	17	16	16
Hispanic	7	7	14	14	16	17	18	19
Asian/Pacific Islander	2	3	4	4	4	4	5	5

American Indian/ Alaska Native															
	I		I		I		I		I		I		I		I

Table 9.4: Percentage of Students Assessed in Fourth-grade NAEP Reading, by Race/Ethnicity for Various Years, 1992–2007 (The Nation's Report Card, 2007, p. 11).

But the data are less important than what comes from these data, and these data have generally been used to pathologize students of color and limit their educational possibilities through the widespread use of low-level, test-driven curricula in overpopulated and underfunded schools. Current federal involvement in education has used national reviews and content assessments to help bring about reform, particularly through initiatives like Reading First that tie performance to federal monetary support. However, Au (2009) and other scholars take a more critical view of large scale assessments, noting as Sheppard, Hammerness, Darling-Hammond, and Rust (2005) have that they are often "used to monitor achievement trends over time, to evaluate educational programs, or to hold districts, schools, and teachers accountable" (p. 307). Ladson-Billings (2009) observes that in schools that serve poor students of color, testing dominates the school curricula, in part because test scores are made public whereas in schools that serve more wealthy students, testing is not as strongly emphasized.

Conclusion

To bring this chapter full circle, let's return to the stories about boiling frogs and miner's canaries I presented at the beginning of this chapter. Much like the boiling frogs story, the traditional and accepted history of the normal distribution of intellect, only seems to be true. Some politicians, researchers, educators, and the general public, however, have been lulled into believing the concept of a normal distribution of intellect, that psychological tests measure innate intellect, and that intelligence is racially/ethnically determined. This chapter points out the fallacy of these ideological assumptions that underpin some educational and reading assessments. The critical and seldom recognized history of normal distribution of intelligence and linkages to educational and reading assessment is much like the miner's canaries; it is true and points to serious dangers ahead.

Beyond the folktales that began this section are several popular media stories that explicate how the notion of normal is a part of our everyday discourse with little thought to how it has been socially constructed, maintained, and used to delimit access and opportunity in a meritocratic educational system. In a nation that prides itself on the idea of independence and celebrates an individual's ability to overcome personal tests and trials; there is a peculiarity in the process that seeks to codify educational progress under notions of normality. As a social construct, the idea of normalness locates its power in the ordinariness/commonsensical/ simple way in which the discourse surrounding the idea is unchallenged.

This chapter is not the first to articulate historical linkages between the ideological assumptions that underpin notions of normalcy and educational and reading assessments. Dominant values and views along with traditions are difficult to break, and the inequities inherent within educational and reading assessment persist, in large part, because of long-held belief in the natural distribution of intelligence. Despite documentation and evidence to the contrary, researchers and policy makers seldom critique or challenge the scholarship that informs curricula, instruction, policy, and research. As the luster of NCLB fades, and as politicians, researchers, and agencies scramble for funding, scientism, positivism, and racism—ideological assumptions that underpin educational and reading assessments—continue unabated. To move forward, we need a new vision of the multiple knowledges that inform our intelligence, a more detailed and precise means of assessing both.

References

Au, W. (2009) *Unequal by design: High-stakes testing and the standardization of inequality.* New York: Routledge.

Bond, H. M. (1924). Intelligence tests and propaganda. *The Crisis, 28,* 63–64.

Bond, G., & Dykstra, R. (1967). The cooperative reading program in first-grade reading instruction. *Reading Research Quarterly, 2,* 5–142.

Cattell, J. M. (1890). Mental tests and measurements. *Mind, 15,* 373–381.

Cattell, J. M. (1896). Address of the president before the American Psychological Association, 1895. *Psychological Review, 3,* 134–148.

Cattell, J. M. (1928). Early psychological laboratories. *Science, 67,* 543–548.

Cattell, J. M., & Farrand, L. (1896). Physical and mental measurements of the students at Columbia University. *Psychological Review, 3*(6), 618–648.

Eugenics Archive. (2005). Image archive on the American eugenics movement. Retrieved July 22, 2005, from http://www.eugenicsarchive.org/eugenics.

Goodman, K. S. (2006). The truth about DIBELS: What it is—What it does. Portsmouth, NH: Heinemann.

Hurd, C. A. (2008). Cinco de Mayo, normative whiteness, and the marginalization of Mexican-descent students. *Anthropology & Education Quarterly, 39*(3), 293–313.

Johnson, C. (1923). The mental testing of Negro groups. *Opportunity, 1,* 21–28.

Karier, C. (1986). *The individual, society, and education: A history of American educational ideas* [2d ed.]. New York: Free Press. (Original work published 1967).

Katzman, M. T., & Rosen, R. S. (1970). The science and politics of National Educational Assessment. *The Record, 71*(4), 571–586.

Ladson-Billings, G. (2009). Race still matters: Critical race theory in education. In M. W. Apple, W. Au, & L. A. Gandin (Eds.), *The Routledge international handbook of critical education,* (pp. 110–122). New York: Routledge.

Lagemann, E. C. (2000). *An elusive science: The troubling history of education research.* Chicago, IL: University of Chicago Press.

Long, H. (1923). Race and mental tests. *Opportunity, 1,* 22–25.

Montagu, M. F. A. (1945). Intelligence in northern negroes and southern whites in the first world war. *American Journal of Psychology, 58,* 161–188.

National Assessment of Educational Progress (2007). The nation's report card. Retrieved from http://nationsreportcard.gov/

National Reading Panel. (2000). *Teaching children to read: An evidence-based assessment of the scientific research literature on reading and its implications for instruction.* Washington, DC: National Institute of Child Health and Human Development.

Popkewitz, T. (1984). *Paradigm and ideology in educational research: The social functions of the intellectual.* London: Falmer.

Richardson, T., & Johanningmeier, E. V. (1998). Intelligence testing: The legitimation of a meritocratic educational science. *International Journal of Educational Research, 27*(8), 699–714.

Rury, J. (1988). Race, region, and education: An analysis of black and white scores on the 1917 Army Alpha Intelligence Test. *Journal of Negro Education, 57*(1), 51–   65.

Samelson, F. (1977). Ware War I intelligence testing and the development of psychology. *Journal of the History of Behavioral Sciences, 13,* 274–282.

Sheppard, L., Hammerness, K., Darling-Hammond, L., & Rust, F. (2005). Assessment. In L. Darling-Hammond & J. Bransford, *Preparing teachers for a changing world: What teachers should learn and be able to do* (pp. 275–326). San Francisco: Jossey-Bass.

Snow, C. E., Burns, S., & Griffin, P. (Eds.). (1998). *Preventing reading difficulties in young children.* Washington, DC: National Academy Press.

Sokal, M. M. (Ed.). (1987). *Psychological testing and American society.* New Brunswick, NJ: Rutgers University Press.

Spring, J. (1972). Psychologists and the war: The meaning of intelligence in the Alpha and Beta tests. *History of Education Quarterly, 12*(1), 3–15.

Terman, L. (1920). *National intelligence tests, with manual of directions.* Yonkers-on-the-Hudson. New York: World Book.

Travers, R. (1983). *How research has changed American schools: A history from 1840 to the present.* Kalamazoo, MI: Mythos.

Willis, A. I. (2008). *Reading comprehension research and testing in the U.S: Undercurrents of race, class, and power in the struggle for meaning.* Mahwah, NJ: Lawrence Erlbaum.

Willis, A. I. (2009). EduPolitical research: Reading between the lines. *Educational Researcher, 38*(7), 528–536.

Willis, A. I., & Harris, V. J. (1997). Expanding the boundaries: A reaction to the first grade reading studies. *Reading Research Quarterly, 32*(4), 439–445.

Yerkes, R. M. (1921). *Psychological Examining in the Unites States Army, Memories of the National Academy of Science, Vol. 15.* Washington, DC: Government Printing Office.

Ten

A Dialogue We've Yet to Have: Race and Disability Studies

Beth Ferri

Johnnella Butler's (1989) call for scholars to more deeply engage in difficult yet necessary dialogues around race, gender, sexuality, and class is also relevant to the ways that scholars have yet to fully account for the overlapping politics of disability and race. As Erevelles, Kanga, and Middleton (2006) write, scholars in "critical race theory and disability studies have rarely explored the critical connections between these two historically disenfranchised groups within educational contexts" (p. 77). Given the longstanding problem of overrepresentation of students of color in special education (Blanchett, 2006; Losen & Orfield, 2002; Ferri & Connor, 2006; Harry & Klingner, 2006), it has become increasingly difficult to ignore these connections. Could it be that, "educators and researchers believe that if they do not name these issues, they will go away" (Blanchett, 2008, p. xii)?

A quick, yet disheartening review of *Dissertation Abstracts* does not bode well for the field. Of the ninety-nine dissertations published in the past five years that include "disability studies" in the title, abstract, or as a key term, only twenty-four include analyses of race or ethnicity, and of those only five are in the field of education. It seems clear that unless we intervene quickly we will likely produce another generation of disability studies scholars willfully ignorant of issues of race. A similar lack of engagement with disability studies is evident in scholarship focused on racial inequity. It is into this absence that I write—hopeful that this chapter serves as an invitation for more sustained and meaningful dialogues among my colleagues in disability studies and race studies.

There are many difficult dialogues that remain to be explored between critical race theorists and scholars in disability studies in education. Working margin to margin, I examine one potential starting point for building a coalitional politic that accounts for and works to eradicate multiple ways that students are "othered" in schools. Specifically, I focus on the entangled histories of racism and ableism embedded in the construction of mental deficiency (and normalcy) as well as the legacies of this history. I begin this conversation with the ways of talking about race and disability that have been less than helpful and then point to the history of feeblemindedness as one of the several promising starting points for moving the dialogue forward. Although I don't focus explicitly on issues of normality or the normal curve, discussions of the intersection of race and disability—or gender and race or race and class and so on—reveal just how simplistic and misleading the construct of normal is.

Speaking for One Another

According to Bakhtin, explanation requires only one consciousness, while understanding requires two (Hohne & Wussow, 1994). Thus, understanding requires that we both orient ourselves to the particular context of the "other" and engage in dialogue across our differences (Morris, 1994)—an engagement infused with multiplicity and productive tension. This does not involve speaking to or for one another—but entering into a more dialogic engagement across difference.

Certainly there are many connections between disability studies and critical race studies. As a group, scholars in both fields are not so much cohesive in terms of focus or methodology as they are committed to a shared interest in social justice (Bell, 2009). Both disability studies and critical race studies place ideology at the center of their analyses—exploring ways that ableism and/or racism are deeply engrained in the very structures of society (Parker & Lynn, 2009). Both reject biological determinism and view race and/or dis/ability as socially constructed, ever shifting in terms of meaning and shaped by intersecting political, social, and historical contexts. Finally, both fields value narrative and counter-narrative (Parker & Lynn, 2009), not simply as expressions of lived experience but as important sites of knowledge production to resist hegemonic representations that valorize individuals, groups, and bodies of knowledge deemed "normal" and marginalize the "other." Yet, despite these and other similarities, scholars in critical race studies and disability studies have yet to engage in any sustained dialogue about the interconnections between ableism and racism. Of course, we should not assume that these groups would agree on either the source of the problem or its solution.

Thus, what is needed is not simply a cursory attending to race or ethnicity but a sustained and careful analysis of the ways racism and ableism are interdependent. Unfortunately, too often, when scholars or activists do attempt to combine analyses of race and disability or gender and disability, they do so by analogizing between the two or placing these systems of oppression in a hierarchy (May & Ferri, 2005). This amounts to placing one type of oppression as overarching or as foundational to all others. A common claim is that disability cuts across all the other forms of oppression. Moreover, because anyone can acquire disability it is therefore thought to be more universal, as opposed to the particular interests of race or gender, I suppose. I admit to being puzzled by these assumptions. Don't race, gender, and sexuality, for example, cut across social class? Moreover, what is universal about disability experience—Is there really one disability experience or isn't it mediated by the particular social, historical, and political context?

A slightly different approach attempts to garner attention to one type of oppression by linking it to another, usually through analogy. Consider a bumper sticker that reads something like, "Black people had to fight for the right to ride in the front of the bus, but we can't even get on the bus." Other examples use terms like being "shackled" by ableism or "crippled" by racism. These analyses ignore the ways that racism and ableism are dissimilar—ways that they cannot or should not be seen as interchangeable or analogous. Moreover, they all but erase those who experience racism and ableism simultaneously—a point cogently raised in the germinal collection of essays, *All the Women Are White, All the Blacks Are Men, But Some of Us Are Brave: Black Women's Studies* (Hull, Scott, & Smith, 1982).

Another approach focuses on the "double jeopardy" of race and gender (Beale, 2008); or, disability and gender (Rousso & Wehmeyer, 2001); or, race/ ethnicity and disability (Fierros & Conroy, 2002); or, the "triple jeopardy" of race, gender, and sexuality (Bowleg et al., 2003; King, 1988); or, gender, race, and disability (Demas, 1993). Although these analyses are preferable to ones that completely ignore the intersection of race and disability, for instance, they run the risk of oversimplifying interlocking and multiple systems of oppression by offering a false sense of equivalency among different forms of oppression (Carbado, 1999). In other words, if we think about various forms of oppression and privilege from this model, anyone can be and often is multiply situated by diverse forms of privilege and oppression. This, however, is not to say that all forms of oppression are equivalent or interchangeable—a form of "conceptual tidiness" that Spelman (1988) rightly critiques. Thus, although one may experience heterosexual privilege, this should not be construed as similar to the ways someone else might experience racial privilege or class privilege. Neither will our experiences of one form of oppression (ableism or homophobia, for example) be analogous to someone else's, particularly if we live in very different circumstances because of race or social class, for example.

Finally, disability studies scholars have yet to grapple with the ways that disability has functioned as a "discursive tool for exercising white privilege and racism", (Blanchett, 2006, p. 24), as well as normative gender and sexual practices. Perhaps it is because of these many ways that attempts to "do" intersectionality can and often do go wrong that scholars have come to see this work as impossible and simply avoid it. It is telling, for instance, to pick up a disability studies book and search the index for terms like race or ethnicity. Even if you find these terms, the analysis will often be brief and superficial—the "embarrassing etcetera" (Butler in Zerilli, 2004) tacked on at the end of a list of more central oppressions. Likewise, you will most likely see a similar dearth of attention to disability or ableism in books that focus on critical race studies, leaving disability to be defined as asocial, apolitical, and ahistorical. Evoking biological determinism and deficit notions of disability, critical race theorists have sought to distance themselves from any association with disability (Erevelles et al., 2006).

The bulk of educational literature examining race and disability has focused on documenting overrepresentation in special education (Harry & Klingner, 2006; Losen & Orfield, 2002). Requiring schools to disaggregate achievement data by race and ethnicity has been "a powerful tool for describing inequity and addressing its causes" (Gibb & Skiba, 2008, p. 2). This said, I think it is safe to say that we have done more describing and documenting the problem than addressing its causes or proposing solutions. Thus, although scholars have begun to address the ways that race and disability intersect (Connor, 2008; Erevelles et al., 2006; Ferri & Connor, 2006; Harry & Klingner, 2006; Watts & Erevelles, 2004), there is much work that remains. As Blanchett (2008) writes,

> A first step in moving forward toward more equitable schooling opportunities and experiences for impoverished African Americans and other students of color identified as having disabilities is to openly discuss these issues, how they play out in educational settings, how practices and policies contribute to these and other educational inequities, and how individuals identified as having disabilities experience the intersections of disability with race and social class in the American educational system. (p. xii)

In the remaining section of this chapter I discuss one of the more difficult dialogues that remain to be explored between critical race theorists and scholars in disability studies in education. I focus therefore on the concept of mental deficiency as it represents a pernicious confluence of ableism and racism.

The Color of Ability

According to Noguera (2006), "innate racial differences rooted in biology have been…the favored explanation for disparities in intellectual performance between students of color and white students" (p. 5). Race and class differences in measures of "intelligence" have been taken for granted as evidence of white, middle class superiority, rather than a cause for questioning the legitimacy of such measures. Prevailing ideas about race, class and ability provide the justification for "otherwise morally indefensible political and economic institutions such as slavery and colonialism" as well as various sorting practices in schools (Oakes, Wells, & Datnow, 1997, p. 487). The history of mental deficiency, therefore, is an obvious place to begin to try to come to terms with the interconnected histories of racism and ableism in education, as well as the legacies of this history in terms of our current practice.

Historically, disability (and particularly mental or cognitive disability), according to Baynton (2001), proved to be an effective tool in justifying discrimination and inequality not just of people with disabilities but also women and racial minorities as well. Mental retardation and all of its related terms is a construction whose "changing meaning is shaped both by individuals…and by the social context to which these individuals are responding" (Trent, 1994, p. 2). At their core, however, cultural meanings of mental deficiency are saturated with eugenic-based racism, which gave the concept the traction it needed in order to be seen as a social and political cause for concern (Danforth, 2009). This explains why mental deficiency only became a crisis once it was associated with a host of "social ills such as crime, unemployment, prostitution, and alcohol abuse" (Danforth, 2009, p. 20). Conveniently, these and other social problems were blamed on the inherited defectiveness of individuals, who were variously characterized as mentally defective, feebleminded, and subnormal. But when did the idea of feeblemindedness get entangled with race, in particular, and why, despite scientific evidence to the contrary, does this supposed relationship between race and ability remain so ingrained? How can retracing this history help us to locate where and when notions of race figured into ideas about dis/ability? And, finally, how does challenging the legacy of this shared history of ableism and racism necessitate a coalitional politic?

The concept of mental deficiency arose as a "response…to serious disruptions and dislocations that resulted from the nation's transformation into an urban, industrial society" (Franklin, 1987, p. 190). The historical context would most likely include two World Wars, the Great Depression, the largest wave of immigration into the U.S., and the vast migration of African Americans from the rural south to the burgeoning urban centers of the north. To say these were tumultuous times would be an understatement. It is against this historical backdrop that we see the earliest facilities designed for individuals who were considered feebleminded which, despite efforts to the contrary, were more custodial than educational, as well as the first college textbook focusing on special education (Franklin, 1987), and the first teacher training programs (Osgood, 1999).

Despite some early optimism that these state schools for the feebleminded would parallel the successful education of individuals who were blind or deaf, the rhetoric quickly shifted, making it clear that these institutions were for the protection of the state, rather than for the education of the individuals who were placed in them. By the time eugenics gained currency in the first two decades of the 20th century, feebleminded women of child bearing age became targets for ever more restrictive interventions. Reformers proposed that, "all women under 30, when arrested for misdemeanors, or upon the birth of a second illegitimate child, should be committed" until they were past child bearing age (Trent, 1994, p. 74). The first of these institutions for women, according to Trent, was opened about sixty miles west of Syracuse, NY for women between the ages of sixteen to forty-five. This particular focus on women reveals the view at the time that feeblemindedness was an inherited trait, which if left unchecked, would pose a serious burden on society.

When it became obvious that institutionalizing every feebleminded individual in the country would be impossible—partly because the term was so ill defined and also because, at the time, the U.S. was facing serious economic hardships—states began to look for alternatives, such as sterilization. Individuals who submitted (either voluntarily or involuntarily) to sterilization could be released back into the community. The most famous example of eugenic sterilization was argued in the *Buck v. Bell* Supreme Court decision of 1927, which upheld a Virginia eugenic sterilization statute. After the Court sided with VA, 30 more states passed similar statutes. Before the practice was overturned, 65,000 Americans (mostly women) were sterilized without their own or their family's consent (image archive). Speeches given by superintendents of state "schools" for feebleminded individuals illustrate the thinking at that time. At an annual conference in Vermont, the superintendent of one institution reported feeling gratified that the state is "beginning to take a marked interest in the study of feeblemindedness" (Russell, 1917, p. 31). He writes that the "burden of feeblemindedness is felt by the entire public and every intelligent person who has considered the subject realizes that this blight on mankind is increasing at an alarming rate" (p. 31). The expressed concern was that birthrates of poor and immigrant women were outpacing white and middle class women. The superintendent claims that rather than waste time and resources trying to train or educate such individuals that a more "rational and progressive policy" for dealing with this "great problem" (p. 32) was "early identification of feebleminded persons" so they could be removed from public schools and placed in "special institutions" (p. 33).

A few years later another superintendent identified the "subnormal mind" as the country's "greatest social burden" (Allen, 1921, p. 3). He named feeblemindedness as "a prolific cause of crime, prostitution, disease, pauperism and human inefficiency" (p. 5). He went on to claim that "every feebleminded person is potentially a criminal and that every feebleminded woman is potentially a prostitute" (p. 6). Reflecting eugenic thinking, he located the abnormal condition of feeble-mindedness in heredity and, therefore, advocated "segregation, specialized train-ing and supervision" in a state school for mental defectives as "the only practical and sensible" course of action (p. 7). He further proposed that males be admitted between the ages of five and twenty-one and females between the ages of five and forty-five. Of course, economic conditions in the U.S. at the time made this vision of almost lifelong incarceration impractical. This vision was soon replaced with other modes of containment, including marriage restrictions and forced (or coerced) sterilization (Danforth, 2009).

Of increasing concern at the time were individuals who were considered "high grade" mental defectives, who could "care for themselves and may present no physical evidence of deficiency," but who were thought to be at risk of be-coming a "pauper, alcoholic, thief, prostitute or graver criminal" (Russell, 1917, p. 32). Over time there was a shift from feeblemindedness being characterized as a burden to it being characterized as a menace (Trent, 1994, p. 141). Because of her supposed ability to pass her defect on to her offspring, "the higher grade men-tally defective girl of child bearing age" was often posited as the greatest threat to the community. The "high grade feebleminded person" (Russell, 1917, p. 31), because of "their resemblance to the normal person," made them all the more dangerous. Individuals in this category, superintendents argued, required clinical diagnosis and specialized training and supervision (Allen, 1921). Of course, the new field of mental measurement quickly established itself as the clinical arbiter of normalcy because it could root out these more subtle differences among indi-viduals that were not obvious to the ordinary—or normal—person.

Yet, even before states began widespread institutionalization of so-called de-fectives, the U.S. passed the "Undesirables Act" in 1882 to ensure that "convicts, paupers, the insane, and idiots" would not be able to enter the country (Trent, 1994, p. 86). These laws reflected a concern about the waves of immigrants coming into the U.S. before and after WWI, particularly from southern Europe (Italians, Jews, and Eastern Europeans). Compared to earlier immigrants from northern and western Europe, latter groups were more often poor and illiterate (Erevelles et al., 2006). Because of their already low status, they were obvious targets for the loose and unformed categories of "unfit" and "feebleminded." Viewed as an inherited trait, feeblemindedness was linked to criminality, devi-ance, or dependence (image archive). Thus, the fact that immigrants were poor or illiterate was not thought to be a reflection of social, political, or economic circumstances but, rather, due to inherited deficiencies. After eugenics fell out of favor, these same groups were seen to be "culturally deficient" products of the negative effects of urbanization or industrialization on our nation (Franklin, 1987). Although often seen as progressive, compulsory education was a natural outgrowth of earlier attempts at social control, such as sterilization, institutional-ization, and marriage restriction.

Viewing this history from a contemporary lens might lead most people to think that the earliest groups associated with mental deficiency were immi-grants and poor people, particularly women, not people of color. For example, Goddard's 1912 infamous study of the Kallikak family as well as similar stud-ies that followed, focused primarily on the rural poor, not on people of color. Moreover, discourse about feeblemindedness rarely mentioned race specifically (Trent, 1994). However, as Guglielmo and Salerno (2003) argue, many of the later waves of immigrants coming into the U.S. were not considered white. Moreover, blacks, already legally segregated in the South under Jim Crow, were migrating to northern cities in great numbers. Yet, unlike other groups that eventually became "culturally absorbed" and granted "white" status, African Americans "contin-ued to remain the denigrated racialized other in U.S. society" (Erevelles et al., 2006). Thus, the answer to the question about when feeblemindedness became entangled with race is that it has been from the very beginning—as long as you understand race to be socially constructed.

But, why do these ideas continue to hold sway, particularly for students of color, and what are the legacies of this history in terms of education? Like the concepts themselves, the educational responses to so-called "backward" children emerged in the political, social, and economic conditions of 20th century America (Franklin, 1987). The first non-custodial classes for students who were considered "backward" emerged in the form of ungraded classes (Franklin, 1987; Osgood, 1999). Patterns of enrollments in these classes are instructive. In Boston, enroll-ment in special classes grew slowly in the first "twelve years of their existence," but between 1912 and 1930 and coinciding with ever-increasing diversity in the city and compulsory attendance laws, enrollments in special classes burgeoned. During the same period in Atlanta, special classes for "deaf, blind, mentally de-fective, socially maladjusted, and backward" children were instituted—at least for white students (Franklin). However, after forced desegregation and compulsory attendance laws, special classes would once again be called upon to serve those students who had been rejected by general education and would again experi-ence burgeoning enrollments, particularly among students of color and English language learners.

If we pay close attention to the history of special education, what we see is a series of attempts to deal with diversity by creating ever more specific categories of otherness, categories which have always been (and continue to be) associated with race, class, and culture/ethnicity. We should not be surprised that today's special education classrooms continue to be overly populated with students of color, particular in those categories that are more subjective (and less obvious, like the "high grade" mentally defective category), that patterns of school disciplinary referrals and placements are disproportionately applied to students of color, or that the achievement gap continues to mirror racial inequalities. What we should be surprised at is the lack of real engagement with these inequities. Does our collective silence, as disability studies scholars, reveal a complicity in this history—are we not surprised because we expect to see these differences? If we link the history of categories, such as mental retardation, and special education more broadly with racist ideologies, do we stop at critiquing only the over-representation of students of color or do we insist on dismantling the whole enterprise? If we, as critical race scholars, take "our" kids out, who do we think still belongs "in there"? What then justifies our current state of affairs and how do we collectively dismantle it?

Conclusion: Is Coalition Possible?

Calls for coalitions often assume, uncritically, that there are shared interests among two separate groups, in this case, those whose work focuses on race and those whose work focuses on disability. Of course, many scholars would find such an assumed dichotomy puzzling—working always from the intersections of these as well as other identity categories. But, for the moment, let us assume that, given the fact that there are programs, journals, book series, and degrees that are demarcated by their particular focus on either race or disability, these are indeed separate fields of study. What then is possible in terms of working margin to margin—of building and sustaining a coalition? What are the conditions that would facilitate disability studies scholars and critical race scholars becoming more reliable allies? Moreover, what would a viable and sustainable coalition require of ourselves and each other?

As Carmichael and Hamilton (2008) write in their chapter "The Myths of Coalition," there are often unexamined assumptions operating in calls for co-alition. First, such calls assume that there are shared interests—that each party stands to benefit from the alliance. However, what this has often amounted to is the belief that what is good for the majority is also good for the minority, advancing an agenda that uncritically equates the dominant group's interests with what is normal universally. In other words, "what is assumed to be good for white people will necessarily be good for black people," is often an unstated assumption operating in calls for coalition. Yet, these groups often operate from different sets of premises and priorities, which can lead to conflicts of interests, rather than shared interests (Carmichael & Hamilton, 2008).

Before we can engage in a shared dialogue or form coalitions, Carmichael and Hamilton (2008) insist that we engage in a serious and self-critical examination of any potential conflicts of interests between our groups. We must also acknowledge and account for differences in political and economic power between ourselves and any potential ally. Finally, we must determine a mutually beneficial goal that we both stand to benefit from the alliance. It is from this position of shared self-interest that fuels a sustainable coalition.

The purpose of this chapter was to open a dialogue about what might be a useful starting point from which to forge a coalition—to begin to outline the points of contact between our various struggles for social change. Such points of contact are not necessarily without conflict or tension. Thus, we must not be satisfied with seeking out the easy places where we walk side-by-side, but rather the more difficult moments where we must face one another eye-to-eye and engage across our differences—to see where our histories entangle and our futures interdepend. If we fail to engage in this more difficult work, we will stay the course but ultimately fail to do the more transformational work that we must do to ensure schools are a place where all students can and do thrive.

References

Allen, T. J. (1921, October 16). Mental defect: Its manifestations, influence, and control. *Proceedings of the Seventh Vermont Conference of Social Work.* (pp. 3–12). Original located at: University of Vermont, Special Collections.

Baynton, D. C. (2001). Disability and the justification of inequality in American history. In P. K. Longmore & L. Umansky (Eds.), *The new disability history: American perspectives* (pp. 33-57). New York: New York University Press.

Beale, F. M. (2008). Double jeopardy: To be black and female. *Meridians: Feminism, race, transnationalism, 8*(2), 166–176.

Bell, C. (2006). Introducing white disability studies: A modest proposal. In L. J. Davis (Ed.), *The disability studies reader* [2d ed.]. (pp. 275–282). New York: Routledge.

Bell, D.A. (2009). Who's afraid of critical race theory? In E. Taylor, D. Gillborn, & G. Ladson-Billings (Eds.). *Foundations of critical race theory in education* (pp. 37–50). New York: Routledge.

Blanchett, W. (2005). Urban school failure and disproportionality in a Post-*Brown* era: Benign neglect of the constitutional rights of students of color. *Remedial and Special Education, 26*(2), 70–81.

Blanchett, W. (2006). Disproportionate representation of African American students in special education: Acknowledging the role of white privilege and racism. *Educational Researcher, 35*(6), 24–28.

Blanchett, W. (2008). [Foreword] Educational inequities: The intersection of disability, race and social class. In D. J. Connor. *Urban narratives: Portraits in progress, Life at the intersections of learning disability, race, and social class* (pp. xi–xvii). New York: Peter Lang.

Bowleg, L., Huang, J., Brooks, K., Black, A., & Burkholder, G. (2003). Triple jeopardy and beyond: multiple minority stress and resilience among black lesbians. *Journal of Lesbian Studies, 7*(4), 87–108.

Butler, J. (1989, February). Difficult dialogues. *Women's Review of Books, 1,* 16.

Carbado, D. W. (1999). Black rights, gay rights, civil rights: The deployment of race/sexual orientation analogies in the debates about the "don't ask, don't tell" policy. In D.

W. Carbado (Ed.). *Black men on race, gender, and sexuality: A critical reader* (pp. 283–302). New York: New York University Press.

Carmichael, S., & Hamilton, C. (2008). The myths of coalition. *Black Power: The politics of liberation in America. Race/Ethnicity, 1*(2), 171–188.

Connor, D. J. (2008). *Urban narratives: Portraits in progress, Life at the intersections of learning disability, race, and social class.* New York: Peter Lang.

Danforth, S. (2009). *The incomplete child: An intellectual history of learning disabilities.* New York: Peter Lang.

Demas, D. (1993). Triple jeopardy: Native women with disabilities. *Canadian Women's Studies, 13*(4), 53–55.

Erevelles, N. (2000). Educating unruly bodies: Critical pedagogy, disability studies, and the politics of schooling. *Educational Theory, 50*(1), 25–47.

Erevelles, N., Kanga, A., & Middleton, R. (2006). How does it feel to be a problem? Race, disability, and exclusion in educational policy. In E. Brantlinger (Ed.). *Who benefits from special education? Remediating [fixing] other people's children* (pp. 77–99). Mahwah, NJ: Lawrence Erlbaum.

Fierros, E. G., & Conroy, J. W. (2002). Double jeopardy: An exploration of restrictiveness and race in special education. In D. Losen & G. Orfield (Eds.). *Racial inequity in special education* (pp. 39–70). Cambridge, MA: Harvard Education Press.

Ferri, B. A., & Connor, D. J. (2006). *Reading resistance: Discourses of exclusion in desegregation and inclusion debates.* New York: Peter Lang.

Franklin, B. M. (1987). The first crusade for learning disabilities: The movement for the education of backward children. In T. S. Popkewitz (Ed.). *The formation of school subjects: The struggle for creating an American institution* (pp. 190–209). London: Falmer.

Gibb, A. C., & Skiba, R. J. (2008). Using data to address equity issues in special education. Bloomington, IN: Center for Evaluation & Education Policy. Retrieved September 23, 2009 from: http://www.iub.edu/~safeschl/Equity/resources.html

Guglielmo, J., & Salerno, S. (Eds.). (2003). *Are Italians white? How race is made in America.* New York: Routledge.

Harry, B., & Klingner, J. (2006). *Why are there so many minority students in special education?* New York: Teachers College Press.

Hohne, K., & Wussow, H. (Eds.). (1994). *A dialogue of voices: Feminist literary theory and Bakhtin.* Minneapolis, MN: University of Minnesota Press.

Hull, G. T., Scott, P. B., Smith, B. (1982). *All the women are white, all the blacks are men, but some of us are brave: Black women's studies.* New York: Feminist Press.

Image archive on the American eugenics movement. Dolan DNA Learning Center, Cold Springs Harbor Laboratory. Retrieved August 5, 2009 from http://www.eugenicsarchive.org/eugenics/

King, D. K. (1988). Multiple jeopardy, multiple consciousness: The context of black feminist ideology. *Signs: Journal of Women in Culture and Society, 14*, 42–72.

Lombardo, P. A. (2008). *Three generations, no imbeciles: Eugenics, the Supreme Court, and Buck v. Bell.* Baltimore, MD: Johns Hopkins University Press.

Losen, D. J., & Orfield, G. (2002). *Racial inequality in special education.* Cambridge, MA: Harvard Education Press.

May, V. M., & Ferri, B. A. (2005). Fixated on ability: Questioning ableist metaphors in feminist theories of resistance. *Prose Studies, 27*(1 & 2), 120–140.

Morris, P. (1994). *The Bakhtin reader: selected writings of Bakhtin, Medvedev, Voloshinov.* London: Edward Arnold

Noguera, P. (2006). *Unfinished business: Closing the racial achievement gap in our schools.* San Francisco: Jossey-Bass.

Oakes, J., Wells, A. S., & Datnow, A. (1997). Detracking: The social construction of ability, cultural politics, and resistance to reform. *Teachers College Record, 98*(3), 482–510.

Osgood, R. L. (1999). Becoming a special educator: Specialized professional training for teachers of children with disabilities in Boston, 1870–1930. *Teachers College Record,* 101(1), 82–105.

Parker, L., & Lynn, M. (2009). What's race got to do with it? Critical race theory's conflicts with and connections to qualitative research methodology and epistemology. In E. Taylor, D. Gillborn, & G. Ladson-Billings (Eds.). *Foundations of critical race theory in education* (pp. 148–162). New York: Routledge.

Roberts, D. E. (1997). *Killing the black body: Race, reproduction, and the meaning of liberty.* New York: Pantheon.

Rousso, H., & Wehmeyer, M. C. (Eds.). (2001). *Double jeopardy: Addressing gender equity in special education.* Albany, NY: State University of New York Press.

Russell, F. J. (1917, January 24). The deficient child. *Proceedings of the Second Annual Vermont Conference on Charities and Correction.* (pp. 31–33). Original located at: University of Vermont: Special Collections.

Spelman, E. (1988). *Inessential woman: Problems of exclusion in feminist thought.* Boston, MA: Beacon.

Spelman, E. (1997). *Fruits of sorrow: Framing our attention to suffering.* Boston, MA: Beacon.

Trent, J. W. (1994). *Inventing the feeble mind: A history of mental retardation in the United States.* Berkeley, CA: University of California Press.

Watts, I. E., & Erevelles, N. (2004). These deadly times: reconceptualizing school violence by using critical race theory and disability studies. *American Educational Research Journal, 41*(2), 271–299.

Zerilli, L. M. G. (2004). The universalism which is not one. In S. Critchley & O. Marchart (Eds.). *Laclau: A critical reader* (pp. 88–110). New York: Routledge.

ELEVEN

Labeling and Treating Linguistic Minority Students with Disabilities as Deficient and Outside the Normal Curve: A Pedagogy of Exclusion

Felicity A. Crawford & Lilia I. Bartolomé

"This population, this population," the new euphemism for inferior, minority, ignorant, illegal immigrant, you pick whichever you want. "This population"—I hear it all the time . . . I am so tired of it. They might as well say "spic" because that's what they mean. "This population" has roaches; "this population" does not speak to their children; "this population" doesn't care about their children; "this population" is neglected; "this population" can't read; "this population" does not honor students; "this population" is low, low, low. This list goes on . . . and writing this exhausts me.

—Reflections of a Latina special educator in a predominantly Spanish-speaking urban elementary school in the Northeast. December 5, 2007

In our land of promised equal opportunity, the quality of schooling provided to the fastest-growing segment of our population—linguistic minority students in high-poverty school districts—is as problematic as schooling for students identified as having disabilities. For instance, in 2008, a mere 58% of Latino high school students graduated within four years (Editorial Projects in Education Research Center, 2008)—a percentage not much higher than the 52% graduation rate for students with disabilities reported in 2002–03 (National Center on Learning Disabilities, 2008). Jim Cummins (2003) noted that, "school failure of subordinated marginalized students is attributed to alleged intrinsic characteristics of the group itself (e.g., genetic inferiority, parental apathy, bilingualism, etc.) or to social and educational programs that are intended to serve the interests of the group" (p. 41). Therefore, linguistic minority children with disabilities often encounter attitudes and beliefs among both pre-service and in-service special educators that have a bearing on the teachers' expectations and on the type of curricula they design for students (Crawford, 2007). For example, while reflecting on her experience as an intern in a substantially separate special education classroom, a student of one of the authors asked, "How are we expected to bring them up when they are on the down escalator?"

The prevailing deficit ideology is based on a number of factors, including an entrenched pseudoscientific theory that defines intelligence as being either fixed or innate, or as one's general or limited ability (see, e.g., Burt, 1955/1973; Galton, 1865). This view depends on the equally powerful dominant ideology that a "normal" group exists and is used as the standard against which all other groups are measured. Although this normal group is not explicitly named or described, it is clear that it is made up of white, middle-class, native English-speaking, and able-bodied students who, by virtue of their class standing, possess the type of cultural capital expected in school.

In our role as teacher educators, we struggle to name and make clear to our students these classist and white supremacist ideologies that influence so much thinking in education. As teacher educators who prepare future special education (SPED), English as a second language (ESL), and sheltered English (SE)[1] teachers, we are well aware that effective teachers require more than technical expertise. While we recognize the need to impart to our students the technical skills they require to competently teach SPED, ESL, or SE students, we argue in this chapter that it is equally important that they understand the ideological dimensions of education. In fact, given that our students will most likely work with non-white, low-socioeconomic-status linguistic minority students, many of them diagnosed as having special needs, it is equally important that current and prospective teachers understand the ideological dimensions of their work that could have an adverse impact on teaching of students from subordinated populations.

We believe that teacher-education programs must include the explicit study of the role ideology plays in shaping the curriculum and of the asymmetrical power relations that often exist between school personnel, students, and their communities. Moreover, current and prospective teachers need to be given frequent opportunities to name and challenge their unacknowledged views of their linguistic minority students with disabilities as being "outside the normal range," and, thus, different from "regular" students, where "different" is a polite euphemism for "deficient" and, ultimately, "inferior" (Finnerty, 2002).

In this chapter, we propose that educators, as part of their teacher-education studies, formally study ideology and learn about the harmful manifestations that various dominant ideologies can have in school contexts. This is particularly urgent in special education and ESL/SE classrooms, where teachers work with student populations that are generally perceived as inferior. Therefore, drawing from well-established literature on the medical model of special education, the social construction of "difference" (Cummins, 2003; Trifonas, 2003), and the politics and economics of failure (Duncan-Andrade & Morrell, 2008), we examine how the ideology of deficit thinking (Bartolomé, 2008; Valencia, 1997) shapes school structures and educators' instructional and assessment practices and portrays linguistic minority students with disabilities as falling on the left-hand tail of the normal curve. We begin by contextualizing our chapter with a discussion of the significance of including the study of ideology in teacher-preparation programs.

What Is Ideology and Why Do Special Education Teachers Need to Study It?

Teacher-education researchers suggest that prospective teachers tend to have uncritical and even unconscious beliefs about the existing social order that reflect dominant ideologies that are harmful to many students (Gomez, 1994; Gonsalves, 2008; Haberman, 1991; Marx & Pennington, 2003). Definitions of ideology include the worldview of a particular social class or group, an officially sanctioned set of ideas used to legitimize a political system or regime, or the ideas of the ruling class (Heywood, 2003, p. 6). Terry Eagleton (1991) emphasizes, as we do in this chapter, the concept of ideology as legitimizing the power of a dominant social group or class. Quoting John B. Thompson, Eagleton explains that, "to study ideology is to study the way in which meaning (or signification) serves to sustain relations of domination" (p. 5). Dominant ideologies are typically reflected in both the symbols and the cultural practices that shape people's thinking, so that people unconsciously accept the current way of doing things as natural and normal.

Gramsci (1971) defined dominant or hegemonic ideology as the power of the ideas of the ruling class to overpower and eradicate competing views and to become, in effect, the commonsense view of the world. Furthermore, "Gramsci emphasized the degree to which ideology is embedded at every level in society, in its art and literature, in its education system and mass media, and its everyday language and culture" (Heywood, 2003, p. 8). Given their pervasiveness, dominant cultural ideologies perpetuated in schools are generally unseen, and if they are perceived, they tend to be viewed as conventional wisdom or common sense. Thus, unquestioningly accepting them can well be construed as legitimate and normal to those who may be less discerning. In fact, Eagleton (1991) explains that dominant cultures use a variety of strategies to legitimize hegemonic ideologies and render them invisible. One key strategy includes portraying such beliefs as natural and universal, thus making them seem self-evident and even inevitable.

Eagleton (1991) further explains that because hegemonic ideologies are perceived by society as natural and self-evident, alternative ideas are perceived as being unthinkable and, thus, are rarely considered. This strategy of naturalizing underlies the belief that human diversity is, in fact, characterized by a bell-shaped curve of the normal, "one of the most powerful ideological tools of modern society" (see Dudley-Marling & Gurn, this volume). The belief that there is an inherently objective and purely scientific way to categorize humans according to intelligence or academic ability is a prime example of a hegemonic ideology, one that is uncritically accepted as conventional truth in the field of education in general and special education in particular.

Only recently, as exemplified in this volume, have efforts been made to go beyond the border of the unthinkable and to confront previously unquestioned "truths" of the "normal distribution of normality." As part of these efforts, we argue that students in teacher-preparation programs must be offered opportunities throughout their course of studies to name and interrogate potentially harmful hegemonic ideologies and to imagine more humane, just, and accurate theories and the resulting practices in their work with linguistic minority and special needs of students.

A Sociohistorical Analysis of Special Education and Linguistic Minority Students

There is a tremendous need for critically thinking teachers who understand the links between ideology, power, culture, and language in educational contexts. This is especially true in special education, given its history of pseudoscience and exclusionary racist and classist practices. A common starting point for helping educators identify hegemonic ideologies includes situating the object of study—in this case, the field of special education—sociohistorically. Taking a sociohistorical perspective gives students the opportunity to contemplate the ideologies inherent in the social, political, and economic structures that, in turn, influence linguistic minority special education. This will help them develop a more comprehensive, dialectical understanding of the field and to study current educational challenges both critically and profoundly.

Paulo Freire (1985) maintains that in order to solve an educational problem, it is necessary to first understand it historically; that is, to comprehensively construct the problem. The second step is to analyze the problem critically—to deconstruct it. The third and final step is to imagine alternatives and to realistically imagine more humane and democratic solutions—in other words, to reconstruct the problem as an opportunity for change that can yield more positive solutions.

To adequately name, analyze, interpret, and then re-envision a pedagogy of possibility, one that serves the best interests of English language learners and students with disabilities, requires that we discuss the social construction of the notion of "difference," the pseudoscientific medical model in special education, racist ideologies and the growth of special education, the politics and economics of failure, and some resulting instructional and assessment practices that reflect deficit thinking and "othering" of black[2] and Latino students.

These topics help educators understand how the notion of difference applies to English language learners with disabilities. This is important because it defines the social and historical landscape that informs educators' practices. Furthermore, as Mannheim (1936) asserts, inherited ideas not only shape how everyone, including educators, responds and operates on a daily basis, they play a role in the plans we develop and then use as a starting point for our own judgment and actions. Later in the chapter, we illustrate what occurred when tacit agreement on inherited ideas led to four special educators' unquestioning use of racist materials in an urban high school classroom, where the students were mostly Spanish-speaking immigrants. We begin, though, with a look at the social construction of difference.

Linguistic minority students and the social construction of "difference" in special education

Dominant groups in countries the world over have deliberately and methodically organized their educational structures in ways that construe human differences (e.g., race, class, language, gender, and culture) as deficits, which, in turn, are viewed as the source of students' academic failures (Cummins, 2003). Arguments to justify this view range from racist claims about genetic inferiority to the influence of family socialization processes, which inevitably point to the victims as the source of their own failures (Ryan, 1992). Cummins (2003) asserts that the "coercive power relations" that emerge from this arrangement permeate the "role definitions of educators (e.g., their mindset, attitudes, expectations) as well as the organizational structure (e.g., curriculum, assessment, language of instruction, etc.) of schooling" (p. 41).

The type of efforts bilingual education opponents make to subordinate linguistic minority student populations have historically also been evident in special education. Lawrence Finnerty (2002) explains, "Throughout the history of special education, the issues of 'difference' versus disability, social class, and bias-free assessment have been problematic for all students but especially for non-white linguistic minority students" (p. 28). "Difference" in special education, he contends, is synonymous with "inferiority." To explain, Finnerty utilizes Martha Minow's (1990) assertion that difference, when ignored or held up to scrutiny as the single identifying characteristic, serves to stigmatize, isolate, and exclude another. By marking "others" with some kind of signifier, the majority is tacitly rendered normal and neutral, with an embedded assumption of sameness or equality.

By contrast, students who fall at the tails of the normal distribution—outside the boundaries of normal—are perceived as being different from the invisible normal population against whom they are compared. Difference thus becomes linked to the notion of inequality and, finally, to inferiority. Therefore, the process of identifying and serving some students based primarily on their perceived differences gives way to a highly ideological and subjective assessment and labeling process. The following section illustrates how the conception of difference in special education was succeeded by a system of service that mirrored what was construed in medicine.

The evolution of special education in the U.S.

From the inception, care for individuals with disabilities in the U.S. was left up to parents and private charitable organizations. By the turn of the 20th century special education became a segregated space in public schools for holding youths with disabilities who were forced into schools because of a newly mandated compulsory schooling law that came to fruition as a result of two competing agendas: social control and humanitarianism (Lazerson, 1983). The need to control the whereabouts of the rapidly growing numbers of non-English speaking immigrants from poor families was spurred on by the prevailing eugenicist ideology, which simultaneously promoted selected parentage and restricted the breeding of "others" (e.g., people with disabilities, immigrants and poor families) deemed inept, "feeble-minded," and "subnormal" (Osgood, 2008, p. 47) with "criminal" (p. 54) and "over-sexed" (p.24) tendencies. The impetus for social control was fuelled by the perceived need to protect so-called "normal" children from contact with individuals with disabilities and to ensure the so-called homogeneous academic grouping of students in regular classrooms (Ferri & Connor, 2006; Johnson, 1967;9; Lazerson, 1983; Osgood, 2008; Tweedie, 1983).

Concurrently, progressive reformers looked to schools to provide the humanitarian space wherein the social needs of immigrant youths were to be addressed alongside the growing need to Americanize an increasingly diverse student population[3] (Lazerson, 1983) consisting of impoverished youth from Eastern and Southern Europe, and to instill in them a common work ethic that would contribute to a growing industrial nation. These two ideas, though divergent, served as impetus for the passage of a law that mandated schooling for all children—which effectively placed very "undesirable" children in the same room with "normal" children (Tweedie, 1983). What followed was the creation of a segregated space in schools—special education. Though ostensibly designed to provide appropriate services to children with disabilities, special education was, from its inception, a holding place for society's deviants who no one wanted to teach (Ferri & Connor, 2006).

The institution of special education gained legitimacy with the advent of intelligence testing. Building on the work of Alfred Binet, intelligence tests were redesigned for the "feebleminded" and promoted by Stanford University psychologist Lewis Terman in 1917 (Lazerson, 1983). Terman, proposed that feeblemindedness, though ever-present, was never given the attention it warranted. He claimed to have examined many individuals from diverse backgrounds and found that feebleminded people were responsible for many of the prevailing ills of the day: alcoholism, criminal behavior, pauperism and venereal diseases (Terman, February 1917, as cited by Lazerson, 1983).

Bolstered by his findings Terman administered thousands of intelligence tests to children in Oakland and published confirmatory reports that touted his success in improving outcomes for students in regular education and a growing efficiency in providing services for students with disabilities (Lazerson, 1983). Intelligence testing soon caught on in other urban settings, and by the 1920s there was exponential growth in the number of students assigned to special education and to the formalizing of the profession. Pennsylvania, for example, led the way in increasing the numbers of children in special education, which it accomplished through the widespread use of the IQ test and published reports (Lazerson, 1983).

By the 1930s, with the U.S. in the midst of the Great Depression and new problems on the minds of its citizens, the cost of the very programs that were aimed at containing society's so-called deviants came under scrutiny. Although that decade proved to be a struggle for advocates of children with disabilities, they nonetheless gained funding for vocational programs for youth with disabilities (Osgood, 2008). The post war (World War II and Vietnam) and Civil Rights eras yielded much more movement in legislation that changed the conditions under which children in special education were to be taught (Tweedie, 1983). On one hand, the post war and civil rights eras brought with them the activism of white middle class families and other advocates (e.g., special educators, legislators, lobbyists and attorneys) who took their cue from the precedent set by the *Brown v Board of Education* (1954) decision (which stipulated that separate schooling was an inherently unequal proposition). Advocates pursued the right-to-education (Tweedie, 1983) argument and through litigation and later through legislation— namely, the *Rehabilitation Act* (1973) and the *Education for All Handicapped Children Act* (P.L. 94-142) (1975)—secured services for and ensured the rights of individuals with disabilities (U.S. Department of Education, 2007).

More recently, the landmark law, now known as the *Individuals with Disabilities in Education Act* (IDEA), was reauthorized in 1990, 1997 and again in 2004, each time extending the level of access to services for students with disabilities. As a result, there are more categories of disabilities; increased parental advocacy; a greater chance of ensuring the right of children with disabilities to a free and appropriate education in the least restrictive environment; access to individualized education program; and, access to due process hearings if services are undercut (Ferri & Connor, 2006). Despite the increased strength of this legislation, the experiences as well as public perceptions of students with disabilities remain largely unchanged (Ferri & Connor, 2006).

Ferri and Connor (2006) propose another reason why the spirit of IDEA is yet to come to fruition: the persistence of the systematic resistance to the desegregation mandates handed down by the *Brown* decision which led to the overrepresentation of vast numbers of black and Latino children in special education. Although the problem of overrepresentation was meticulously documented for more than four decades after being brought to national attention by Dunn (1968) and later, by other scholars and members of Congress (Artiles Rueda, Salazar and Higareda, 2002; Ferri & Connor, 2006; Johnson, 1969; Oswald, Coutinho, & Best, 2002; U.S. Congress House Committee on Education and Workforce, 2002), the problem has since grown progressively worse. Artiles et al. (2002), for example, report that English language learners (ELL) at the secondary level are more than twice as likely as their English speaking peers to be placed in self-contained settings and are more often than not identified as having mental retardation (MR) and speech and language impairments.

Another reason for the persistence of disappointing gains made as a result of IDEA lies in the paradox that making provisions for individuals with disabilities yields. As far back as the 1960s, little, if any, attention was paid to the fact that entitlements like Title I, III, VI of P.L. 88–164 (1963), which supported the development of special education also inadvertently provided a perverse incentive for black and Latino youths to be placed in disproportionate numbers in special education (Johnson, 1969). Title I, part C of P.L. 88–164, for example, provided federal grants to aid in the construction of public or nonprofit clinical facilities, as well as services and training to professionals who worked with individuals with mental retardation (see, for example, Pennsylvania Office of Mental Retardation, 1967). These monies were dependent on the number of individuals with disabilities who needed services (U.S. Department of Education, 2007).

Coupled with the established culture of resistance to educating children with disabilities in regular classrooms, black and Latino youths, regardless of socioeconomic status, when compared to their white peers, continue to be disproportionately placed in restrictive, self-contained settings with minimal access to grade-level curriculum—a condition that subverts their chances for gainful employment or post-secondary opportunities (Ferri & Connor, 2006; Fierros & Conroy, 2002; Florian & McLaughlin, 2008; Harry, Klingner, Sturges, & Moore, 2002; Harry &

Klingner, 2005; Osgood, 2008). In sum, the legislative history of special education has a well-entrenched race-based deficit ideology and culture of resistance
that has gained strength since *Brown v. Board of Education* (1954) and the civil rights
era (Hilliard, 2001). Other issues that plague the effectiveness of the outcomes
for students with disabilities have to do with the stigma that comes along with
labeling children.

The pedagogy of labeling

Hobbs's 1975 landmark report, which synthesizes the research about the consequences of inappropriately classifying and labeling children in education, reveals
a complex and ambiguous process that is fraught with problems. According to
Hobbs, student labels are typically constructed to convey specific technical information. With time, however, the listeners change, as do the intent and meaning
of classifications that rely on clinical judgment instead of verifiable data that are
indicative of a disability. Thus, Hobbs concedes, labels originally designed to help
students often wind up becoming the source of discrimination and denigration.
As noted earlier, special education has become the dumping ground for black and
Latino students, who are often identified by categories of disabilities that rely on
clinical judgment rather than data that point to disabilities with physical manifestations (Harry et al., 2002). Blacks and Latinos, for example, are more frequently
identified as having emotional disturbances than their white counterparts (Harry
& Klingner, 2005).

The problem of classification in special education is, of course, not new. Using ethnographic methods, Mehan, Hartwick, and Meihls (1986), for example, set
out to learn how children with disabilities are classified. Mehan and his colleagues
followed students' progression through the special education process: referral,
consideration, appraisal, assessment, reappraisal, evaluation, and placement. They
found that students were referred for a variety of reasons, all of which were
based on perceived behavioral, academic, or physical deficits. In the process, they
found discrepancies between educators' stated "interview reasons" and "official
reasons" for why students were referred. For example, when teachers responded
to their video-taped accounts, they referred more to the "official" or academic,
behavioral, psychological, and social issues. Moreover, when demonstrated by
students without disabilities, the same behaviors, regardless of frequency, did not
elicit the same reaction. The strength in Mehan et al.'s (1986) study comes from
their agreement that institutional practice is a form of cultural practice and that
the two are not inseparable. We would add that cultural practices, even when represented as institutional practice, represent the values, beliefs, and perspectives of
those who have the power to shape practice. Once institutionalized, these practices take on a life of their own and become normal operating procedure.

Racist ideologies, a deficit view of nonwhites in special education

The deficit notion cannot be separated from the theories of inferiority that parallel the growth of this nation and the actions of its founding members. In fact, the notion of deficits was at the center of the nation's founding ideology, and white America has struggled to justify its exploitive economic policies as it addresses the demographic shifts resulting from immigration (Harry & Klingner, 2005; Valencia, 1997). According to the prevailing deficit thinking, students who fail do so because of "alleged internal deficiencies (such as cognitive and/or motivational limitations) or shortcomings socially linked to the youngster—such as familial deficits and dysfunctions" (Valencia, 1997, p. xi). Similarly, the trend of disproportionately negative outcomes for non-white students is preceded by a long history, which continues today with the high rates of school failure, dropout, and imprisonment among African American and Latino students in special education programs (Losen & Orfield, 2002; Valencia, 1997). In fact, Valencia (1997) suggests that high levels of school failure and overrepresentation in special education among non-white students is in large part due to the fact that special educators continue to use the self-perpetuating "description-explanation-prediction-prescription" (p. 7) cycle that operates within a deficit paradigm. Valencia's four-stage cycle begins by identifying students' shortcomings, followed by educators' explanations that attribute students' deficits to limited intellectual capabilities or dysfunctional family backgrounds. Students so described are inevitably labeled deficient.

Over time, labels for students who are viewed as deficient have included: ineducable, handicapped, culturally and linguistically deprived, semilingual, and, more recently, at-risk (Flores, 1982, 1983). Moreover, the explanations educators supply, even today, have become the basis on which they make predictions about how the deficits they identify will impact students. Although the mission of schools across the country reflects the notion that "all children can learn," what happens in practice runs counter to that statement. Students with low socioeconomic status—blacks and Latinos in particular—are often tracked in lower-level classes and identified for special education that is delivered in settings separate from the general—or normal—classroom (Harry & Klingner, 2005; Oswald, Coutinho, & Best, 2002; Valencia, 1997). The deficit paradigm persists, in part, because schools continue to rely on it to diagnose disabilities. Each case comes with a label that enables educators to pathologize, track, place, and serve students in a prescriptive manner. Culturally and linguistically subordinated students of color in urban schools are most often tracked into lower-level classes, where they tend to receive inadequate instruction and a substandard curriculum. Another reason the notion of deficit persists is that many of the assessment procedures for referring and placing students remain unchanged. Models are still premised on diagnostic tests that are set up to attribute failure to problems within children that need remedy (Harry et al.,

2002). After being referred, students are sorted according to supposed behavioral and cognitive inabilities, which become the basis upon which they are labeled and placed in self-contained special education classrooms (Mehan et al., 1986; Rist, 1970).

The persistence of failure

Our examination of the social construction of difference as deviant, particularly as it relates to linguistic minority students with disabilities, would be incomplete without identifying racist, classist, and ableist ideologies and understanding why they exist in the first place. Duncan-Andrade and Morrell (2008) assert in a recent book that urban school failure persists because the U.S. collectively subscribes to the belief that "someone has to fail in school" (p. 2). Duncan-Andrade and Morrell propose that the idea that some will fail is substantiated with statistical calculations—suggesting a seemingly irrefutable expectation—that reflect a so-called normal distribution. With such "evidence," the system of grading, testing, and sorting students continues uncontested, thereby guaranteeing the same result. Although thoroughly refuted by rigorous scholarship (e.g., Trifonas, 2003; White, 2006), the prevailing discourses of deficit and cultural deficiency have been repeatedly used as justification for why schools fail some children more than others. Herrnstein and Murray (1994), for example, proposed that blacks and Latinos are intellectually inferior to their white counterparts. The nature of an individual's schooling is also instrumental in determining their economic future (Duncan-Andrade & Morrell, 2008). Those who fulfill the least economically viable roles in society do so because the sorting mechanism of school—which provides better educational opportunities for those with the requisite social, economic, and political capital, and the inverse for those without—justifies their place in society (Bowles & Gintis, 1976).

Another reason failure persists among students who fall outside the boundaries of normality is the endurance of powerful myths, such as the idea that opportunity exists for anyone who wants it, which is often the lynchpin in rags-to-riches stories and in the notion that competition will ensure the rise of the best among us. The fact is that there is not much room at the top, and sorting has replaced the more overt racist and classist policies (Duncan-Andrade & Morrell, 2008) that continue to weigh heavily on how teachers, including special educators, define their students, organize their classrooms, and implement lessons.

Below we discuss a type of "methods fetish" (Bartolomé, 1994) that occurs in special education classrooms, whereby teachers treat high school students as they would much younger children by using activities and materials normally meant for elementary school. Similar to what Bartolomé (1994) discusses in her article regarding the technical and methodological focus in the linguistic minority literature, we maintain that in special education, especially in regard to linguistic minority education, the common belief that the educational challenges of special education linguistic minority students is in finding the "right" teaching method or strategy that will magically work with these students. Another similarity in this belief system is that the "problems" all lie within the students, as teachers or other school experts show little consideration for contextual factors or the social construction of disability. A final similarity has to do with the belief that what works best with special needs students is direct, basic skills instruction and that the unilinear curriculum they use resembles that offered to younger students. For example, if special needs students test at a particular grade level, a common response by teachers is to use materials designed for that particular grade level, no matter how infantile or insulting the students may find the materials. Typically, the students are not allowed to skip the sequence employed by the particular basal series or program. In essence, what often occurs in special education (and in English-only classrooms with students limited in English) is that teachers begin with "easy" materials such as those used in kindergarten and proceed through the curriculum in a lock-step manner, knowing fully well that given the numbers of days in the school year, students will never catch up no matter how hard they work. In addition, when teachers follow a unilinear curriculum, even if students master more advanced concepts, they are often not allowed to work on those concepts until they demonstrate mastery of most basic skills. Shirley Brice Heath (1983) discovered this unilinear curriculum fetish in her research on mainstream teachers who worked with lower socioeconomic status African American students. She explained that although the students could be highly creative linguistically (e.g., they played with words, puns, rhymes, told rich and varied stories, etc.), teachers felt obligated to have them slog through an entire basal workbook that focused on low-level skills like letter-sound activities, even though the students demonstrated their well-developed phonemic awareness skills during informal activities. These teachers, like so many special educators who work with black and linguistic minority students, translate their unacknowledged deficit views of their students into basic, unchallenging, and often irrelevant instruction.

Instructional and Assessment Practices That Reflect Deficit Thinking and the "Othering" of Black and Latino Students

There seems to be an uncritical acceptance of a unilinear curriculum in special education in which no matter how old the students, teachers tend to begin with the alphabet, phonics, and other simplistic concepts. Illustrating this point, in Crawford's (2007) study of teacher attitudes and practices, she observed and interviewed four veteran special educators in an urban high school. Their tenth-grade students, who had moderate disabilities, included a majority of blacks and

Latinos. The goal of Crawford's study was to learn how the teachers planned and implemented curricula for these special education students. The findings indicate that these teachers consistently used beginner-level curricular material instead of the state-mandated high school curricula. The history teacher, for example, used a textbook by Bernstein (1997) that was intended for grades 4 to 8. The three-page chapters included large pictures, text that was typeset in an oversized (18-point) font, and assignments that required students to "fill in the blanks; match column A with column B; and put a check next to each sentence" (p. 20). When compared to the expectations in terms of depth of knowledge and understanding for the regular ninth-grade history curriculum, this teacher's materials fell far short. The teacher never used any exercises, for example, that promoted the study of pivotal political, economic, or social events that shaped the specific period under study, as mandated by the state of Massachusetts (Massachusetts Department of Education, 2001).

Crawford (2007) argued that the language teachers use shapes and reflects the expectations they have in any situation (Gee, 2002). In this case, the infantile "simplicity of the foregoing passage construed an elementary school reality in a high school classroom" (p. 19), with assignments that promoted "writing without composing" (Nagin, 2003, p. 39), a practice that advances "skill-based instruction and negates opportunities for students to engage in higher order cognitive processes, such as reflecting and analyzing, which are essential aspects of critical thinking" (Crawford, 2007, p. 19).

During this study, Crawford discovered disturbing materials one of the teachers was using in an English class. Coming from a series entitled, *Power English: Book I: Basic Language Skills for Adults* (Rubin, 1999), this brightly covered text featured images of culturally diverse people, characters with names such as José and Maria. Below is a sample of one of the exercises in Rubin's text:

Fill in the blank with a word from this list. Use each word only once. Be sure the completed sentences make sense.

how	where	who	why
when	what	husband	
jail	police	shelter	

1. _____ is she so frightened?
2. Her _____ beat her yesterday.
3. My friend called the _____.
4. _____ told you all this?
5. _____ did they take him?
6. They took him to _____.

7. _____ happened next?
8. She slept in a _____.
9. _____ is she coming home?
10. _____ long have they been married? (p. 43)

This particular exercise was saturated with beliefs and expectations that instanti-ated the teachers' deficit and racist assumptions and reflected a skills-based in-structional approach that did not afford students any opportunities to develop or practice the higher-order skills required for achieving high school competencies. This pattern has been repeatedly characterized as problematic by scholars (see Tyack, 1976, 1996; Tyack & Cuban, 1997, for example) who portray school as a socializing agency that transmits biased societal beliefs and expectations. These findings reflect James Gee's (2002) assertion that educators provide the level of communication that they believe "fit" (Gee, 2002, p. 11) the context within which students operate, which, in this case, also reinforced biased perceptions of chil-dren (Crawford, 1997).

A similar outcome was evident in a classic study by Diaz, Moll, and Mehan (1986) which investigated the learning experiences of English language learners in the English language component of a southern California bilingual program. Diaz et al. (1986) found that, regardless of their existing native-language literacy abilities and experiences in school, English language learners were typically treat-ed like kindergarteners or beginners in school in the English language component classroom. The English language teacher in this study consistently began his Eng-lish language arts instruction by teaching the students phonics, with the rationale that the students failed to "sound out" specific words "naturally" (i.e., these chil-dren spoke English with an accent). The teacher continued to bore them with phonics lessons because, in a unilinear and lock-step approach to the language arts curriculum, teachers erroneously expect students to master letter-sound cor-respondence before they are perceived as capable of reading for comprehension or meaning. Yet, when the English language teacher observed his students in the Spanish language component during Spanish language arts, he quickly discovered that they could read above grade level and, in fact, demonstrated high levels of comprehension when reading in their stronger language. The English teacher deduced that if the students could read above grade level in Spanish, then they obviously had mastered letter-sound correspondence (phonics). He also realized that his focus on having his English language students sound out the letters in English with native-like pronunciation was incorrect and distracting to their com-prehension. This teacher adjusted his instruction to reflect what he eventually found out about his students' level of native language literacy. Subsequently, he allowed his students to read English silently and to discuss the readings with their peers in both English and Spanish.

What is hopeful about this second study is that the teacher adjusted his instruction to reflect a more appropriate starting point for his students' learning experiences in English. However, in the two studies described, educators initially began with a unilinear, "infantile" approach to teaching that relied solely on a direct, basic skills approach rather than providing students opportunities to build on their existing language and literacy skills or life experiences to enhance their learning of critical thinking skills that are integral to the 21st-century educational experience.

While it is clear that the prevailing use of a unilinear, lock-step, and exclusively basic skills approach taken by the educators in the examples put forth in this chapter does little to enrich students' understandings, there are a variety of approaches and principles that, if applied, offer much more promising results. These include Culturally Responsive Pedagogy (Gay, 2000), Differentiated Instruction (Tomlinson & McTighe, 2006), Understanding by Design (Wiggins & McTighe, 2005), and Universal Design for Learning (Rose & Mayer, 2006). A culturally responsive approach to instruction, for example, is ideal in situations where the teacher is unfamiliar with his or her students and runs the risk of viewing and treating them as deficient and incapable (as the Crawford research example so powerfully and painfully demonstrates). The focus of this approach is to tap into and build on students' life experiences and their existing knowledge and skills as both a strategy for learning about their students and for "hooking" students into learning conventional academics (Villegas & Lucas, 2002). Much like the English language teacher in the Diaz et al. (1986) study, teachers who subscribe to a culturally responsive approach create a variety of learning activities during which they learn about their students' lives and previous educational experiences, which also challenges teachers' implicit beliefs that their students don't know anything that is of value or relevant to their school learning. Culturally responsive pedagogy requires that educators begin with the belief that every child can learn, and with the expectation that they have the knowledge and skills to provide students all that they need, including knowledge of how to use a variety of technologies in order to access and make significant progress in the general curriculum. Taken together, these approaches ensure that educators know how to weigh their own biases and take into account the ways their students are impacted by the social and cultural positions they occupy as members of subordinated groups. Moreover, regardless of students' circumstances, educators who take these approaches seriously will not only seek to ensure that they teach to and through students' strengths, they will use a variety of critical thinking tools and strategies to facilitate their participation as knowledge producers and their in-depth understanding of content. Moreover, given their focus on meeting the needs of all students, educators who embrace the principles previously described will create space in their curricula to recognize and honor their students' unique learning styles; provide them choices in constructing, deconstructing, and reconstructing knowledge (Freire, 1985); and, utilize technology to enable students to use what they know to create new, hopeful opportunities for themselves as learners and leaders.

Conclusion

The thrust of this chapter has been to help teacher educators begin to see that teachers' daily practices (e.g., their plans and actions in a classroom), particularly with linguistic minority students who have disabilities and are typically identified as falling outside the boundaries of normality, are powerfully shaped by received, uncontested beliefs about normalcy that are mistakenly but powerfully substantiated by decontextualized and biased statistics and pseudoscientific thinking. Such ideas can take up residence in educators' psyches and become the basis from which they operate (Darder, Baltodano, & Torres, 2003). To prepare educators who can appropriately name, examine, and reconstruct alternative ways of teaching begins with a pedagogy that nurtures hope, innovation, and successful intervention and instills a sense of humanity in learning environments currently occupied by students whom we recognize only by their differences or deviances. This type of pedagogy requires that educators, particularly those who serve English language learners and children with disabilities, learn how to responsibly identify, analyze, contest, address, and then monitor the ways in which they perpetuate current dominant ideas that have proven detrimental to students identified as falling outside the boundaries of normality.

Endnotes

1. Sheltered English instruction refers to English-only instruction that is treated as being synonymous with content-based ESL. It is defined as follows: "[Sheltered English instruction] teaches English and its components (vocabulary, discourse style, and syntax) using the core curriculum as the means. . . . The primary goal of sheltered instruction is to teach academic subject matter. . .using comprehensible language and context, enabling information to be understood by the learner. Sheltered instruction functions as a support until the student is ready for mainstream classes" (Echevarria & Graves, 2003, p. 8). Unfortunately, despite the fact that SE was envisioned for intermediate ESL students, often, even newcomers with little or no English proficiency are enrolled in SE classrooms. In 2002, the state of Massachusetts outlawed the use of non-English languages in classroom, dismantled bilingual education, and mandated sheltered English instruction for students identified as limited English proficient.

2. The term "black" in this chapter represents youths from across the African Diaspora and not just African Americans.

3. It is important to keep in mind that at this historical moment in time, non-white caste minorities such as African Americans, Mexican Americans, and Native Americans

were excluded from participation in integrated public schools. Thus, any discussion of "diversity" in the literature that deals with this time period typically refers to Eastern and Southern Europeans.

References

Artiles, A. J., Rueda, R., Salazar, J. J., & Higareda, I. (2002). English-language learner representation in special education in California urban school districts. In D. J. Losen & G. Orfield (Eds.), *Racial inequity in special education* (pp. 117–136). Cambridge, MA: Harvard University Press.

Bartolomé, L. I. (1994). Beyond the methods fetish: Toward a humanizing pedagogy. Cambridge, MA: *Harvard Educational Review, 64,* 173–194.

Bartolomé, L. I. (2008). Introduction: Beyond the fog of ideology. In L. I. Bartolomé (Ed.). *Ideologies in education: Unmasking the trap of teacher neutrality* (pp. ix–xxix). New York: Peter Lang.

Bernstein, V. (1997). *World history and you. Book 1.* Orlando, FL: Steck-Vaughn.

Bowles, S., & Gintis, H. (1976). *Schooling in capitalist America: Educational reform and the contradiction of economic life.* New York: Basic.

Brown v. Board of Education (1954). 347 U.S.C. 483.

Burt, C. L. (1973). The evidence for the concept of intelligence. In S. Wiseman (Ed.). *Intelligence and ability.* Harmondsworth, England: Penguin. (Original work published 1955).

Crawford, F. (2007). Why bother? They are not capable of this level of work: Manifestations of teacher attitudes in an urban high school self-contained special education classroom with majority Blacks and Latinos. In P. Chen (Ed.), *E-yearbook of urban learning, teaching and research* [American Educational Research Association Special Interest Group] (pp. 12–24) [Online]. http://www.aera-ultr.org/Web%20Site%20Files/Images/PDF%20files/2007_eYearbook_final.pdfCrawford, J.

Cummins, J. (2003). Challenging the construction of difference as deficit: Where are identity, intellect, imagination, and power in the new regime of truth? In P. P. Trifonas (Ed.). *Pedagogies of difference: Rethinking education for social change* (pp. 41–60). New York: RoutledgeFalmer.

Darder, A., Baltodano, M., & Torres, R. D. (2003). *The critical pedagogy reader.* New York: RoutledgeFalmer.

Delpit, L. (1995). *Other people's children: Cultural conflict in the classroom.* New York: New Press.

Diaz, E., Moll, L., & Mehan, H. (1986). Sociocultural resources in instruction: A context specific approach. In California State Department Bilingual Education Office (Ed.), *Beyond language: Social and cultural factors in schooling language minority students* (pp. 187–230). Los Angeles: California State University, Los Angeles Evaluation, Dissemination, and Assessment Center.

Duncan-Andrade, J. M. R., & Morrell, E. (2008). *The art of critical pedagogy: Possibilities for moving from theory to practice in urban schools.* New York: Peter Lang.

Dunn, L. M. (1968). Special education for the mildly retarded: Is much of it justifiable? *Exceptional Children, 35,* 5–22.

Eagleton, T. (1991). *Ideology: An introduction.* London: Verso.

Echevarria, J., & Graves, A. (2003). *Sheltered content instruction: Teaching English language learners with diverse abilities.* Boston: Allyn and Bacon.

Editorial Projects in Education Research Center. (2008). *1.23 million students will fail to graduate in 2008: New data on U.S. Congressional districts detail graduation gaps* [Online]. http://www.edweek.org/media/ew/dc/2008/DC08_Press_FULL_FINAL.pdf

Ferri, B. A., & Connor, D. J. (2006). *Reading resistance: Discourses of exclusion in desegregation and inclusión debates.* New York: Peter Lang.

Fierros, E. G., & Conroy, J. W. (2002). Double jeopardy: An exploration of restrictiveness and race in special education. In D. J. Losen & G. Orfield (Eds.). *Racial inequity in special education* (pp. 39–70). Cambridge, MA: Harvard Education Press.

Finnerty, L. (2002). *Cultural and linguistic diversity: Difference or disability? An exploratory case study of the team evaluation process* (Vol. 1). Unpublished doctoral dissertation, University of Massachusetts, Boston.

Flores, B. M. (1982). *Language interference or influence: Toward a theory for Hispanic bilingualism.* Unpublished doctoral dissertation, University of Arizona, Tucson.

Flores, B. M. (1993). *Interrogating the genesis of the deficit view of Latino children in the educational literature during the 20th century.* Paper presented at the annual meeting of the American Education Research Association.

Florian, L., & McLaughlin, M. J. (2008). *Disability classification in education: Issues and perspectives.* Thousand Oaks, CA: Corwin.

Freire, P. (1985). *The politics of education: Culture, power, and liberation.* New York: Bergin & Garvey.

Galton, F. (1865). Hereditary talent and character. *Macmillan Magazine, 12,* pp. 157–166.

Gay, G. (2000). *Culturally responsive teaching: Theory, research and practice.* New York: Teachers College Press.

Gee, J. P. (2002). *An introduction to discourse analysis: Theory and method.* New York: Routledge.

Gomez, M. L. (1994). Teacher education reform and prospective teachers' perspectives on teaching "other people's children." *Teaching and Teacher Education, 10,* 319–334.

Gonsalves, R. E. (2008). Hysterical blindness and the ideology of denial: Preservice teachers' resistance to multicultural education. In L. I. Bartolomé (Ed.). *Ideologies in education: Unmasking the trap of teacher neutrality* (pp. 3–28). New York: Peter Lang.

Gramsci, A. (1971). *Selections from the prison notebooks* (Q. Hoare & G. Smith, Trans.). New York: International. (Original work published 1935)

Haberman, M. (1991). Can culture awareness be taught in teacher education programs? *Teacher Education, 4,* 2–31.

Harry, B., & Klingner, J. K. (2005). *Why are so many minority children in special education?: Understanding race and disabilities in schools.* New York: Teachers College Press.

Harry, B., Klingner, J. K., Sturges, K. M., & Moore, R. F. (2002). Of rocks and soft places: Using qualitative methods to investigate disproportionality. In D. J. Losen & G. Orfield (Eds.). *Racial inequity in special education* (pp. 71–92). Cambridge, MA: Harvard Education Press.

Heath, S. B. (1983). *Ways with words.* New York: New York University Press.

Herrnstein, R., & Murray, C. (1994). *The bell curve: Intelligence and class structure in American life.* New York: Free Press.

Heywood, A. (2003). *Political ideologies: An introduction* [3d ed.]. New York: Palgrave Macmillan.

Hilliard, A. G. (2001). Race, identity, hegemony, and education: What do we need to know now? In W. H. Watkins, J. H. Lewis, & V. Chou (Eds.). *Race and education: The roles of history and society in educating African American students* (pp. 7–33). Needham Heights, MA: Allyn & Bacon.

Johnson, J.L. (1969). Special education and the inner city: Challenge for the future and another means of cooling the mark out? *Journal of Special Education 3*(3) 241–251.

Lazerson, M. (1983). The origins of special education. In J. G. Chambers & W. T. Hartman (Eds). *Special education policies: Their history, implementation and finance.* Philadelphia, PA: Temple University Press (pp. 15–47).

Losen, D. J., & Orfield, G. (Eds.). (2002). *Racial inequity in special education.* Cambridge, MA: Harvard Education Press.

Mannheim, K. (1936) *Ideology and Utopia,* New York: Harcourt Brace Jovanovich.

Marx, S., & Pennington, J. (2003). Pedagogies of critical race theory: Experimentations with white preservice teachers. *International Journal of Qualitative Studies in Education, 16,* 91–110.

Massachusetts Department of Education. (2001). *Massachusetts history and social science curriculum framework.* Malden, MA: Author.

Mehan, H., Hartwick, A., & Meihls, J. (1986). *Handicapping the handicapped: Decision-making in students' educational careers.* Palo Alto, CA: Stanford University.

Minow, M. (1990). *Making all the difference: Inclusive, exclusive and American law.* Ithaca, NY: Cornell University Press.

Nagin, C. (2003). *Because writing matters: Improving student writing in our schools.* San Francisco: Jossey-Bass.

National Center on Learning Disabilities. (2008). Graduation rates of students with disabilities [Special issue]. Paper prepared for Editorial Projects in Education, Diplomas Count 2006: An Essential Guide to Graduation Policy and Rates special issue, *Education Week,* January 10–11, p. 20.

Osgood, R. L. (2008). *The history of special education: A struggle for equality in American schools.* Westport, CT: Praeger.

Oswald, D. J., Coutinho, M. J., & Best, A. M. (2002). Community and school predictors of overrepresentation of minority children in special education. In D. J. Losen & G. Orfield (Eds.). *Racial inequity in special education* (pp. 1–13). Cambridge, MA: Harvard Education Press.

Pennsylvania Office of Mental Retardation (1967). The 1967 Pennsylvania State plan for the construction of facilities for the mentally retarded (title I, part C, P.L. 88–164). Harrisburg, PA: Dept. of Public Welfare, Office of Mental Retardation and Division of Planning, Evaluation, and Community Programs, Office of Mental Health. [Online] Library of Congress Online Catalog http://lccn.loc.gov/a%20%2068007508

Rist, R. C. (1970). Student social class and teachers' expectations. The self-fulfilling prophecy in ghetto education. *Harvard Educational Review, 40,* 411–451.

Rose, D. H., & Meyer, A. (2006). *A practical reader in universal design for learning.* Cambridge, MA: Harvard Education Press.

Rubin, D. (1999). *Power English: Book 1: Basic language skills for adults.* Upper Saddle River, NJ: Prentice Hall.

Ryan, W. (1992). *Blaming the victim.* New York: Vintage.

Tomlinson, C. A., & McTighe, J. (2006). *Integrating differentiated instruction and understanding by design.* Alexandria, VA: Association of Supervision and Curriculum Development.

Trifonas, P. P. (2003). *Pedagogies of difference: Rethinking education for social change.* New York: RoutledgeFalmer.

Tweedie, J. (1983). The politics of legalization in special education. In J. G. Chambers & W. T. Hartman (Eds). *Special education policies: Their history, implementation and finance* (pp. 48–73). Philadelphia, PA: Temple University Press.

Tyack, D. B. (1976). Ways of seeing: An essay on the history of compulsory schooling. *Harvard Educational Review*, 46, 3, 355-89

Tyack, D. B. (1996). What are good schools and why are they so hard to get? *Journal of Business Administration and Policy Analysis*. 24(26), 172.

Tyack, D. B., & Cuban, L. (1997).*Tinkering toward utopia: A century of public school reform*. Cambridge, MA: Harvard University Press.

U.S. Department of Education (2007). Special education and rehabilitative services. Archived: A 25 year history of the IDEA [Online] http://www2.ed.gov/policy/spe-ced/leg/idea/history.html

U.S. Congress, House. Committee on Education and Workforce (2002). Overidentification issues within the Individuals with Disabilities Education Act and the need for reform: hearing before the Committee on Education and the Workforce, House of Representatives, One Hundred Seventh Congress, first session: hearing held in Washington, DC, October 4, 2001. [Online] http://frwebgate.access.gpo.gov/cgi-bin/getdoc.cgi?dbname=107_house_hearings&docid=f:80039.pdf

Valencia, R. R. (1997). *The evolution of deficit thinking: Educational thought and practice*. London: Falmer.

Villegas, A. M., & Lucas, T. (2002). Preparing culturally responsive teachers: Rethinking the curriculum. *Journal of Teacher Education 53*(1), 20–32.

White, J. (2006). *Intelligence, destiny and education: The ideological roots of intelligence testing*. London: Routledge.

Wiggins, G., & McTighe, J. (2005). *Understanding by design* [2d ed.]. Upper Saddle River, NJ: Prentice Hall.

TWELVE

Sex Education and Young Adults with Intellectual Disabilities: Crisis Response, Sexual Diversity, and Pleasure

Michael Gill

In this chapter, sex education for individuals with intellectual disabilities in the United States is explored; historical changes, contents, and overall messages about appropriate sexuality are discussed.[1] Generally, battles around providing comprehensive sex education for school-age children and adolescents illustrate ideological divisions in the U.S. stemming from different viewpoints regarding appropriate (read: normal) expressions of sexuality. The Christian Right, comprised of conservative Catholics and Christian evangelicals, has rallied against comprehensive sex education in their rise to political power in the U.S. over the last 40 years (Irvine, 2002, p. 3). In contrast, since the 1960s the Sex Information and Education Council of the United States (SIECUS) has argued for more comprehensive sex education including a discussion of sex as pleasurable and not merely reproductive (Irvine, 2002, pp. 17–34). This chapter takes up the historical debate about sex education as the background to discuss sex education for people with intellectual disabilities. While at times the content of sex education for individuals with intellectual disabilities can look quite different than education aimed at a non-disabled cohort, a comparison between sex educations for both populations of individuals allows for a nuanced understanding of sexuality for people with intellectual disabilities. Abstinence-only education has become the most widely used approach for non-disabled and disabled students in classrooms across the U.S. (Fields, 2008; Irvine, 2002; Tepper, 2000). Sex education that meaningfully incorporates a discussion of homosexuality and bisexuality is rare, especially in special education classrooms. Sex education remains a location in which morality, religion, notions of normality and abnormality, and ableism work to endorse and reinforce non-reproductive heterosexual expressions while distancing discussions about sex away from notions of pleasure.

As a whole, the chapter does not seek to determine the educational effectiveness of the various sex educational materials, but rather, considers what meanings and messages are reinforced in these materials.[2] Since professionals in educational and residential settings frequently use these curricula, an analysis provides an understanding of how sex is managed and taught in group homes and classrooms across the U.S.[3] I suggest that, historically, sex education for individuals with intellectual disabilities has failed to address the multiple and varied ways in which people express their sexuality both inside and out of all kinds of relationships. Rather, sex education is used to instruct people with intellectual disabilities that sexual expression is best done by either self-pleasuring through masturbation or with heterosexual partners without the possibility of reproduction. Non-disabled students are taught in sex education that sexual activity and reproduction ought to occur within the bounds of traditional family, an option that is not widely pursued for people with intellectual disabilities because professionals and sex educators do not envision parenting as a viable option. The way of conducting sex education shows the struggles of liberal ideology versus religious conservatism, while the pleasures of sex for individuals are lost in a discourse of abuse and disease prevention. The collective weight of these two competing ideological camps serves as a normalizing discourse that obscures the desires and rights of individuals that do not fit within this dichotomous framing.

Education that centers on individuals with intellectual disabilities as passive receptors as opposed to active agents in their own sexual development helps to disguise how individuals make operative choices as sexual beings. All people, including those with intellectual disabilities, are "agentic sexual subjects," being able to contribute to the development of sex education materials that reflect their experiences and desires (Fields, 2008, p. 171). Sex education for people with intellectual disabilities can equip individuals with self-respect, respect for other people, sexual knowledge that facilitates their sexual expression as well as a comfort in expressing non-dominant ways of sexuality.

Professional Literature on Sex Education

In the 1960s, two events led to a greater focus on sexuality for individuals with intellectual disabilities. The first involved the growing influence of the philosophy of normalization which advocated an increased level of control by people with intellectual disabilities over their daily life choices, and of the notion of "dignity of risk" (Kempton & Kahn, 1991, p. 98), which recognizes the rights of all people as self-determining individuals to take risks and make mistakes. Constant protection, regardless of impairment or disability, limits individual potential to make decisions that can result in failure. Normalization and dignity of risk appreciate that equipping individuals with knowledge of sexuality still affords the responsibility to determine individual sexual decisions. Alongside these philosophical developments within the profession and society, deinstitutionalization resulted in larger numbers of individuals with intellectual disabilities living in the community. Professionals and families were, however, concerned that those outside of the institution would experience sexual abuse and manipulation (Kempton & Kahn, 1991, pp. 98–99). The promotion of sex education offered one way to equip individuals with the tools needed to recognize sexual abuse. Since its inception, a primary function of sex education in the United States has been preventing sex abuse and exploitation. The dominant discourse of sexual education delineates sexuality as a non-pleasurable, potentially dangerous public health activity. In the exploration of sex education for people with intellectual disabilities, the rhetoric of harm reduction is significant throughout. Reducing the potential for sexual abuse and to a lesser extent sexually transmitted disease is a primary goal in sex education for people with intellectual disabilities.

Since the 1970s, many prominent professionals and educators have upheld the belief that individuals with intellectual disabilities have the right to sex education. This abiding belief motivates their work to create a sex education curriculum (Craft & Craft, 1982, 1983; Johnson, 1973; 1975; McCarthy & Fegan, 1984). However, it is questionable if the education materials, their delivery, and the educational outcome of learning can ensure the right-to-have-sex of people with intellectual disabilities, in part, due to constraints of the broader social and institutional settings where they are situated. A close examination of sex education materials and its changes not only provides a gauge to ascertain what professionals and educators think about sexuality in relation to the norms of their times but also illustrates what types of sexuality and expressions of sex are seen as appropriate, or normal, for this population. By extension, we can infer how these professionals define the rights and freedoms of sexuality for people with intellectual disabilities and what these estimations tell us about the sexual status of people with intellectual disabilities.

In 1971, Warren Johnson, one of the earliest advocates for comprehensive sex education for people with intellectual disabilities, delivered a treatise on the characteristics and subject matter of successful sex education programs. Johnson aimed to dispel myths about the sexuality of people with intellectual disabilities and stressed the importance of educators putting aside their moral beliefs about sex in general and people with intellectual disabilities in particular.[4] Historically, individuals with intellectual disabilities were seen as "sexually promiscuous," especially fecund, and that their offspring would also be intellectually disabled and potential criminals (Kempton & Kahn, 1991, p. 95). Sex education, Johnson argues, is "tangled up with moral theology parading as virtue, and with misconceptions parading as matters of health or decorum" (1973, p. 62). Historically, however, the Christian Right has endlessly tried to connect a sense of conservative morality with any public discussions and education about sexuality (Irvine, 2002).[5] Alternate moralities are ignored, marginalized, and disrespected in this discourse. In contrast, Johnson argues that sex education can equip individuals with intellectual disabilities with the tools necessary for "their guilt-free enjoyment of life, their personal and social awareness, their ability to contribute to a world that "cares" for them—cares not in the custodial sense of the word, but in the rationally loving sense of concern" (1973, p. 65). It is worth noting that Johnson contrasts sexual freedom against feelings of guilt and moral beliefs as well as discourses of health and decorum. The desire to distance sex education from morality and public health concerns highlights the complicated relationship that exists between health, morals, and sexuality.

The themes of morality, health, and autonomy are not easily delineated in discussions of sexuality and sex education. Certainly, champions of sex education as empowering individual autonomy gladly link being sexual as a sign of good health and morality, while the argument that sexual relations outside of heterosexual marriage are an assault on Judeo-Christian morality still has traction in U.S. society. Sexuality itself is often coded as immoral or moral, healthy or unhealthy, celebrated or repressed. The rights of people with disabilities to express their sexuality can also clash with the discourse of protectionism that sees disabled people as vulnerable to exploitation and abuse. Normalization theory and social role valorization pose long-standing critiques of this type of conservatism (Osburn, 2006; Wolfensberger, 1983), and I argue that an individual stakeholder's view of sexuality influences the delivery of education about sex.

The basis for the claim for comprehensive sex education made by Johnson and others is that individuals with intellectual disabilities are not given or allowed access to knowledge about reproduction, sexual gratification, and other aspects of sexuality. However, when it comes to sexuality and sexual expression for people with intellectual disabilities, it is generally agreed that one of three approaches can be taken: (1) eliminate sexual expression; (2) tolerate and accept sexual expression; or, (3) cultivate sexual expression (Johnson, 1975, pp. 7–8; McCarthy & Fegan, 1984, pp. 2–3). When we turn our attention to more recent research around sexuality and sex education for people with intellectual disabilities, these philosophical approaches to sex are seen as influencing the day-to-day programming that occurs in educational and residential facilities. Johnson contends that members of "special groups" are treated as somewhat like children and "have tended to occupy a somewhat less than adult status even though chronologically adult" (1975, p. 48). People in these special groups are often on the receiving end of charity, assistance and/or are pathologized by medical and allied related fields. The position of receiving assistance or diagnoses can help to contribute to a child-like dependency or treatment. The discriminatory concept of mental age also helps to create this dependency.

Developing and promoting sex education is one of the primary ways of tolerating and even equipping individuals with knowledge for sexual expression and not violating public sentiment about sexuality. The problem arises when the promotion of sex education mimics harm reduction, essentially preparing individuals with intellectual disabilities to protect themselves from being manipulated or abused without addressing any other aspect of sexuality. My point is not to criticize education that helps prevent abuse and manipulation. Rather, individuals with intellectual disabilities are capable of not only understanding education that facilitates a reduction of abuse but also a more comprehensive understanding of sexuality that equips them to lead diverse sexual lives.

These three philosophical approaches to sexuality illustrate varying degrees of regulation and repression of the sexuality of certain groups of individuals. Punitive approaches to sexuality including sterilization and segregation highlight a type of sexual paranoia that is attached to groups of people including those with intellectual disabilities. Individuals with intellectual disabilities living in institutions were often sterilized "in a futile effort to eliminate the evil of masturbation, that dire source of further mental, physical and moral deterioration" (Johnson, 1975, p. 49).[6] If all individuals are supposedly sexual beings, then active management of sexuality is an effort to prevent unwanted or unnecessary sexual expression.[7] In this way, professionals usurp the sexual agency of individuals with disabilities (Siebers, 2008, p. 136). Additionally, promotion of sexuality for groups of individuals deemed "special" becomes a political endeavor in which the answer to repression becomes facilitation of sexuality through comprehensive sex education and other measures. Sex education becomes a tool that can either be withheld or promoted depending upon negative or positive assessments of sexuality. Educator unease about sex can determine what is contained in sex education materials. Ideologies of sex education reveal more about the teachers than the learners.

The body of literature on the sexuality of people with intellectual disabilities is substantial, and these materials reveal how cautiously sexuality is viewed and how it is believed to require structural and professional surveillance.[8] The major finding is that the population does not have an adequate knowledge about sex and sexual practices. Outside of the field of intellectual disability, similar conclusions have been reached about the lack of knowledge of sex for adolescents (Giami et al., 2006). For example, in a study conducted by Weaver, Smith, and Kippax (2005) comparing sex education in the United States, the Netherlands, France, and Australia, they found that young people in the United States report higher levels of personal shame around sex and have higher numbers of sexually transmitted infections and terminated pregnancies than their peers in the other countries. Arguably, abstinence-only sex education limits sexual knowledge, promoting incorrect peer-to-peer knowledge, which contributes to more negative attitudes toward sex and unhealthy outcomes. Abstinence-only sex education is "successful" insomuch that students refrain from sexual activity prior to marriage, which largely does not happen. Young people in the U.S. have sex regardless of the current culture of abstinence. The problem arises when sexually active individuals are not exposed to a more comprehensive understanding of sexuality. Additionally, abstinence-only education often capitalizes on the assumption that individuals need sexual knowledge that facilitates harm reduction (e.g., consistent use of condoms) without acknowledging the sexual lives of students. There is also a belief that "appropriate sex education should assist to protect those with an intellectual disability from exploitation and lack of choice" (Cuskelly & Bryde, 2004, p. 261). Some researchers point to an increasing risk of manipulation for this population, especially at the hands of non-disabled peers, often in the context of pornography, prostitution and stylized sex (e.g., sadomasochism) (Cambridge & Mellan, 2000). As Craft and Craft (1983) point out, educating individuals about sex can provide knowledge about what constitutes sexual abuse with the goal being that individuals are able to comprehend when they are in abusive situations. With knowledge comes an understanding of how to avoid abuse if possible and report it to staff members and other professionals who can assist in obtaining the appropriate remedy. The lack of education and access to education is a major theme in the research on sexuality and intellectual disability. Access and exposure become the "solution." Access and exposure should not, however, mimic abstinence based approaches but rather include sex education that incorporates multiple forms of pleasure, same sex practices as well as a discussion on safer sexual habits.

In sum, the research advocates for consistent approaches to sex education for individuals that not only teaches people about basic anatomy but also about how to recognize and avoid potential sexual abuse and manipulation. However, I believe that this approach misses the idea of sexuality altogether. Focusing on abuse primarily results in a crisis response approach to sexuality. For example, when person with an intellectual disability becomes pregnant or is diagnosed with a sexually transmitted infection, then a response to the situation is initiated. This approach fails to recognize an individual's right to sexual freedom. Additionally, inclusion of reproduction and genital-to-genital intercourse is generally suggested to be included in sex education programs for adults. Proposals to include non-heterosexual and non-genital practices in sex education programs are not as forthcoming, despite the implication that individuals in gender-separate congregate living settings engage in same-sex sexual practices. Some researchers contend that when people with intellectual disabilities live in same-sex living situations they become "gay by circumstances," often resorting to sexual rela-tions with people of the same-sex because it is most convenient (Craft, 1983, pp. 46–48).[9] Not only does this hypothesis deny that some people with intellectual disabilities are gay or bisexual, but also if a staff member or professional ob-jects to same-sex relations because of moral or other reasons, using the "gay by circumstances" ideology can result in removing individuals from their same-sex partner because the staff member thinks the relationship is merely one of conve-nience. Despite heteronormative ideals in relation to sexuality, some individuals with intellectual disabilities identify as gay, lesbian, bisexual, and transgendered (Allen, 2003). So, while comprehensive sex education may increase people with intellectual disabilities knowledge about sexuality, it rarely addresses issues related to non-reproductive sexual activities. In the next section, I examine sex education curriculum that promotes learning about anatomy and colloquial terms for sex as a way to facilitate increased sexual knowledge.

What's Dirty in a Word?

Sex educators discuss the importance of utilizing what is often called "street language" in their sex education sessions with adults with intellectual disabilities. Knowing a variety of names for sexual organs not only apparently offers a level of defense against ridicule from an individual's non-disabled peers but also allows the educator, be she a parent, teacher, or staff member to utilize language or con-cepts that might be familiar to an individual when more clinical language might not be comprehended (McCarthy & Fegan, 1984, p. 11). Frequently, using medi-cal terminology and expressions to describe sexuality and anatomy can place the learner at a disadvantage when trying to understand the message (Johnson, 1973, p. 59). Being open to the use of more colloquial terms can facilitate a level of comfort and desensitization allowing for the opportunity to advance education beyond a simple anatomy lesson (Monat, 1982, p. 31). The irony, however, is that individuals with intellectual disabilities already know many colloquial terms for sexual practices and genitalia, so efforts to incorporate these terms illustrate how some aspects of sex education may have more to do with making professionals more comfortable and avoiding pretension around sex. Johnson and Kempton make the argument that being more comfortable using "street" or "vulgar" lan-guage allows for more effective communication between the learner and educator (1981, pp. 125–131). An assessment of vulgarity is entangled with notions about class, in which "gentility is positioned against its opposite, vulgarity, viewed in sexual and classed terms" (Sanders, 2001, p. 192). Even the language of sex is programmed with class-based assessments of "respectability." The amount of educational labor to make sex education relevant to individuals with intellectual disabilities points to one way in which sex education is not only about delivering

knowledge but also about educators confronting their own biases and preconceived notions.

Promoting "street language," however, is not a simple solution where a diversity of words equals successful outcomes. I would argue that individuals hear
and learn the meaning behind words such as "blow job" and "giving head" before they know the term "fellatio." However, I also recognize that many slang
terms, often in relation to the female anatomy or sexual practices between lesbian
or gay individuals, include a complex and oppressive history. The use of these
terms perpetuates that history of oppression. Jessica Fields in her observations
of sex education classrooms in North Carolina comments that, "Jokes about
homosexuality and silence in the face of harassment contribute to sex education
classroom curricula that are homophobic (encouraging a fear and loathing of
one's own and others' same-sex desires, behaviors, or identities) and heteronormative (reasserting straight sexuality as normal, expected, and dominant)" (2008,
p. 72). Some consider that insult and shame are the key power dynamics within
various expressions of sexuality (Eribon, 2004; Pascoe, 2007). Discussions of
sexuality in the classroom often are accompanied by jokes between students and
the exchange of derogatory language. Despite efforts to reclaim words like queer,
there are still words that continue to be associated with a lexicon of intolerance.
It would benefit all students if educators were equipped to recognize situations in
which these words come up in the sessions and address the discriminatory meaning behind such words with the students.

An example of what seem to be effective ways to utilize "street language"
in sex education programs is illustrated in the film *What's Dirty in a Word?* (1980).
The film, created by the Institute for the Study of Mental Retardation and Related Disabilities at the University of Michigan, is part of the Human Fulfillment
Series, an eleven-episode series that addresses the sexuality of individuals with
intellectual disabilities. The film uses a variety of techniques to not only make
educators more comfortable with the use of more vulgar terminology but gives
examples of activities that can be used including something referred to as "Fuck
You Bingo" (FYB). FYB is fashioned after traditional bingo with cards and a call-
er but, instead of numbers, slang terms are used. When a person has a bingo on
their card they are supposed to yell, "fuck you" to indicate the end of the game.

Shot entirely in black and white, the film teaches professionals how to utilize sexual jargon, described as the "language of the people," and advocates that
"dirty words are not dirty." The film opens with two people playing scrabble,
but instead of spelling more conventional words to score points, the board is
filled with sexual words including "cock," "hump," and "jiz." This opening scene
is illustrative of the tone of the film; medical terminology has no place in this
film, rather *What's Dirty in a Word* celebrates colloquial language with the hope of
desensitizing the teacher and students to the effect that the words hold as well as

increasing sexual knowledge. Desensitizing about sexual morals and taboos can reduce some sexual guilt that students might experience. Additionally, throughout the film, songs from the sexual musical, *Let My People Come*, are incorporated throughout.[10]

Besides FYB, the film also suggests an activity called "Language Bombardment" (LB), where a facilitator calls out a sexual term or body part and the pupils then shout out alternative terms for the previously named word. In the film, the facilitator lists "void in the jar," and some of the words that were suggested included "peeing" and "wet." This was followed by a round where anal sex and homosexuality were suggested. Some of the the participants' responses reinforce heterosexual privilege and homosexual oppression, thus highlighting the complex oppressive history that language can bring. D'Emilio and Freedman discuss how at the end of the 1970s "conservative proponents of an older sexual order had appeared," which led to a great incorporation of sexuality into U.S. national politics with the emergence of HIV/AIDS, and the sustained interests of feminism and gay liberation (1997, pp. 343–345). *What's Dirty in a Word* is a reminder of these historical times in which discussions about sexuality and sex education were largely dominated by the Reagan-influenced New Right and the Christian Right (Irvine, 2002, pp. 81–90). This historical context points to the need for facilitators to be especially adept at navigating the complicated phraseology that can be "street language"—what do various words mean and what is their relation to sexuality, anatomy, minority identities, etc? And how are certain words used to perpetuate discrimination and oppression? LB and FYB can be effective activities that release socially imposed tension and awkwardness around sexual language, but the potential exists for reproducing hate speech in these same activities.

Another approach in sex education activities to facilitate sexual knowledge is the use of explicit drawings and dolls to teach people about anatomy. Some researchers contend that the use of pictures and images, even explicit ones, is more effective than utilizing language alone (Fischer et al., 1973, p. 1). Eliciting information, with the aid of images and pictures, can gauge the sexual knowledge of an individual and what kind of education might be needed or be beneficial to a particular group of learners. These images and pictures, however, are most likely "pink-skinned, slender, able-bodied, and conventionally modest female bodies" that affirm "normatively racialized and gendered ideas about a girl's and women's sexuality" (Fields, 2008, p. 102). Clitorises are routinely absent on these representations of female bodies, while "discussions of erections and ejaculation support men's and boy's claims to pleasure" (Fields, 2008, p. 103). The result being that female sexuality is more closely associated with discussions of reproduction while male sexuality incorporates pleasure and reproduction. Women with intellectual disabilities have historically been constructed as especially fecund, thus supposedly warranting eugenic sterilization (Garland-Thomson, 2005, pp. 581–582;

Razack, 1998; Snyder & Mitchell, 2005). This attention to controlling women's regulatory abilities is reflected in sex education. While men with intellectual disabilities are also not encouraged to reproduce, contemporary efforts to sterilize or control their sexuality are not as evident. Women with intellectual disabilities, on the other hand, are placed on birth control, often without their knowledge as one way to limit their reproduction (McCarthy, 1993). While sex education materials are heavily dependent on visual representations of male and female bodies, there remains the potential of distancing discussions of pleasure, especially for female students, in favor of a more reproductive focus on anatomy.

Other materials suggested the use of anatomical dolls to illustrate male and female reproductive organs. At the very least, these dolls act as tactile tools that can be used to educate people about anatomy. However, the dolls require a certain amount of abstraction since a plush doll, no matter how lifelike, is not sufficiently representative of a nude male or female body without some sort of generalizability occurring. Additionally, any choice of doll reinforces a type of anatomy that might not apply to all individuals especially those with atypical sexual organs. Fausto-Sterling (2000) comments that mixed-gender bodies challenge the constructed "normal" dichotomous gender system:

> Bodies in the "normal" range are culturally intelligible as males or females, but the rules for living as male or female are strict. No oversized clits or undersized penises allowed. No masculine women or effeminate men need apply....If we choose, over a period of time, to let mixed-gender bodies and altered patterns of gender-related behavior become visible, we will have, willy-nilly, chosen to change the rules of cultural intelligibility. (pp. 75–76)

The seemingly benign use of dolls to teach anatomy reinforces the process of gender hegemony by illustrating the "ideal" (i.e., normal) body for students. Those without the ideal normal body are made invisible in the representational silencing of the intelligible bodies. Finally, using a doll can mask other features of identity, which are not tied to sex; for example, an agency serving a diverse clientele would require multiple dolls representing the palette of humanness.

Educational uses of dolls to teach sex can facilitate creative understandings of sex and desire that foster children's imaginations and playful ways to disrupt heteronormative regulation (Addison, 2008, p. 274). However, as with any sex education materials, there is also a strong chance that hegemonic understandings of sexuality can be reinforced. Addison argues that dolls can be "used not only to reinforce stereotypical notions of heteronormative culture but also to invade and police the imaginative spaces that playing with dolls once afforded" (2008, p. 273). Additionally, there appears to be little flexibility for family structures not based on blood relations, thus limiting the strength of alternative kinship that queer life brings (Halberstam, 2005). For instance, transvestite dolls are generally absent as are the use of props with dolls that signal fetishes.

Outline drawings of male and female bodies are often used to assess the sexual knowledge of individuals with intellectual disabilities. However, such drawings can reinforce the dichotomous sex system, with male and female bodies represented generally; however, since the intricacies of the various reproductive systems are left blank, individuals are, potentially, able to use these outlines to represent their own anatomy. Less prescriptive curricula where female genitalia are not represented as designed to receive male genitalia allow for a type of re-imagination and counter-narrative to more dominant understandings of the sex-gender system. There is a sense of hope in allowing students the opportunities to personalize sexuality instead of subjecting them to educator-approved ways of expressing sexuality.

Conclusion: Moving Toward Pleasure and Agency

This chapter traces the various ways in which sex education activities for individuals with intellectual disabilities prescribe what is seen as appropriate or "normal" expressions of sexuality. Some efforts like *What's Dirty in a Word* give individuals an increased lexicon of words that can be used to describe sexuality, reproduction, and anatomy. Knowing the multiple and varied names for "penis" might not provide increased opportunities for sexual interactions, but it might allow for comprehension of a joke of sexual nature on a television sitcom. A knowledge of colloquial sexual terms helps to facilitate a discussion of sex and sexuality. Likewise using graphic images or models can give tangible examples to individuals of a certain kind of anatomy—that which is photographed and reproduced in the materials. The problem is that this type of activity capitalizes on representing the "typical" vagina, albeit with a missing clitoris. What makes it possible to include diverse bodies in sex education, such as those without typical genitalia, including those undergoing gender transitions, intersex individuals, and persons with smaller or larger genitalia? By promoting "street language" and images of anatomy, sex education lays out a very particular view of sexuality for individuals with intellectual disabilities—one where that same knowledge can perpetuate discrimination of atypical bodies and queer individuals and allow dominant expectations of heterosexuality to prevail.

Within the reviewed educational materials, sexuality is calculated and deliberate. All spontaneity has been replaced with lengthy discussions of appropriateness and reduction of risk. The underlying message is that individuals with intellectual disabilities are not able or willing to participate in spur-of-the-moment passionate sexual activity; best to leave that to their non-disabled peers. But spontaneity in sex is also absent in sex education curriculum in general education classes, despite research which indicates that adolescents continue to have intercourse earlier and more frequently than cohorts from earlier generations (Weaver, Smith, & Kippax, 2005; Smylie, 2008; Giami et al., 2006).

Desire and pleasure are also missing in these sex education materials. As Michelle Fine discussed two decades earlier, "a genuine discourse of desire would invite adolescents to explore what feels good and bad, desirable and undesirable, grounded in experience, needs and limits" (1988, p. 33). Allowing students to access their own experiences of what feels "good and bad" in discussions of sex mirrors research findings that students often supplement what is learned in sex education classrooms with their own experiences and discussions with peers (Sprecher, Harris, & Meyers, 2008). Sexual pleasure can challenge gendered aspects of power "by introducing women's capacity for self-determination" (Fields, 2008, p. 160). For example, feminist-based sex education that not only addresses gender inequality but discusses desire and pleasure separate from male heterosexuality serves as examples of the transformative potential of sex education (Askew, 2007). Sex education can empower individuals as well as provide them with the tools to avoid sexually transmitted infections. Traditionally, public health promotion in sex education has overshadowed discussions of pleasure in sexuality (Ingham, 2005). Pleasure and desire often include alternatives to vaginal intercourse including mutual masturbation (Ingham, 2005, p. 381). Allowing a discussion of pleasure back into sex education classrooms "would release females from a position of receptivity, enable an analysis of the dialectics of victimization and pleasure, and would pose female adolescents as subjects of sexuality" (Fine, 1988, p. 33). Sex education has the potential to reinforce gender inequality; a discourse of pleasure that allows for alternative sexualities to be discussed is one way to mitigate this inequality. Unfortunately, even when specific sexual activities like masturbation are discussed for people with intellectual disabilities, aspects of pleasure get lost. Sex education can meaningfully incorporate discussions of pleasure and sexual agency alongside equally compelling discussions of remaining safe and healthy in sexuality.

Instead of merely advocating for increased exposure and access to sex education, an examination of the content of sex education is needed in order to envision what can be taught. This chapter offers one attempt to historically examine the contents of sex education curricula. Additionally, protectionism as an end goal denies the reality that individuals are already and always active sexual agents. Gender and heteronormative assumptions in sex education should be re-examined. The notion of power that comes from age, ability, gender, class, and race differences should be named in order to facilitate negotiations among individuals. Integrating sexual pleasure into sex education is a worthwhile endeavor largely absent up to this point. An incorporation of pleasure has the potential to make unpleasant sexual experiences visible while respecting individuals with intellectual disabilities as sexual agents with diverse—but normal—sexual needs and interests as well as a range of strengths, not solely vulnerabilities.

Acknowledgments

For the thoughtful suggestions and helpful assistance, I thank Scot Danforth, Lennard Davis, Curt Dudley-Marling, Judith Gardiner, Alex Gurn, Eunjung Kim, Sarah Parker, Mark Sherry, Tobin Siebers, and Virginia Wexman. Each individual has provided valuable comments and suggestions on the multiple versions of this chapter. I am in debt to each of you for your generosity and guidance.

Endnotes

1. I have no proprietary interest in any of the sex educational materials analyzed in this chapter.
2. There are already studies conducted to determine the educational effectiveness of sex education materials. These include Garwood and McCabe (2000); McCabe (1999); and Whitehouse and McCabe (1997).
3. I am unsure how often these particular sex education materials are used. The publisher for *CIRCLES* advertises that their materials are used in over 10,000 facilities across the U.S. The other materials are representative of the typical content of sex education materials for people with intellectual disabilities.
4. Johnson also challenged the utility of using "mental retardation" as a diagnostic characteristic: "Labels like 'mentally retarded' tend both to create and to conceal *individuals* under them. It is, therefore, hazardous to suppose that such a label necessarily provides any useful information with dealing with any given person, either with regard to his capacity to learn or his interest in sex" (1973, p. 58, emphasis original). Challenging the usefulness of "mental retardation" points to the problems associated with the diagnosis—mental retardation means one thing to a group of professionals, educators, and physicians; it means something else to the general public and in reality the limitations in intellect and functioning associated with the impairment might not apply to individuals. Or put another way, "The fact that someone is mentally retarded tells us little about the sexuality of that person (McCarthy and Fegan, 1984, p. 1)."
5. Irvine explains how the success of groups like Jerry Falwell's Moral Majority and the John Birch Society depended in part by attacking the SIECUS and advocates of comprehensive sex education as corrupting the traditional values and morals of U.S. society (2002, p. 63-68). "In historically unprecedented coalitions, conservative Catholics, conservative Jews, along with Christian evangelicals, fundamentalists, Pentecostals, and even some Muslim allies abrogated denominational loyalties to fight for 'traditional values'—a move which united opponents of sex education" (2002, p. 65).
6. The process of sterilization continues today, under different legislative and political frameworks. Currently, it operates in a context where eugenic tendencies operate at the individual, rather than state, level. Effectively, eugenic practices have been privatized (Kerr and Shakespeare, 2002).
7. People with disabilities are often considered asexual by others. Shakespeare, Gillespie-Sells, and Davies assert that, "Stereotypes of disability often focus on asexuality, or lack of sexual potential or potency. Disabled people are subject to infantilization,

especially disabled people who are perceived as being 'dependent.' Just as children are assumed to have no sexuality, so disabled people are similarly denied the capacity for sexual feeling. Where disabled people are seen as sexual, this is in terms of deviant sexuality, for example inappropriate sexual display or masturbation" (1996, p. 10). There is a tension between being labeled as asexual and actively choosing an asexual lifestyle. Celibacy and temporary asexuality also complicate this tension. The Asexuality Visibility and Education Network is largely an online forum where people across the globe discuss asexual identity and orientation.

8.   Examples include Cambridge and Mellan, 2000; Christian et al., 2001; Coleman and Murphy, 1981; Cuskelly and Bryde, 2004; Dotson et al., 2003; Galea et al., 2004; Heyman and Huckle, 1995; Walcott, 1997; Wolfe, 1997.

9.   Institutionalization places people into living situations often without their consent. Lack of choice in living situations is another violation of rights for individuals with intellectual disabilities.

10.   *Let My People Come* was an off-Broadway musical that debuted in 1974. It ran until 1980, ending with a brief and ultimately unsuccessful run on Broadway and showings in London, Philadelphia and Toronto. The title of *What's Dirty in a Word* comes from a song in the musical, *Dirty Words*.

References

Addison, N. (2008). The doll and pedagogic mediation: teaching children to fear the 'other.' *Sex Education. 8*(3), 263–276.

Allen, J. (2003). *Gay, lesbian, bisexual, and transgender people with developmental disabilities and mental retardation: Stories of the rainbow support group.* Binghamton, NY: Harrington Park.

Askew, J. (2007). Breaking the taboo: An exploration of female university students' experiences of attending a feminist-informed sex education course. *Sex Education. 7*(3), 251–264.

Cambridge, P. & Mellan, B. (2000). Reconstructing the sexuality of men with learning disabilities: empirical evidence and theoretical interpretations of need. *Disability and Society. 15*(2), 293–311.

Christian, L., Stinson, J., & Dotson, L. A. (2001). Staff values regarding the sexual expression of women with developmental disabilities. *Sexuality and Disability. 19*(4), 283–291.

Coleman, E.M. and Murphy, W.D. (1981). A survey of sexual attitudes and sex education programs among facilities for the mentally retarded. *Applied Research in Mental Retardation. 1*, 269–276.

Craft, M. (1983). Sexual behaviour and sexual difficulties. In *Sex education and counseling for mentally handicapped people*. Ann Craft and Michael Craft. (Eds.). Baltimore, MD: University Park Press.

Craft, M. & Craft, A. (1982). *Sex and the mentally handicapped: A guide for parents and careers.* London: Routledge and Kegan Paul.

Craft, A. & Michael C. M. (Eds.). (1983). *Sex education and counseling for mentally handicapped people.* Baltimore, MD: University Park Press.

Cuskelly, M. & Bryde, R. (2004). Attitudes towards the sexuality of adults with an intellectual disability: parents, support staff, and a community sample. *Journal of Intellectual and Developmental Disability. 29*(3), 255–264.

D'Emilio, J. & Freedman, E. (1997). *Intimate matters: A history of sexuality in America*. [2d ed]. Chicago: University of Chicago Press.

Dotson, L. A., Stinson, J., & Christian, L. (2003). "People tell me I can't have sex": Women with disabilities share their personal perspectives on health care, sexuality and reproductive rights. *Women and Therapy*. *26*(3/4), 195.

Eribon, D. (2004). *Insult and the making of the gay self*. (Translated by Michael Lucey) Durham, NC: Duke University Press.

Fausto-Sterling, A. (2000). *Sexing the body: Gender politics and the construction of sexuality*. New York: Basic Books.

Fields, J. (2008). *Risky lessons: Sex education and social inequality*. New Brunswick, NJ: Rutgers University Press.

Fine, M. (1988). Sexuality, schooling, and adolescent females: The missing discourse of desire. *Harvard Educational Review*. *58*(1), 29–53.

Fischer, H.Q., Krajicek, M.J., & Bortheck, W.A. (1973). *Sex education for the developmentally disabled: A guide for parents, teachers, and professionals*. Baltimore, MD: University Park Press.

Galeaa, J., Butlera, J., Iaconoa, T., & Leightonb, D. (2004). The assessment of sexual knowledge in people with intellectual disability *Journal of Intellectual and Developmental Disability*. *29*(4), 350–365.

Garland-Thomson, R. (2005). Integrating disability, transforming feminist theory. In *Feminist Theory: A Reader*. Wendy K. Kolmar & Frances Bartowski.(Eds.). (2005) Boston, MA: McGraw-Hill.

Garwood, M. & McCabe, M. (2000). Impact of sex education programs on sexual knowledge and feelings of men with a mild intellectual disability. *Education and Training in Mental Retardation and Developmental Disabilities*. *35*(3), 269–283.

Giami, A., Olrichs, Y., Quilliam, S., Wellings, K., Pacey, S., & Wylie, K. (2006). Sex education in schools is insufficient to support adolescents in the 21st century. *Sexual and Relationship Therapy*. *21*(4), 485–490.

Halberstam, J. (2005). *In a queer time and place: Transgender bodies, subcultural lives*. New York: New York University Press.

Heyman, B. & Huckle, S. (1995). Sexuality as a perceived hazard in the lives of adults with learning difficulties. *Disability and Society*. *10*(2), 139–155.

Ingham, R. (2005). "We didn't cover that at school": Education against pleasure or education for pleasure? *Sex Education*. *5*(4), 375–388.

Irvine, J. (2002). *Talk about sex: The battles over sex education in the United States*. Berkeley, CA: University of California Press.

Johnson, W. (1973). Sex education of the mentally retarded. In *Human sexuality and the mentally retarded*. Felix de la Cruz & Gerald LaVeck (Eds.). New York: Brunner/Mazel.

Johnson, W. (1975). *Sex education and counseling of special groups: The mentally and physically handicapped, ill and elderly*. Springfield, IL: Charles C. Thomas.

Johnson, W. & Kempton, W. (1981). *Sex education and counseling of special groups: The mentally and physically disabled, ill, and elderly*. [2d ed.]. Springfield, IL: Charles C. Thomas.

Kempton, W. & Kahn, E. (1991). Sexuality and people with intellectual disabilities: A historical perspective. *Sexuality and Disability*. *9*(2), 93–111.

Kerr, A. and Shakespeare, T. (2002) *Genetic politics: From eugenics to genome*. Gretton: New Clarion Press.

McCabe, M. (1999). Sexual knowledge, experience and feelings among people with disability. *Sexuality and Disability*. *17*(2), 157–170.

McCarthy, M. (1993). Sexual experiences of women with learning difficulties in long-stay hospitals. *Sexuality and Disability. 11*(4), 277.

McCarthy, W. & Fegan, L. (1984). *Sex education and the intellectually handicapped: A guide for parents and caregivers.* Balgowlah, Australia: ADIS Health Science Press.

Mohr, M. (1991). *The CIRCLES program: Is it effective in teaching appropriate social distance skills to mild, moderate and severely mentally retarded adults.* Unpublished Master's Thesis. Shippensburg University.

Monat, R. K. (1982). *Sexuality and the mentally retarded: A clinical and therapeutic guidebook.* San Diego, CA: College Hill Press.

Osburn, J. (2006). An overview of social role valorization theory. *The SRV Journal. 1*(1),4–13.

Pascoe, C. J. (2007). *"Dude, you're a fag": Masculinity and sexuality in high school.* Berkeley, CA: University of California Press.

Razack, S. (1998). *Looking white people in the eye: Gender, race, and culture in courtrooms and classrooms.* Toronto: University of Toronto Press.

Sanders, L. S. (2001). The failures of the romance: Boredom, class, and desire. In George Gissing's *The Odd Women* and W. Somerset Maugham's *Of Human Bondage. Modern Fiction Studies. 47*(1), 190–228.

Shakespeare, T., Gillespie-Sells, K., & Davies, D. (1996). *The sexual politics of disability: Untold desires.* London: Cassell.

Siebers, T. (2008). *Disability theory.* Ann Arbor, MI: The University of Michigan Press.

Smylie, L. (2008). *The influence of social capital on the timing of first sexual intercourse among Canadian youth.* Doctoral dissertation, University of Windsor.

Snyder, S. L. & Mitchell, D. T. (2005). *Cultural locations of disability.* Chicago, IL: University of Chicago Press.

Sprecher, S., Harris, G., & Meyers, A. (2008). Perceptions of sources of sex education and targets of sex communication: Sociodemographic and cohort effects. *Journal of Sex Research. 45*(1), 17–26.

Tepper, M. (2000). Sexuality and disability: the missing discourse of pleasure. *Sexuality and Disability. 18*(4), 283–290.

Walcott, D. D. (1997). Family life education for persons with developmental disabilities. *Sexuality and Disability. 15*(2), 91–98.

Walker-Hirsch, L. (2007). Six key components of a meaningful comprehensive sexuality education. In *The Facts of Life...and More: Sexuality and Intimacy for People with Intellectual Disabilities.* Leslie Walker-Hirsch (Ed.). Baltimore, MD: Paul H. Brookes.

Weaver, H., Smith, G., & Kippax, S. (2005). School-based sex education policies and indicators of sexual health among young people: A comparison of the Netherlands, France, Australia and the United States. *Sex Education. 5*(2), 171–188.

What's Dirty in a Word? (1980). Institute for the Study of Mental Retardation and Related Disabilities: University of Michigan.

Whitehouse, M. & McCabe, M. (1997). Sex education programs for people with intellectual disability: How effective are they? *Education and Training in Mental Retardation and Developmental Disabilities. 32*(3), 229–240.

Wolfe, P. S. (1997). The influences of personal values on issues of sexuality and disability. *Sexuality and Disability. 15*(2), 69–90.

Wolfensberger, W. (1983). Social role valorization: a proposed new term for the principle of normalization. *Mental Retardation. 21*(6), 234–239.

THIRTEEN

The Sirens of Normative Mythology: Mother Narratives of Engagement and Resistance

Jan Valle & Susan Gabel

I stand here ironing, and what you asked me moves tormented back and forth with the iron. "I wish you would manage the time to come in and talk with me about your daughter. I'm sure you can help me understand her. She's a youngster who needs help and whom I'm deeply interested in helping." "Who needs help," . . . even if I came, what good would it do? You think because I am her mother I have a key, or that in some way you could use me as a key? She has lived for nineteen years. There is all that life that has happened outside me, beyond me. And when is there time to remember, to sift, to weigh, to estimate, to total? I will start and there will be an interruption and I will have to gather it all again. Or I will become engulfed with all I did or did not do, with what should have been and what cannot be helped.
— Tillie Olsen (1961)[1]

And so begins the narrator's monologue in Olsen's (1961) short story, *I Stand Here Ironing*. Acclaimed by second wave feminists for its introspective depiction of a working-class single mother, *I Stand Here Ironing* grants the reader access into a nameless mother's stream-of-consciousness response to a seemingly innocuous, yet impossible question. Within the visiting official's presumably well-intentioned desire to help, this mother hears insinuation of blame and judgment (i.e., if you tell me what you have done or not done, I may be able to fix the child you have broken)—an indictment all the more jarring juxtaposed among the endless domestic demands that do not cease even for a visitor. The monologue that comprises the entirety of the short story provides a window into a mother's interiority, revealing how her response is not just about how she mothers but also about the larger cultural, political and social context within which her mothering takes place.

Nearly fifty years have passed since the publication of Olsen's short story. In the interim, a profound re-shaping of American culture has taken place. The women's movement of the 1960s and 1970s, with its focus upon civil liberties for women (e.g., legal rights; workplace rights; protection from domestic violence, sexual harassment, rape; and reproductive choice), led to professional, economic, and personal opportunities that women today regard as natural—opportunities that Olsen's narrator would find simply unimaginable. Yet, we pose the question—just how different is motherhood in the 21st century?

In this chapter, we examine the contemporary context within which American motherhood takes place, the normative discourse of schooling that envelops mothers and their children within this context, and what happens when disability—or the threat of disability—interrupts the cultural script for motherhood. Lastly, we conclude with a discussion of the material consequences for mothers that result from our culture's allegiance to normative mythology.

The Context of American Motherhood

In *Perfect Madness: Motherhood in the Age of Anxiety* (2005), journalist Judith Warner examines the general culture of American motherhood and concludes that it is, quite simply, driving mothers to madness. Having become a mother herself while living in France, Warner returns home to experience American motherhood as oppressive in comparison—describing how "the pressure to perform, to attain levels of perfect selflessness was insane" (p. 16). In an effort to make sense of American motherhood, Warner interviews nearly 150 women (the majority white, middle-class, and college educated) about their experiences as mothers and examines their narratives within the context of both historical and contemporary American culture. Having made the choice to limit her study to this particular, and relatively privileged, segment of American culture, it is worth noting that Warner finds it impossible to write about the middle class without also referencing the cultural influence of upper middle-class families who are, after all, "our reference point for what the American good life is supposed to look like and contain" (p. 20). And it is this decidedly American conceptualization of "the good life" (propagated endlessly by our media) that Warner identifies as an underlying impetus for what she terms "the craziness" of contemporary motherhood—particularly for white, middle-class mothers.

Mothering in the age of anxiety

More so now than ever, American culture might be characterized as The Ultimate Competition for Rapidly Shrinking Resources. Within the current context of economic downturn, ordinary citizens—who worry about job security and stability of family finances and who contemplate the long-term effects of government bailouts of banks and corporations upon our country's economic future—are the mainstay of daily news features. As a nation, it seems we are becoming more and more collectively anxious about the individual futures of ourselves and our families.

Writing from a perspective that pre-dates the significant economic events of the last year, Warner (2005) offers a rather prescient explanation of a growing sense of unease among middle-class mothers even during the earlier years of this decade.

> To many of us today, it feels as though the pie of life—the ultimate rewards spelling success and happiness in adulthood—is becoming ever smaller, and if we don't prepare our children well now to seize their piece, they may end up going hungry altogether. (p.162)

In response to this sense of unease, Warner claims that many mothers (particularly those in the middle class) feel compelled to add strategic planning to their maternal duties in hopes of giving their children a competitive edge in the race for success. The thinking goes something like this—I am expecting; I need to get myself on a waiting list now for the best pre-school or my unborn child will begin life at a disadvantage; I need to start reading about how to prepare my unborn child to enter the best pre-school as a rising star because my child's performance there will determine whether or not we get accepted into the best kindergarten program— and so on and so forth throughout the course of childhood and beyond. In fact, this kind of thinking is the subject of the documentary, *Nursery University* (2008), that follows five Manhattan families in competitive pursuit of admission into pre-schools believed to set toddlers upon a trajectory to the Ivy League. One misstep along the way and a mother risks condemning herself to guilt and public shame over not having done the very best for her child. Even mothers who instinctively recoil from this kind of thinking still engage in it because the risks seem simply too high not to do so. Warner asserts that "supermothers" (herself included) have been convinced

> …that every decision we make, every detail we control, is *incredibly important*… Ergo: soccer and violin and public service and weekends of baseball practice become *vitally important* because if we don't do everything right for our children, they may be consigned, down the line, to failure, to loserdom. (2005, p. 33, italics in original)

And lest a mother allow herself to believe that she can control the outcome of her child's life, our media-drenched culture performs its daily duty to report every possible danger that might befall even the most well-tended child. Cautionary tales such as those of JonBenet Ramsay, Elizabeth Smart, and Jaycee Lee Dugard live in our collective imagination as examples of what can happen to beautiful children of parents "just like us." (The influence of race and class upon the media attention given to these cases is another topic in and of itself.) The likes of Dr. Phil, Oprah, and Geraldo Rivera regularly inform the viewing public about the panoply of threats lurking about our children—food additives, environmental toxins, autism, over-the-counter medications, obesity, the internet, music, vaccines, drugs, television, cancer, video games, and so on. Should you miss one of these TV segments, you can be sure to read about it in the endless array of popular magazines and/or internet sites. Television dramas (e.g., *CSI, House, Law and Order*) and popular fiction (e.g., *Lovely Bones, My Sister's Keeper*) feed our already over-active imaginations about the vulnerability of children. In a recent *New York Times Magazine* article (June 21, 2009), Ginia Bellafante describes the cultural phenomenon of "the endangered or ruined child" as

> ...a media entity within a culture that has idealized the responsibilities of parenthood to a degree, as has been exhaustively noted, unprecedented in human history. The more we seek to protect our children, the more we fear the consequences in an inability to do so. (p. 36)

In other words, it appears that the more we fear for our children, the more anxious we become. And the more anxious we are, the more protective we become. The more protective we are, the more we believe in our capacity to keep our children safe from the ills of the world. Is it little wonder that the 21st century "helicopter parent" emerged out of this media-saturated culture of anxiety? Television and print media blame helicopter parents (so-dubbed for their tendency to hover above even college-aged offspring) for creating a generation of overly dependent children who have experienced little challenge or failure in life. Lisa Belkin, a mother of older children, defends helicopter parents on a *New York Times* parenting blog (March 4, 2009):

> I try not to be as extreme as some...I am purposely sitting on my hands, biting my tongue and reining myself in, because I understand that independence (theirs) is a muscle that needs exercise. I can understand how parents can go from helpful to hovering. For years the message we're given is "the world is scary and complicated; your kids need you to navigate." Then one day (Their 18th birthday? The day they leave for college?) we are told: "Time is up. Pencils down."

And just who is doing the telling to which this mother refers?

The Sirens of Normative Mythology

It is written in Greek mythology that the hypnotic song of the island-dwelling sirens (part female and part bird) lured many an unsuspecting crew to shipwreck upon their rocky shores. And much like sailors of Greek mythology, unsuspecting mothers in our anxiety-ridden culture seem unable to resist the Siren song of *normativity*—the compelling cultural message that calls to all good mothers and defines what they and their children should be doing to be considered successful. It is worth noting that the bar for normativity is set higher than ever within our increasingly competitive culture, luring many a mother to shipwreck herself in pursuit of an ideal. Reflecting upon her own quest for perfection as a mother, Warner describes the all-encompassing self-doubt that came to consume her.

> There was so much pressure to always be doing something with or for [my children]. And *doing* it right. And I was increasingly feeling that I was doing everything wrong. As a mother. As a woman. As a human being. (2005, pp. 25–26)

In much the same way that Olsen's narrator is unable to articulate a response to what essentially is an unanswerable question for her, Warner likewise suggests that many women experience a "caught-by-the-throat feeling" about motherhood that defies expression. Yet, what is unarticulated somehow circulates invisibly within our culture as something right and natural—and often contradictory.

Laying claim to the good mother

In 2003, Cathy Hanauer published her *New York Times* best seller, *The Bitch in the House*—a collection of tales about conflicted motherhood (as well as work and marriage) told by women of the Have-It-All generation. In this era of third wave feminism, it seems that we have yet to "kill the Angel in the House" (a reference to Victorian poet Coventry Patmore's idealized notion of self-sacrificial womanhood)—as Virginia Woolf (1966) so famously quipped. In fact, "she" figures centrally within the current-day politics of "family values" as well as the ongoing Mommy Wars that pit working mothers and stay-at-home mothers against one another (Hays, 1998; Peskowitz, 2005). And at the epicenter of political, religious, and cultural discourses of motherhood sit science and its minion, the media. Television and print media (as well as the internet) serve up a daily diet of scientific studies to support and/or contradict nearly every choice in motherhood.

Beginning with the notion of "scientific mothering" in the 1920s, mothers have been a continual subject of scientific study and ostensible cause of childhood disorders (Simpson, 2002; Apple, 1995). From Freud to Bettelheim to Brazelton, it seems that what a mother does and does not do or what she says and does not say determines her child's developmental outcome. Consider, for example, recent scientific research that points to the importance of brain development from birth to age three. In response to the media attention given to this research, many mothers stimulate their little ones in every way imaginable (assisted by an endless offering of mommy and me classes as well as a thriving industry of early education DVDs, toys, and books), in hopes of nurturing each precious brain synapse to fruition. While this is not to suggest that early childhood stimulation is in any way inconsequential, we do argue that our culture's saturation in numerous (and often contradictory) scientific findings escalates maternal anxiety about "doing it right." In light of the cultural authority afforded to science within American culture, it is nearly impossible for mothers to ignore its proclamations (Valle, 2009). What kind of mother would not do everything she could to ensure a positive outcome for her child—especially that which is deemed to be "good mothering" by science?

> It is as though, through the power of our prodigious mental energies, we feel we can erect a protective force field around our children, sheltering them against fat, lack of focus, immaturity, lack of muscle tone…failure. And if all this doesn't work, then the fault lies with us. So we must try harder. Do better. *Be there* more—and more perfectly. (Warner, 2005, p. 192)

And nothing makes a mother try harder to be there more perfectly than the education of her child. After all, a child's success in school leads to success in life—the ultimate confirmation that one is indeed "a good mother."

Normative Mythology as a Device of Schooling

The formal schooling of children provides yet another—and highly significant—stage upon which motherhood is enacted. It is a long-running performance spanning childhood, adolescence, and, in many instances, young adulthood. When mothers engage with schools, they do so within a particular culture that is public education—a culture, like all others, defined by patterns of human activity, and social structures that embody its history, beliefs, attitudes, practices, and values (Valle & Connor, in press).

The pressures of "normalcy" that many mothers experience during their children's pre-school years do not stop with the advent of formal schooling; in fact, such pressures intensify as children becoming increasingly defined in terms of their relationship to an established "norm" of academic performance. A primary feature of public school culture is its allegiance to a concept of normality that assumes a predictable distribution of student abilities along a bell-shaped curve. From the way students are organized into age-based grades (based upon the belief that most same-aged children fall into an "average" range of performance) to the current standards-based education reform, the normal curve is the tool by which students become defined and categorized. And at the center stands the mythical normal child—that paragon of desirability and expectation to which all others are compared and known (Baglieri, Bejoian, Broderick, et al., in press). In fact, it has become so natural to think of schoolchildren in this way—neatly lined up side-by-side in their designated spots along the normal curve—that little thought is given to the sensibility of it all. This is, after all, how we do school here in America—scientifically and efficiently.

Reliance upon the normal curve as a sorting tool is certainly not a new educational practice. The marriage of science and public education has long endured. With the emergence of the IQ test in the early decades of the last century, psychologists assumed authority to sort public school students by IQ score into corresponding curriculum that would best prepare them for their eventual roles in society—an educational caste system of sorts (Spring, 1989; Kliebard, 1995; Ferri & Connor, 2006). Moreover, given that the IQ test came out of America's revered scientific tradition, its legitimacy was not called into question nor was the accompanying practice of sorting children for educative purposes. What naturalized these ideas and gave them momentum was their association with the methods of natural science (Thomas & Loxley, 2008). And the normal curve remains with us—despite the fact, as noted in the Introduction to this volume, that "human traits do not tend to cluster about the mean in a bell-shaped distribution."

And nowhere has the normal curve had more of an impact than within the institution of special education. In light of the historical relationship between medicine and disability, public schools readily embraced "the medical model" for understanding and responding to disability (Gabel, 2005; Gallagher, 1998). As conceptualized within special education, disability is understood to be a pathological condition intrinsic to the individual, identifiable through scientific assessment (e.g., IQ tests, individually administered standardized tests of achievement, social and behavioral scales), and presumably responsive to remedial instruction that seeks to restore or approximate normalcy (Brantlinger, 2004; Linton, 1998; Davis, 1997). This particular way of understanding and responding to disability gave rise to the notion that there are two types of children—normal and not normal—who require qualitatively different instruction and differently trained teachers (Reid & Valle, 2004). Now more than thirty years since the inception of special education, it has become so naturalized to think in these terms that a parallel system of education for children with disabilities is regarded not only as unproblematic but also necessary.

The four r's: Reading, 'riting, 'rithmetic, and rank

So enchanted is our culture by the Siren song of normative mythology that its application to education continues to increase. Having established high standards and measurable goals as the means by which to improve student learning outcomes, the federally legislated *No Child Left Behind Act of 2001* (NCLB) (U.S. Congress, 2001) requires every state, for example, to develop and administer basic skills assessments to all students in certain grades. Based upon student test performance (as defined by the normal curve), teachers now choose and apply evidence-based practices (meaning instructional approaches grounded in "scientifically based research") within their classrooms.

In the spirit of leaving no child behind, we now strive toward newer and more ubiquitous ways to identify and categorize schoolchildren in relation to one another. All manner of rankings—from state tests to classroom-based rubrics—position children along pre-determined standards. It seems we are intent on rooting out and exposing all differences in relation to an established norm—an institutionalized practice that Baker (2002) notably named "the hunt for disability."

Let's consider, for example, a recent educational reform, response to intervention (RTI), becoming increasingly present within public schools. RTI is a three-tiered process that delivers preventive, supplemental intervention for students in general education who do not meet grade level standards (Vellutino, Scanlon, Small, & Fanuele, 2006). Once targeted as deficient relative to the norm, these students are instructed by teachers who carry out "evidence-based practices"—i.e., instruction grounded in scientific studies that (a) identify and control variables in the classroom and (b) indicate the level of confidence with which outcomes and results can be associated with those variables (NCLB, 2001). Such instruction presumably generates "measurable results" that can be used to determine whether or not a student is improving or needs to move to a more intensive tier of intervention. A referral to special education occurs only upon the occasion that a student fails to respond to the last intervention tier (Fuchs & Deshler, 2007). Thus, it seems we are bent on creating more opportunities to label children beyond what has been established by special education—a curious choice at best given the well-documented deleterious effects of labeling (Brantlinger, 2006). Yet, it is worth noting that this now-continual "swarming" (Baker, 2002) around children (e.g., testing, identifying the "not normals," designing and implementing interventions, eventual referral)—although perhaps different in quantity and quality than in the past—has been happening for decades. NCLB has merely increased the stakes in response to global trends.

Mother Narratives of Engagement and Resistance

Educational literature is rife with studies that document both intended and unintended outcomes for children classified as different from the norm; however, we know far less about the effect of labeling upon the mothers of labeled children. It stands to reason that the relentless focus upon normativity within schools contributes to maternal anxiety already induced by our culture. There is no denying the judgments that come with our endless rankings. In this age of competition, there is social cachet that comes with a child whose performance falls on the desirable side of the bell curve (e.g., the ubiquitous bumper stickers that proclaim My Kid is a Honor Student) and conversely, social stigma associated with a child's position on the undesirable side of the bell curve (e.g., the notable absence of bumper stickers that proclaim My Kid is in Special Education).

Mothers have no choice but to participate within the school structures that uphold normative discourse, i.e., the grammar of schooling. In the current educational climate, it is believed that science is the answer to leaving no child behind. Plug a measured and categorized child into the appropriate curriculum and instructional business is done. Education is, of course, a far more complex and messy endeavor than science might suggest; moreover, the privileging of science within education functions in a way that invalidates other ways of knowing (Valle, 2009). And if women in our culture, as Warner (2005) suggests, already feel pressured and consumed by maternal expectations and responsibilities, it is worth considering how they might experience the normative discourse that defines both their children and the meaning of academic success—particularly when the cultural script for motherhood is interrupted by disability or the threat of disability.

I stand here feeling blamed: Alexandra's story

The narrative account that follows grants us access into the interiority of a middle-class mother, Alexandra, who describes how normative mythology has impacted her mothering. Reminiscent of the narrator's internal monologue in *I Stand Here Ironing* (1961), this contemporary mother speaks aloud thoughts and feelings most often left unsaid and unheard by educators. We acknowledge that Alexandra's story is partial and situated. It is not meant to be a representation of all mothers' experiences nor are we making a claim for any grand generalization; yet, there is much to consider within Alexandra's lived experience about the unintended material consequences of normative discourse upon contemporary motherhood.

Alexandra, a married, middle-class professional, emigrated from eastern Europe as a young adult. She is the mother of two young children, Marc, who is five years old, and Maria, who is two and a half years old. Alexandra's narrative opens with an account of how she, a good and vigilant mother, brings her concerns about Marc's development to the attention of his teacher. By doing so, Alexandra explains how she unwittingly activates an institutional process that not only assumes control over her child's education but also becomes impossible to deactivate.

> Working with special ed people often starts with the mother. And that's why I blame myself so much about why my child is this way—maybe it is because of my *own* stress. You would think, you would hope—*naïve* me—that they would help you rather than end up messing you up. You just *share* a concern like my child may not be working as well as my neighbor's child or talking as well as my neighbor's child or dancing or whatever or smiling as much. And then they say, "Oh sure. Let's do some tests." And before you know it, then you have social workers in your house, right? So you start this process and you are in the process and they *blame* you. And it *is* partly your fault because *in the process* you lose control of this whole situation. And you try *so* hard to gain it back, but the whole thing is like checking yourself into a mental institution and then finding out that as soon as you walk in, you cannot walk out.

As a result of sharing concerns with the teacher, Alexandra feels as though she is blamed (not unlike Olsen's narrator) for not being the kind of mother that the "special ed people" expect her to be (whatever that is) and blames herself for having invited this loss of control over her mothering. She experiences the sanctioned and institutionalized response to difference as the kind of "hunt for disability" that Baker (2002) describes. In comparing her experience with special education personnel to that of checking herself into a mental institution and not being able to check out, Alexandra offers a compelling metaphor for the way she, as a mother, likewise feels captured and restrained by the normative discourse that now defines her child.

Upon declining a subsequent recommendation to place Marc in a segregated special education classroom, Alexandra discovers how daunting it can be to resist normative discourse, despite her legal right to do so. She is highly disoriented by the questioning of her capacity to make a rational decision—an act she performs daily in regard to every other aspect of her child's life as she has since the day he was born.

> It has a way of making you feel *guilty* that maybe you *have* been hurting your child or they *do* convince you at times—you go back and forth, I think. There are days that you want to say, "No. This is all *crazy*. My child is just fine." And there are days that you feel that—but I *have* to—it is at the *core* of your mothering that you want to make sure that you're providing the *best* for your child. And they are making sure that you understand that you may be *hurting* him in ways that are irreversible because you did not address these things or have sessions

with him or whatever they want…And they come back to you and they *push*—so that's when [the teacher] told me, "I'm really *worried* about your child." At which point, something clicked. "*You're* worried? *You* are worried about the decisions I am making for my child?" "Yes because I *care* about him." And I wanted to say, "You are such a hypocrite! How can *you* care *more* than *I* do? It's *my* child. *You worry more?* How can you say that with a straight face to me? Everything *I am* is for that child!"

Despite Alexandra's conviction that she is acting in the best interest of her child, the questioning of her decision "moves tormented back and forth" like the iron in Olsen's short story. She relates how the teacher's assessment of her decision as worrisome induces a maddening wave of self-doubt that runs to the core of her motherhood. The teacher, responding from her professional position within the normative discourse, is no doubt well-meaning in her desire to persuade Alexandra otherwise. Yet, she enrages Alexandra with the subtext beneath her expression of care (i.e., if you cared as much about your child as I do, you would follow my recommendation). Moreover, Alexandra appears unable to articulate what she really wants to say in response—perhaps because of that "caught-by-the-throat feeling" that defies expression (Warner, 2005).

It is worth noting that school professionals regard Alexandra as being in denial about her son because she disagrees with their recommendations about how to best educate him. The idea that she might hold a different worldview about child development is not considered.

But this *whole* issue of this early intervention and all these concerns that we have to address and catch *early on* before they become a big issue—before they lose any more IQ points [laughter]—children there are still being raised by their grandmothers. Not so many children go to daycare. Most women of my age are working. I would say 99% are in the workforce—much more than the United States. People don't give up their jobs to stay home. But it's a grandmother, it's a great-aunt—many end up having a couple of children from the family—and watching them. What I'm seeing with children back home is that the child is expected to participate in the day-to-day activities with Grandma and go to the neighboring house and have coffee together and play with other grandchildren. If a child does not really talk as much, or is awkward in their jumping or whatever, it will come. They believe that children grow at different paces. And when they are with an adult, they are in a *mentoring* situation—like with Grandma cooking together. There is no Grandma sitting them down and saying, "Now roll the ball. Roll the ball. Roll the ball." My friend is more concerned about *me* than the child. She's concerned. "Those Americans. What are they doing to you? They're driving you crazy!"

From her bi-cultural perspective, Alexandra recognizes that there is more than one way to understand, nurture, and respond to children. The American conceptualization of child development seems unnecessarily intense and rigid in expectation to her—a view similarly expressed by Warner (2005). Alexandra does not hold the same value for science applied to child development, evidenced in her wry derision of early childhood intervention and the numerous (and, to her, seemingly contrived) therapies available to American children. Yet, it is assumed by school professionals that she shares the values inherent within American schools.

The degree to which normative discourse erodes Alexandra's confidence as a mother is reflected in her poignant admission of having had conflicted feelings about having a second child.

> I am so thankful to my husband for wanting to have another child, a second child. Because I felt so overwhelmed with the fact that my first child was "all these *things*" that I didn't want to have another one. But it's only because I have a *second* one that I realize there's nothing wrong with me. It's not my mothering. It's just that my first child was not *exactly* the same as everybody else. But at the same time, it also gives me reference to see how my mothering is so different with my first child than my second one because *she* has not been labeled. I don't have to worry about her as much.

Although she resists the normative discourse that so narrowly defines her son, Alexandra simultaneously engages with the discourse by attributing "all these *things*" about her son to something being "wrong" with her mothering—to the point of questioning whether or not she is a "good enough" mother to have a second child. Within an educational context that understands and responds to difference as deficit, it is somewhat unsurprising that the mother of a child so-labeled or constructed might likewise see herself as "missing something" that other mothers innately possess.

Alexandra goes on to explain how labeling continually constructs her son— even though he does not bear a special education label. It appears that once targeted by normative discourse, it becomes nearly impossible to escape the surveillance of well-intentioned professionals intent upon observing, documenting, analyzing, and categorizing his behaviors (Baker, 2002).

> *Everything* my child does goes under the microscope. Everything. His choice of words. His choice of games. Who he is going to interact with? What he does? Whether he naps. Whether he doesn't. Whether he likes certain foods. Whether he doesn't. Whether he is tired. *Everything.* Everything is under the microscope. While with my daughter, *she* gets a free pass with everything because she has never been labeled.... *Because* of all these concerns, I never give him a break. He *never* has a break. He always has an adult in his face questioning and putting

under a microscope *everything* that he does. If he is running around with other children doing those wild sounds, it's because he has *problems*. Another child? It's because he is *playing*. If he doesn't want to focus in circle time at school, it's because he has problems. Another child? It's because he had a rough night or he didn't have breakfast or whatever. *This* child—it's because he has *issues*.

And so it seems that all of Marc's behaviors are suspect and nearly always attributed to the label he has been given—despite the fact that he is *not* classified as a special education student. In fact, Alexandra suspects that school personnel may attribute more significance to Marc's behaviors than is warranted because of a conscious (or perhaps subconscious) desire to amass additional evidence to support their assessment. Significantly, Alexandra observes how her daughter is free to behave in childlike ways without fear of being pathologized because of any label—a freedom no longer available to her son.

Alexandra goes on to share an anecdote that illustrates how the impact of normative discourse burrows its way into her daily mothering. Having had a professional recently express concern that Marc might be having small seizures because he sometimes seems to "space out" in class, Alexandra describes how she over-focuses upon Marc while driving with both children in the backseat.

> They are sitting in the back of the car and I am driving. I'm always checking in the mirror to see if the kids are okay. And at some point, my son is spacing out. And of course, I panic and I say, "What are you doing? What are you thinking? Marc? Marc? *Talk* to me what are you thinking? What are you doing right now?" And he sort of ignores me and before you know it, my other child starts crying. And I am checking the mirror to see if everything is okay. And I say, "What's wrong? What's wrong, Maria?" And she says, "Ask me, too! Ask *me*, too, what am *I* thinking?!" So I ask her, "So what are you thinking, sweetie?" And she says, "I'm thinking about princesses!" And he really hasn't answered. But I didn't want to have to stop the car and question him because he would probably say, "I was looking out the window and thinking about dinosaurs."… It brings you back. You have to stop and say, "What am I *doing* here? What is going on with me?" But clearly, here I am, you can see that I am paying more attention to *him* and ignoring my daughter. Because they *make* me—I am *always* concerned about him.

This small incident illustrates Alexandra's simultaneous engagement with and resistance to normative discourse. Although she rejects the continual attribution of Marc's behaviors to pathology, Alexandra cannot completely rid her thoughts of the possibility that the "experts" could be right—after all, what if her instincts are incorrect and she fails her son and ultimately fails as a mother? Observing her son "space out" while riding in the car, Alexandra is unable to risk ignoring what she sees as daydreaming and begins to pepper him with questions to assure herself that he is not having a seizure—despite the fact that she does not believe that this is the case. Her daughter's plaintive plea to be acknowledged causes her to refocus and ask herself, "What am I doing here?" In this moment, Alexandra recognizes how the normative discourse—whether she subscribes to it or not—significantly impacts her mothering. The power of this discourse to shape how she sees and responds to her son is reflected in her closing comment: "Because they make me—I am always concerned about him." It appears that Alexandra has resigned herself to never being released from the grip that normative discourse has upon her motherhood.

In reflecting upon Marc's demonstrated abilities at a young age as well as his more introverted temperament, Alexandra considers that her daughter (with lesser demonstrated abilities at a comparable developmental stage) is constructed as "normal" largely because of her more social personality.

> And yet, if I compare notes of what they were doing at any given age, Marc was doing a lot of *other* things that we never want to give *him* credit for—like at 2 ½, Marc knew his alphabet, he knew his shapes, he could do patterns, he could do puzzles, he could do *all* these things. She does *not* do any of this, but she is *normal* because she is more of a social little butterfly! And *she's* not allowed to be this more shy and introverted child because then we will start worrying that she may have all these other issues, right?

Once measured, defined, and categorized by school officials, it seems that Marc can no longer be seen in any other way. He is the sum of his identified deficits—documented and recorded upon the normal curve. Yet, Alexandra is unable to reconcile this construction of Marc with the abilities that she knows he possesses. She questions why Marc is not recognized for what he can do and contemplates how much his introverted disposition may have to do with how he has been constructed at school. It is not lost on Alexandra that her daughter may be regarded as "normal" by school personnel in large part because of her more amiable disposition.

In light of Marc's identified language delays, Alexandra recalls how she was advised by school personnel not to speak her native language in the home. In her effort to be A Good Mother, Alexandra takes this advice in hopes of giving her son the best opportunity to develop his language skills.

> I do regret taking some of their advice like they definitely very strongly advised me to stop the bilingual environment in my house—which affected both him *and* her. I think I missed a very important window of opportunity for my children to be bilingual. But because he was having difficulty with language, I had

to put the brakes on bilingualism. And now he is having difficulty—and she too—interacting with the entire family because he doesn't speak the language. Language is a tool of culture, a vehicle of culture—via language, you understand certain ways, certain things, expressions or ways of being—they are reflected in the language. If you don't learn the language early on, you're always going to be an outsider and a *guest* of that language.

From the standpoint of the present, Alexandra reflects upon the consequences of having taken this advice. Given that there is no way to know what kind of effect a monolingual home environment may have had upon Marc's language development, she wonders if the "trade-off" was worth the result. In other words, Alexandra contemplates whether or not the decision to raise her children as monolingual in hopes of possibly enhancing Marc's language development makes up for the limited interactions both of her children now have with extended family. In her effort to "fix" Marc (as she was advised to do), Alexandra realizes that she inadvertently withheld the means by which he (and his sister) could develop meaningful relationships and engage in their cultural heritage—a poignant illustration of the influence of normative discourse within family life.

It is clear that Alexandra has not yet succumbed to the Siren song of normative mythology; however, resistance has taken its toll upon her as a woman, mother, and wife.

> I think that if my husband and I don't divorce because of fights that we've had—because the days that they really *get* me and make me feel as an insufficient mother and as a *failure* mother—those are the days we have fights. The *father* is a *little* more disconnected from the whole process—they *always* call the mother. And also because he's a father and he's at work and you are usually the one who interacts with the teachers and gets all this crap from the teachers. Because you are a mother or maybe it's a personality thing that I am a little more over-stressed person. Or just being a mother. I may get in fights with my husband about—maybe I *have* done something wrong, maybe he *should* be on medication or something or after all *what* is wrong? Whatever, whatever—maybe we are not doing what we *should* be doing for our child.... What *they* don't realize is that they push me so hard and I get into fights with my husband and feel all kinds of thoughts and things about myself.

In referencing fights with her husband, Alexandra reveals the extent to which her struggle with normative discourse has disrupted their marriage. It is noteworthy that Alexandra, also a full-time professional, bears responsibility for their son's education as his mother—a cultural expectation reinforced by both school personnel and her husband. We might revisit our question posed at the beginning of this chapter—just how different *is* mothering in the 21st century? It is Alexandra who feels like "an insufficient mother and as a failure mother" in contrast to her husband whose cultural privilege allows him to be "a little more disconnected from the whole process." Much like Olsen's narrator, Alexandra laments what "they don't realize" about the complexities of being Marc's mother—the cultural pressures to mother perfectly, the self-blame for all things imperfect, the feelings of failure as a mother and wife, the overwhelming anxiety about not ever being good enough or doing it right. And how does a mother begin to explain it all?

Exposing the Myth of Normativity

There is an irony inherent in the myth of normativity, particularly as it plays out in the lives of mothers and their children. Based on the bell curve, the myth holds that normal is average yet the pressure cooker we have described seems to expect mothers to strive for above average, even outstanding, or what *Prairie Home Companion's* Garrison Keillor says about the people of fictional Lake Wobegon: "all the women are strong, all the men are good looking and all the children are above average." Davis (2006) describes the hegemony of normalcy (p. 241) as a symbolic regression to the mean where "the middleness of life, the middleness of the material world, the middleness of the normal body" (Davis, 2006, p. 11) and many other middlenesses reproduce the abnormal. What happens, then, when the good mother's child fails to meet expectations of middleness or above averageness? Alexandra's loss of control over mothering is one example of what happens. Her identity as a good mother is called into question; Marc's middleness is quickly disposed, and the family's cultural connections (through language) are disrupted. The institutional surveillance of Marc filters into the family's everyday life as when Alexandra is driving while worrying that Marc might be having a seizure.

"What is a parent to do?" asks Baker (2002, p. 691), when "caught in the loop" (p. 692) of the hunt for disability? After all, the loop is self-perpetuating. It can be difficult to recognize that one is in the loop, that one has bought into the myth of normativity and sometimes it is only in retrospect that a mother can see it for what it is. While Alexandra's story is disheartening, it is also hopeful in that she has jumped off the speeding train long enough to stand still and clearly see the landscape. What of the other mothers who find no time to "remember, to sift, to weigh, to estimate, to total" as Tillie Olsen once asked? What of them?

Endnote

1.   Olsen, T. (1961). *Tell Me A Riddle*. New York: Delta, pp. 1–2.

References

Apple, R. D. (1995). Constructing mothers: Scientific motherhood in the nineteenth and twentieth centuries. *Social History of Medicine, 8,* 161–178.

Baglieri, S., Bejoian, L., Broderick, A., Connor, D. J., & Valle, J. W. (in press). [Re]claiming "inclusive education" toward cohesion in educational reform: Disability studies unravels the myth of the normal child. *Teachers College Record*.

Baker, B. M. (2002). The hunt for disability: The new eugenics and the normalization of schoolchildren. *Teachers College Record, 104*(4), 663–703.

Belkin, L. (2009). In defense of helicopter parents. Retrieved from *Parenting.blogs. nytimes.com./page/16*.

Bellafante, G. (2009, June 21). Jodi Picoult and the anxious parent. *New York Times Magazine*. Retrieved from http://www.nytimes.com/2009/06/21/magazine/21picoult-t.html

Brantlinger, E. (2004). Confounding the needs and confronting the norms: An extension of Reid and Valle's essay. *Journal of Learning Disabilities, 37*(6), 490–499.

Brantlinger, E. (Ed.). (2006). *Who benefits from special education? Remediating (fixing) other people's children*. Studies in Curriculum Theory Series. Mahwah, NJ: Lawrence Erlbaum.

Davis, L. J. (2006). *The disability studies reader*. New York: Routledge.

Davis, L. J. (1997). Constructing normalcy: The bell curve, the novel, and the invention of the disabled body in the nineteenth century. In L. J. Davis (Ed.), *The disability studies reader* (pp. 9–28). New York: Routledge.

Ferri, B., & Connor, D. (2006). *Reading resistance: Discourses of exclusion in desegregation and inclusion debates*. New York: Peter Lang.

Fuchs, D., & Deshler, D. D. (2007). What we need to know about responsiveness-to-intervention (and shouldn't be afraid to ask). *Learning Disability Research and Practice, 2*(2), 129–136.

Gabel, S. L. (Ed.). (2005). *Disability studies in education: Readings in theory and method*. New York: Peter Lang.

Gallagher, D. J. (1998). The scientific knowledge base of special education: Do we know what we think we know? *Exceptional Children, 64*(4), 493–502.

Hanauer, C. (2003). *The bitch in the house*. New York: HarperCollins.

Hays, S. (1998). *The cultural contradictions of motherhood*. New Haven, CT: Yale University Press.

Kliebard, H. M. (1995). *The struggle for the American curriculum, 1893–1958* (2nd ed.). New York, NY: Routledge.

Linton, S. (1998). *Claiming disability: Knowledge and identity*. New York: New York University Press.

No Child Left Behind Act of 2001, P. L. 107-110 20 U.S.C. 6301 et seq.

Peskowitz, M. (2005). *The truth behind the Mommy Wars: Who decides what makes a good mother?* Berkeley, CA: Seal.

Reid, D. K., & Valle, J. W. (2004). Learning disability as the intersection of competing discourses: Implications for classrooms, parents, and research. In B. Wong (Ed.) *Learning about learning disabilities. (3rd edition)*. San Diego, CA: Elsevier Academic Press.

Simon, M., & Makar, M. (Directors). (2008). *Nursery university* [documentary film]. United States: Docuramafilms.

Simpson, D. E. (Director). (2002). *Refrigerator mothers* [documentary film]. United States: FACETS.

Spring, J. H. (1989). *The sorting machine revisited: National educational policy since 1945*. New York: Longman.

Thomas, G., & Loxley, A. (2008). *Deconstructing special education and constructing inclusion*. Philadelphia, PA: Open University Press.

Valle, J. W. (2009). *What mothers say about special education: From the 1960s to the present.* New York: Palgrave.

Valle, J., & Connor, D. (in press). *Rethinking difference: A disability studies approach to inclusive practices.* New York: McGraw-Hill.

Vellutino, F. R., Scanlon, D. M., Small, S., & Fanuele, D. P. (2006). Response to intervention as a vehicle for distinguishing between children with and without reading disabilities: Evidence for the role of kindergarten and first-grade interventions. *Journal of Learning Disabilities, 39*(2), 157–169.

Warner, J. (2005). *Perfect madness: Motherhood in the age of anxiety.* New York:Riverhead.

Woolf, V. (1966). Professions for women. In L. Woolf (Ed.), *The collected essays (Vol. 2).* London: Hogarth.

FOURTEEN

Living on the Edge of the Normal Curve: "It's Like a Smack in the Head"

Bernadette Macartney

Introduction

The construction and privileging of the "norm" through medical and (special) education knowledge and practices deny children with disabilities access to many life opportunities that "normal" children and families receive as a matter of routine. Normalising discourses, and the disciplinary mechanisms such as surveillance, diagnosis, and the sorting of people into the categories of normal/not normal in education and society limit the opportunities of children with disabilities and their families to contribute, participate, learn, achieve, and feel good about themselves. This chapter presents and explores the processes and effects of being labeled as disabled —and therefore "not normal"—on the experiences, opportunities and lives of two young children, Maggie-Rose and Clare, and their families living in Aotearoa, New Zealand. In response to this case study, I suggest that we must consciously identify, challenge and reject, in all forms, a worldview of "disability," "difference," and "diversity" as deviations from "the norm." As an emancipatory alternative to normalising deficit discourses I advocate a sociocultural and rights orientation to education and diversity.

Narrative and the Importance of Context

One of the hallmarks of a medicalised, normalising discourse of disability is its commitment to decontextualising and minimising the importance and value of the identities, relationships and experiences of children with disabilities and their families. Identity and experience are treated as irrelevant through an expert discourse that assumes it understands the "problem" by discretely measuring deviation from the norm and how to "fix" it. I argue that situating the "problem" of disability within the lived contexts that are played out in people's lives is crucial if we are to understand, resist and challenge socially constructed deficit orientations to difference. Ferguson and Ferguson (1995, p. 107) suggest that telling and interpreting people's stories on a micro level can impact on power relations because:

> it gives voice to those not usually asked to describe anything. Complete description challenges power, because an important part of being powerful is the ability to limit description, to define terms, to set the agenda.

The experiences and stories of families of children with disabilities are situated within a landscape of competing discourses about disability and difference (Raymond, 2002). The unique position of family members presents an opportunity to explore, deconstruct and understand disability from the "inside" (Macartney, 2005, 2008a; Raymond, 2002). Parents of disabled children often become politicised, develop advocacy skills and a knowledge of inclusive education practices as a result of experiencing barriers to securing an inclusive education for their children (Barrkman, 2002; Brown, 1999). Ferguson (2009) describes an enduring professional portrayal of "the resistant family" (p. 51), referring to the historical resistance of many families to the segregation of their disabled child either through institutionalization or through being separated pedagogically, and sometimes physically, from their non-disabled peers within their education. Families are in a unique position to critique social, cultural and educational responses to disability, and their stories provide insights for others into the negative effects of normalising beliefs, knowledge and practices on disabled people. The ways that families interact with deficit discourses and readings of their disabled children give insight into how disabled people's lives are governed as well as the subject positions that are denied, and available to them.

The (Re)-Shaping and -Presenting of Experience

Each of the two families interviewed for this year-long study has a young child with disabilities and a non-disabled younger sibling. The first family consists of Fran and Mark, who are the parents of Clare, who was four years old, and Amber, who was one, at the time interviews were carried out. Clare is "officially" described as being disabled, although Fran prefers to describe her daughter as "special" (Macartney, 2005). My partner Tony and I were the other participants in this study. At the time of the interviews, Maggie was seven and eight years old and Sally was two and three. The interviews of our family were facilitated by other researchers. Our family's data also include documents from medical and special education professionals, a prior published account about our family (Macartney, 2002), excerpts from Maggie-Rose's family baby book, narrative assessments from her early childhood education centre, and personal recollections and reflections.

Multiple Contexts, Positioning, and Narratives

Ferguson (2009) describes a typology of four different kinds of narratives used in research for exploring family experiences and perspectives: received, generated, found, and inferred. *Received narratives* are accounts that family members have written and published. The authors of these narratives write for the particular purpose of sharing their stories and perspectives with others. *Generated accounts* are sought and facilitated by researchers who are interested in listening to, interpreting and representing the stories of family members. *Found narratives* are personal documents written by family members not intended to be shared with a public audience. Ferguson describes *inferred narratives* as the "unspoken" narratives of families that can be inferred through the critical reading of professional documents, correspondence to, and accounts of disabled children and their families. A further narrative within this research and chapter is an *autobiographical narrative*. These "multi narratives" provide a rich, contextualised and complex representation of the intersections between normalising discourses and lived experience, including how families make sense of their lives. This approach allows for a complex and in-depth exploration of the construction and consequences of normalcy from the context of lived experience.

The Problem of "Normalcy"

This chapter explores the social construction of normalcy by inferring and naming its underlying assumptions and beliefs through the narratives of families and professionals. I am interested in the ways that normalising assumptions interact with and shape experience to deny the access and participation rights of persons with disabilities and their families. In particular I highlight the workings and effects of disciplinary mechanisms such as surveillance, diagnostic description and classification through the privileging and legitimation of the "norm" as the ideal, true and valid description of reality (Foucault, 1977, 1980).

Diagnosis as a tool for legitimising, requiring, and constructing normalcy

In the remainder of this chapter I represent and interpret a selection of the narratives that focus on the process, experience and meanings of "diagnosis." I have chosen to focus on diagnosis because, alongside (special) educational assessment, diagnosis is perhaps the most honest and overt process for exposing the social construction of disabled identities in relation to the myth of the normal curve.

Fran & Clare: "Give Us the Full Clobber"

To validate and perpetuate their knowledge base, medical and special education discourses of disability and their associated social institutions and arrangements rely on mechanisms that classify and separate "normal" and "abnormal" children. When Clare was four years old, Fran sought medical acknowledgment from a paediatrician that Clare was not going to "catch up" to other (normal) children. A specific diagnosis of Clare's "condition" would provide grounds to apply for the government's on-going reviewable resource scheme (ORRS) funding, which is used to pay for additional part-time teacher hours to support the classroom teacher, teacher aide hours, and the on-going involvement of special education services while the child is at school. Fran wanted written confirmation from the paediatrician that Clare was disabled and would not "catch up" to include in the ORRS application. Fran spoke to the paediatrician on the phone two weeks before their appointment:

> And I said to him, "Now, look, I'm coming in two weeks' time with Clare and we've got ORRS reports to fill out and we think it's time that you should, you know, give us the full clobber." We're actually going to the paediatrician on Friday to put the hard word on, because we've got to start filling out ORRS funding forms in October, for school. And the only way you can get the most funding we can get is to make her out to be as bad as possible. But we also want to say to him, "Look." We haven't seen him for a long time because she's not a sick child. We don't see him very often, because there's nothing to see him about...

There is a close relationship between "diagnosing" or officially naming "the problem" of disability and access to special education funding and resources (Macartney, 2008a, 2008b). In order to access the resources and funding that Fran felt Clare needed for her education, Fran was encouraged, maybe even required, to comply with a deficit view of her child as less than "normal." At the same time, Fran notes that there wasn't really anything to see the paediatrician about because there was nothing wrong with Clare. Throughout our interviews and Fran's sense-making of her life, she subscribed to two seemingly incompatible ways of viewing Clare. On the one hand, Fran described Clare as being abnormal and equated this with losing her dream of having a "perfect child." She felt that she had missed out on a "normal life" as a parent and that instead life was a struggle because her child was "special":

So I guess some people—I mean, you're probably the same with Maggie-Rose
—we just cruised along thinking that she would maybe come right one day, and
we just took one day at a time, and we do take one day at a time, and integrate it
but all of a sudden we've been, it's like a smack in the head, you know, you have
got a—it's the coming out of the closet thing. We have got a "special" needs
child. So yeah, that's probably the difficult part of that.

On the other hand, Fran often spoke in terms of feeling angry with people for
acting and implying that something was wrong with her child:

> We had a thing at preschool—a picnic at preschool the other night, and I was
> talking to a lady whose wee girl was very friendly with Clare, and she said to me,
> "Well, what is wrong with Clare?" And I said, "Nothing." And she looked at me
> as if to say "What?" And I said "Nothing. She's had muscle biopsies; she's had
> MRI scans. There's nothing wrong with her." She went, "Ohh." So, yeah, that
> was a, so I guess my "nothing's wrong with my girl" is actually out there when
> she's in a wheelchair.

This encounter exemplifies the complexity of power relations and dynamics that
are operating at the level of lived experience and interactions. For example, at the
same time as she challenged the dominant view that children classified as abnormal have something wrong with them, Fran used a medical discourse to support
her claim that there is nothing wrong with Clare. The other parent's surprised
response communicates the taken-for-grantedness of the assumption that if you
are different, there has to be something wrong with you.

Clare as "Moderately Intellectually Disabled" with "Splinter Skills"

Fran was in a position where she was requesting, perhaps demanding, that Clare
undergo the disciplinary gaze, observation examination and judgement of a
medical and quasi (special) educational "expert" involving documented, normalising judgements about Clare's deviation from the norm (Foucault, 1977).
Foucault (1977) suggests that normalising judgements and the documentation
that accompanies them transform a person into a "case." Becoming a "case"
involves the exercise of disciplinary powers through which a person "receives as
his status, his own individuality, and in which he is linked by his status to the features, the measurements, the gaps, the 'marks' that characterize him" (Foucault,
1977, p. 192). Tremain (2002) argues that this process of objectification attaches
disabled people to particular socially ascribed identities, a process exemplified in
Fran's comments:

He (the paediatrician)…for the first time he's actually said that Clare is moderately intellectually disabled. So we've never had that before. All previous to that he's always said, "Oh, she'll catch up one day." . . . This actually means she'll catch up to what everybody else is doing, but she's not going to get to the same level as them.…He called it, because it starts at mildly intellectually, goes to severely (Fran is referring to a graph that the paediatrician was showing her). So he's put it "moderately" which is in the middle of the line. So he described it as the "cone effect" of learning. So that meant that a normal child's line goes straight up, and a severely disabled child's line goes sort of very flat, and Clare's is going through the middle. He put her at the middle, so he said when Clare— he put her at about two, two and a half, which is what our early intervention teacher put her at, although she does have splinter skills, so she's good at some things and not others, but he said like when she's at the level of a two-year-old she's actually four, so when she gets to be the level of a three-year-old, the other children, she'll actually be six. And same, when she gets to four, she'll actually be eight. So her curve is always going to keep going up, but at a very slow rate. So she's going to be…she's not ever going to…ever gonna really catch up…I knew that. So, but it was just this moderately intellectually disabled, was probably the word…But, you know, he was very good. He was blunt and to the point… but he's actually said she is moderately intellectually disabled.

Fran seemed to fully accept the paediatrician's explanation of what "moderate intellectual disability" meant and that this label was appropriate for Clare. I couldn't help thinking that such a diagnosis could work to a person's advantage much later in life. For example, when Clare reaches seventy years old, she will only really be thirty five. The paediatrician's contention that Clare would have "splinter skills" illustrates how the use of the normal curve is justified, even in response to contradicting evidence. By framing learning skills as "splintered," actual or potential strengths are transformed into deficits. The use of the term "splinter skills," which refers to spikes in particular measures on a standardized academic or cognitive test that a "disabled" person may demonstrate, explains away anomalous behaviours or attributes, pathologising them as deficits. Since these attributes do not coincide with the person's overall ability profile, they are interpreted as outliers and considered unrelated to the person's average ability. A potential strength or positive learning attribute becomes a "splinter skill" invoking a deficit interpretation of Clare's abilities. It is unlikely that the same learning and skills displayed by a "normal" child who was not under medical/special education surveillance would be constructed in this way. Having a "moderate intellectual disability" and "splinter skills" were characteristics ascribed to Clare in the process of her being documented and separated out as a "case" (Foucault, 1977). Although ORRS funding was approved for Clare, Fran and Mark were rejected by four schools before they found one that would enroll Clare. The fifth school required Clare to attend school part-time for her first year, and the family paid, in addition to school fees, money to top up the teacher aide funding to full-time. In New Zealand all children "have" a legal right to attend school full-time from the age of five. This right, and the opportunities that accompany it, were denied to Clare because of her label and identity as "disabled."

Bernadette, Tony and Maggie-Rose: "This Is Our Little Baby, of Course She's Perfect."

In this section, I juxtapose family narratives with written materials from a medical, quasi-special educational professional to critically recount our family's experiences of that period in our life. The device I have used to counter-balance medical/special educational and family narratives is split text, divided into two columns, one medical/special educational, and the other family. Each column can be read as separate but related pieces of writing. The purpose of juxtaposing the data this way is to identify and explore the differences and relationships between medical/special education and developmental approaches to disability and our family's views and experiences (Macartney, 2008a). It is intended to highlight the characteristics of each worldview and to take the reader on a journey through the discursive terrain that our family has covered through living life on the edge of the normal curve (Table 14.1).

The Initial Impacts of "Diagnosis"—A Personal Tragedy or a Force to Be Resisted?

Tony and I were very upset when we left the paediatrician's office. It was also a relief to feel like we were able to talk about what had been a pretty much unacknowledged concern for both of us for many months. We had arranged to visit a friend after the paediatrician visit, but we just wanted the three of us to be together and that's what we did. We decided that we would go away together for a few days, to "collect" ourselves before having to tell friends and family about Maggie's diagnosis. When we got up the next morning in our motel, we went to get Maggie out of her cot, as we did every morning. There was Maggie, cute as ever, awake and happy to see us as usual. It was at this moment that Tony and I realised that nothing had changed, or at least the most important things hadn't changed. Maggie was still the person she had been the morning before and we were still her doting mum and dad.

This realisation that Maggie hadn't changed might appear obvious. But it was significant for Tony and me because it helped us to recognise what had changed. What had changed was how Maggie would be viewed and positioned by "others" as a result of having this new label of "developmental delay" as well as the trepi-

Table 14.1: Diagnosis: "A Whole Layer of Doubt"

Medical/Special Educational	Family
	A friend from the College of Education came to visit us at home one day when Maggie was about 7 months old. She rang me that night and told me that she was concerned about Maggie's development and thought we should have her examined by a specialist:
	Excerpt from interview with Tony and Bernadette, 2005: B. I was quite upset when I got off the phone. Int. Can you remember what those feelings were about? B. Yeah, I think it... it's feeling protective. Just feeling really protective of Maggie and thinking, "Oh, God. What are we in for?" And I suppose in some ways I probably felt relieved as well, because I'd been going through months of—you know, in the circle that I move in, although, because I was at home and it was winter with a little baby, I wasn't out and about heaps, but whenever I sort of spent time with my early childhood friends.... Well, I was very aware of people being concerned about her development and things. T. And you do feel defensive about that, don't you? It's like... this is our little baby, of course she's perfect. B. Yeah, yeah—"Butt out." And: She is perfect, thank you very much."
"Assessment" & "Diagnosis" *The abridged letter below was written by the paediatrician to our family doctor, not to us. We received a copy a few days after our appointment:* "Thank you for referring Maggie who is delayed with her development and is of short stature as well.... Maggie was a floppy baby and she was also jaundiced, she was slow to suck and establish breast feeding which did not really get going until she was 3–4 weeks old. After that weight gains have been steady and have taken off recently with a marked increase in weight so that now Maggie is quite obese. This is accentuated by her short limbs and short length.... She did not smile until 9 weeks old and this was only occasional, more smiles came at 12 weeks of age, but she has been slow in her social development, not interacting with other people and not showing a great deal of eye regard even to her parents....	**Journal excerpts from Maggie's Baby Book (7 months):** We took Maggie to a paediatrician a couple of weeks ago because we have been concerned about the slowness of her development, e.g., she is not as responsive socially as many infants, does not roll, or lift her head easily when placed on her tummy, is not reaching for objects.... The paediatrician was quite concerned after meeting and examining Maggie-Rose and she will be having tests soon to x-ray her skeleton, scan her brain and check out her chromosomes. Apparently her limbs are disproportionately short and as a whole she is very short for her age (60 cm). Of course, she is still our lovely wee Maggie-Rose.... We will start checking out early intervention services for her and have been talking to family and friends about her having a/some disabilities. She may have an intellectual impairment of some sort too because her social, motor, and intellectual development are delayed. She'll certainly get every opportunity to reach her potential and is a motivated wee possum. Maggie is turning into a rough and tumble girl—loves flying up in the air, being bounced etc.... Also loves music—especially Tony playing the guitar—she stops whatever she is doing, eyes open wide and she listens. **8 months:** Maggie-Rose is enjoying making "silly" noises like frog sounds and other animal sounds—the ones that tickle her fancy change each day and when you "hit the spot"—she giggles. Saying "mummm-mummm-mum" a lot in the last few days. Talks to us and to herself. *We talked in our interview about how we felt about Maggie and her future:* B. And so, did you, like after Maggie-Rose, after we went to the paediatrician, did you feel differently about her?

She is not able to hold her head up when prone and she is certainly not sitting, she does not support her weight when held upright.... Maggie shows significant delay in her development, motor, social and cognitive. She is also short, she needs further investigations...."	**T.** No, because I, like you, when we went away to Hanmer, we sort of had that epiphany the next day, it was just like, well, nothing's changed. I do feel—I shared that feeling. But it was just, the question marks, there were just suddenly a million question marks that weren't there before—maybe they kind of were there before, but if Maggie-Rose had been "normal" those question marks wouldn't be there. So it just sort of adds a whole layer of doubt. **Int.** A different layer. Did you feel differently once you'd been to the paediatrician? **B.** Ummm, I don't think I felt—I didn't feel differently toward Maggie, but I think that in some ways nothing had changed and in some ways everything had changed. And it was to do with, I suppose in some ways, sort of like having to share her more, having her being the... **T.** The subject. **B.** Yeah, the subject, or the object of other people's interest and intervention and all of that sort of thing. It made me feel a bit tired.... **T.** And we both knew, because of our work, you know, because I had worked in mental health, how badly the world treats people with disabilities. So immediately as well as all those questions about what she's going to be like when she's 21 was, "How's the world going to treat her?" and being aware of the crap the world deals out towards people with disabilities. That sort of adds some anxiety that you don't necessarily... **Int.** that you wouldn't have had otherwise.

dation and sadness we felt about how people would view and treat Maggie from now on and throughout her life and what impact this would have on her. We also experienced uncertainty and anxiety about how she would develop, particularly the "big" things like: "Will she walk?" and "Will she talk?" Tony and I both found that this anxiety reduced over time, as some of our questions were answered through seeing her develop and through getting to know and understand her more as a person. I tried to relax and not worry about what the future might hold. I made a conscious effort to trust Maggie's processes of development and to enjoy and value who she was rather than constantly comparing her to "normal" children and wanting her to be more like them. It was my experience that there was a lot to like, love and enjoy about Maggie-Rose and I tried to communicate that to everybody else.

Deficit Discourses and the Making and Breaking of Silence

Our feelings of relief about being able to talk about Maggie's development and the relative silence that had existed before it indicates that we were at some level keeping her differences a secret. This raises questions about why we felt that it was necessary or best to keep such a secret. I think that one answer lies again in the "fact" that, in the dominant discourse, to be identified as developing differently in our society is equated with being lacking, damaged, deficient, delayed and not as good as "normal" children. This negative positioning and subjectifying are invoked when the labels of "impaired" and "disabled" are used to describe and classify particular groups of children and adults. This abiding relationship between disability and deficit is observed in the language that I used to talk about

Maggie having disabilities in her baby book. My entry is full of negative comparisons to "normal" infants and development. I used this language of comparison and "lack" even though I explicitly disagree with deficit views of disability which points to the deeply ingrained nature of this ideological stance.

Classifying, labeling and pathologising

The paediatrician's letter, and Fran's description of Clare's diagnosis, read as chronicles of Maggie and Clare's perceived deficits, replete with markers of the particular ways in which they were deemed to be different from "normally" developing children. Any of Maggie and Clare's positive qualities and achievements were either absent or reinscribed as deficits. One example of this re-inscription process that I found particularly upsetting was the paediatrician's contention that Maggie was, "quite obese." At the time we took Maggie to the paediatrician, breast milk was her sole source of nutrition. I had never thought and didn't believe that it was possible for a fully breastfed infant to be obese. As the paediatrician pointed out, Maggie (and I) took a while to establish successful breastfeeding. Working hard on and succeeding with breast feeding was one of my first challenges and triumphs as a mother. I was very proud of Maggie's ability to feed from my breasts, thrive and grow into what I believed was a chubby, healthy baby. Breastfeeding was also the major process through which Maggie and I engaged in loving, mutual interactions.

Medical testing—marking out the differences

The initial diagnosis led to several months of regularly going to the hospital with Maggie for tests. Initially, neither of us thought to question the need for medical tests. In fact, Tony was relieved to have "the experts on the case." None of the results from the tests found anything that could medically explain Maggie's differences or point to any "treatment" that she might benefit from. Secretly, Tony and I enjoyed the fact that they couldn't find a label for Maggie or a pigeon hole to fit her into. For a while we coined the term "Maggie Syndrome" until we decided that we couldn't think of any benefits of having a syndrome. Eventually, the paediatrician suggested that Maggie have an MRI scan on her brain under a general anaesthetic. When Tony and I asked why the paediatrician thought that this procedure would be useful or was necessary, he said that they may be able to come up with a prognosis about her potential to develop language by looking at her brain. We were very sceptical about any prognosis being valid and we didn't want to hear a prognosis since we had decided that we weren't going to believe it anyway. We didn't want an opinion that we mistrusted to be spoken, written down or niggling away at the back of our minds. Tony then asked him if the results from an MRI scan would lead to any treatment or suggestions for ways in which we could intervene to support Maggie's development and learning. The paediatrician's answer was, "No." After that we couldn't see any benefits and only risks for Maggie in such a procedure. This was when the penny dropped for us in relation to what we were doing at the hospital. We began to question why we were having all these tests when Maggie obviously wasn't sick or in need of a cure. We realised that what we wanted was to let Maggie's development unfold "naturally" without medical intervention or opinions influencing her future and how other people perceived her and her capabilities. Even though we had doubts and questions about her future, we preferred living with uncertainty to having it all sewn up. That's when we ceased going to the hospital for tests and stopped looking for a label.

Disabled by the Discourse

I argue that the notion and privileging of the norm through medical and special education knowledge and practices denies disabled children's access to many life experiences the children and families who do not live on the boundaries of the normal curve receive as of right. Normalising discourses in education and society limit the opportunities of children with disabilities to contribute, participate, learn, achieve and feel good about themselves. Instead, children and families are expected to accept and cope with the "fact" that their child is lacking in intelligence and/or ability and will lag behind their "normal" peers throughout their lives. This worldview sets the stage for narrow, low and limiting expectations of learning, participation and behaviour within education and society. The "disabled child" becomes an object of normalising knowledge and practices rather than a learner with agency who has a range of diverse qualities and subject positions to draw from. Instead, they are perceived through their fixed status as "disabled" and, therefore, "other" (Macartney, 2008b). The privileging of normalcy in education and society translates into beliefs and practices that require disabled children and adults to fit into existing arrangements and expectations or be separated from people who would otherwise be considered part of their peer group or community. There are many ways that a normalising discourse acts to exclude disabled children within so-called "regular" or "mainstream" educational environments. The problem of the exclusion, marginalization and limiting educational opportunities of disabled children is not about placement but about an unquestioned assumption that divergence from the norm represents a deficit (Macartney, 2009b).

Family resistance and normalising discourses of development and disability

There are perhaps three key cultural concepts and assumptions in western society that help produce parents' feelings of defensiveness and desires to hide or ignore children's perceived deviations and differences from the norm. The first assumption is that there is one proper, preferred, normal timeline and pathway for babies and children to develop. The second is that, if a child does not conform to these normal developmental expectations, there is something wrong with them, and the child is, therefore, objectified as a problem. The third is that the "impaired" child is a tragedy—for them and their family. Yet, who wants their precious children, maybe especially their first child, to be viewed as impaired, a tragedy and a problem? Tony and I certainly didn't. Our defensiveness and protectiveness can be read as a reaction against those dominant constructions or "truths" about difference in a situation where those views threatened our experience of and aspirations for our child and family. Similarly, although Fran described her struggle as being due to having a "special" child, she was equally resistant to the unrelenting view that, because Clare was "special," there was something wrong with Clare.

Medical and special education professionals working from traditional developmental, psychological perspectives construct resistant, defensive or contrary parental reactions as a normal response to their child's impairment rather than as resistance to limiting deficit views, interventions and practices. Through this lens, parental responses are viewed as stemming from a process of "grieving." Stages of denial, hostility, sorrow, and anger are constructed as phases on the way to "accepting" what the medical and psychology profession assume to be a personal tragedy for the child and family (Ferguson & Ferguson, 1995). Defensiveness that is motivated by love and protectiveness against negative views of disability and difference are easily dismissed by professionals or redefined to fit a personal tragedy view. This repositioning of parental resistance as an individual problem with "acceptance" of their children's deficits maintains normalising professional knowledge and practices by ensuring that knowledge is unchallenged and remains intact.

An alternative interpretation of parental resistance is that these feelings embody a reaction against professionals' attempts to cast a child and family into a negative light and the negative consequences associated with such a diagnosis (Ferguson, 2001, 2009). Unfortunately, normalising discourses are pervasive throughout society and are not peculiar only to professional domains that embrace reflexivity in practice. In addition, many popular cultural assumptions and responses to "disability" draw from deficit and personal tragedy discourses (Purdue, 2004), underscoring the commonsensical and tacit operation of deficit orientations.

Resisting "the norm"

I suggest that we consciously identify, challenge and reject in all forms a worldview of disability, difference and diversity as deviations from "the norm." I argue that the place to do this work of resistance is in lived contexts where deficit-based, normalising discourses are being played out and affecting real people in real situations. Adherence and loyalty to the notion of the norm are pervasive and seductive. Being able to identify and recognise normalising thinking and practices in our daily settings is crucial to resisting and dismantling normalising mechanisms in our lives. We must also continually develop and use alternative, transformative discourses as a path to challenging the notion of the norm and its exclusionary effects (Macartney, 2009a). A transformative discourse must work to reveal practices and thinking that rely on deficit explanations of diversity. One possible framework for a transformative discourse lies in critical and socio-cultural approaches to education and society that adopt a view of knowledge and reality as socially co-constructed and situated in particular social, cultural, historical, and political contexts. Working from this perspective, one remains committed to questioning beliefs and practices in terms of their intended and actual effects on groups and individuals, rather than uncritically accepting the status quo (Davis, Gunn, Purdue, & Smith, 2007; MacNaughton, 2005; Macartney, 2007, 2009b). Rather than appealing to a value free, objective neutrality to justify inequalities and then passing them off as unfortunate, but necessary, critical approaches position ethics and morality at the centre of human practice (Dahlberg & Moss, 2005; Macartney, 2009a). Within a critical pedagogical approach lies a responsibility to consider and continually develop ethical sites of practice with an orientation based on an acknowledging, accepting and valuing diversity in meaningful ways (Dahlberg & Moss, 2005). Such ethical environments work so as not to minimize or colonise the interests and subjectivities of some people in the interests of others (Bishop, Mazawi, & Shields, 2005; Dahlberg & Moss, 2005; Macartney, 2009a; Rinaldi, 2006).

Conclusion

There should be no doubt that the normal curve and its associated regime of truth continues to have serious, lifelong consequences for many groups of people in society, including children and adults with disabilities and their families. There are strong professional industries and fields of science built on an adherence to the normal curve and the notion of normal/not normal. The existence of the norm and the normal has become an accepted—given or fact—in mainstream culture. At the same time, the exclusionary impacts of norms-based industries and fields of knowledge are not widely recognised, reported, disputed or seen as problematic to society with the exception of fields such as disability studies and inclusive education. Deep understandings can be gained through listening to and reflecting on the diverse voices and experiences of people with disabilities and their families. People with disabilities and their families are uniquely positioned by and position themselves in relation to normalising discourses. Their biographies need to be at the forefront of co-constructing understandings of and alternatives to living on the edge of the normal curve.

References

Barrkman, J. (2002). *Daring to dream…: Stories of parent advocacy in Queensland.* Brisbane, Australia. Queensland Parents for People with a Disability Inc.

Bishop, R. Mazawi, A., & Shields, C. (2005). *Pathologizing practices: The impact of deficit thinking on education.* New York: Peter Lang.

Brown, C. (1999). Parent voices on advocacy, education, disability and justice. In K. Ballard (Ed.), *Inclusive education: International voices on disability and justice* (pp. 28-42). London: Falmer.

Dahlberg, G. & Moss, P. (2005). *Ethics and politics in early childhood education.* London: RoutledgeFalmer.

Davis, K., Gunn, A., Purdue, K., & Smith, K. (2007) Forging ahead: Moving towards inclusive and anti-discriminatory education. In L. Keesing-Styles & H. Hedges, (Eds), *Theorising early childhood practice: Emerging dialogues* (pp. 99–120). New South Wales, Australia: Pademelon.

Ferguson, P. (2009). The doubting dance: Contributions to a history of parent/professional interactions in early 20th century America. *Research practice for persons with severe disabilities, 33*(1–2), 48–58.

Ferguson, P. (2001). Mapping the family: Disability studies and the exploration of parental responses to disability. In K. Albrecht, K. Selman & M. Bury (Eds.), *Handbook of disability studies* (pp. 373-395). Thousand Oaks, CA: Sage Publications.

Ferguson, P., & Ferguson, D. (1995). The interpretivist view of special education and disability: The value of telling stories. In T. Skrtic, (Ed.), *Disability & democracy: Reconstructing (special) education for postmodernity* (pp. 104–121). Denver, CO: Love.

Foucault, M. (1977) *Discipline and punish: The birth of the prison.* (2d ed.). Translation (1977) Alan Sheridan. New York: Vintage, Random.

Foucault, M. (1980) Truth & power. In C. Gordon (Ed.), *Michel Foucault power/knowledge: Selected interviews and other writings 1972–1977* (pp. 109–133). Brighton, UK: Harvester.

Macartney, B. (2002). Maggie-Rose: A parent's story. *The First Years/Nga Tau Tua Tahi, 4,* 29–31.

Macartney, B. (2005). Opportunities and challenges of being both researcher and coparticipant in openly ideological, emancipatory research. *Qualitative Research Journal, 5*(2), 58–76.

Macartney, B. (2007). What is normal and why does it matter? Disabling discourses in education and society. *Critical Literacy: Theories and Practices Journal, 1*(2), 29–41. Retrieved January 20, 2008 from: http://www.criticalliteracy.org.uk/journal/table2.html

Macartney, B. (2008a). Disabled by the discourse: Some impacts of normalising mechanisms in education and society on the lives of disabled children and their families. *NZ Research in ECE Journal, 11*(1), 33–50.

Macartney, B. (2008b). "If you don't know her, she can't talk": Noticing the tensions between deficit discourses and inclusive early childhood education. *Early Childhood Folio, 12,* 31 –35

Macartney, B. (2009a). *Teaching through an ethics of belonging, care and obligation as a critical approach to transforming education.* Paper presented at the 9th second city conference on disability studies in education. Syracuse University, Syracuse, NY, May 1–3, 2009.

Macartney, B. (2009b). Understanding and responding to the tensions between deficit discourses and inclusive education. *SET: Research information for teachers, 1(1),* 19–27.

Mac Naughton, G. (2005). *Doing Foucault in early childhood studies: Applying poststructural ideas.* London: Routledge.

Purdue, K. (2004). *Inclusion and exclusion in early childhood education: Three case studies.* Unpublished doctoral thesis. Dunedin, New Zealand: University of Otago.

Raymond, H. (2002). *A narrative inquiry into mothers' experiences of securing inclusive education.* Edmonton, Alberta: University of Alberta.

Rinaldi, C. (2006). In dialogue with Reggio Emilia: Listening, researching and responding. In G. Dahlberg & Moss, P. (Eds.), *Contesting early childhood series.* London & New York: Routledge.

Tremain, S. (2002) On the subject of impairment. In M. Corker & T. Shakespeare, (Eds), *Disability/Postmodernity: Embodying disability theory.* (32–47). New York: Continuum.

FIFTEEN

Practitioner Research as Resistance to the "Normal Curve"

Gerald Campano & Rob Simon

"To create one world that encompasses many worlds"—*Zapatista phrase*

Introduction

At a large public elementary school in a midsized city in California, 1% of the student population is designated as "gifted and talented." Another school, located near a major midwestern university, designates roughly 80% of their students as "gifted and talented." Both are neighborhood schools mainly serving the surrounding communities. At the California school, a pressing concern is acquiring more diagnostic resources to test students and, if necessary, to reclassify them as learners with "special needs." At the midwestern school, officials are pressed by parents of the "non-gifted" who are often upset that their children aren't counted in the ranks of the "gifted."

These two schools and their respective institutional constructions of "gifted and talented" and "special needs" illustrate the power of the normal curve. It is perhaps no surprise that the disparities between the schools map onto deeply entrenched social stratifications. The midwestern school, recognized for its high test scores, serves predominantly middle-class and affluent students, many of whom come from families with ties to the nearby university. The students from the California school are predominantly from poor and working-poor families; many have parents who labor in migratory, factory, or low-wage service jobs. There would be bountiful evidence of students' gifts and talents in either community, for those who cared to look. Sixth graders in the California school, many of whom are bilingual and even multilingual, have repeatedly placed in a highly competitive academic pentathlon. Despite severe overcrowding and inadequate facilities, a number of the students have test scores equal to or surpassing their peers across the nation.

There is simply no satisfactory way to justify ethically how students in these two communities—and in many others like them—have been disproportionately categorized, sorted, and offered a disparate set of educational experiences and resources. Yet there is little public outcry. One reason for the lack of protest is that what is constituted as normal varies from context to context. In one school it is "normal" to be remedial. In the other school "normal" is considered the exception, despite marginal—if any—differences in the potentials and capacities of the respective children in these two schools. We suggest that the power and intractability of the idea of "normal" in the two schools are the result of a socially produced and locally instantiated phenomenon (school achievement) masquerading as inevitable reality, an ideology that serves to reproduce social inequalities. Consciousness of inequality, however, is only the starting point for resistance. There lingers a set of more material questions: What would an alternative vision of justice with respect to the normal curve look like in educational contexts? Is it a matter of a more equitable distribution of "gifted and talented" designations across schools and zip codes? Does it involve a more capacious and generous understanding of talent or "intelligences?" How might we re-envision the variance of student potentials, in a way that is not organized around a hierarchy of academic ability or essentialized notions of intelligence?

This chapter examines the role that practitioner research might play, especially when co-articulated with insights from literacy and critical theory and from disability studies, in helping to resist the normal curve and enact alternatives. We build our argument by first suggesting that this resistance must be premised on considering the ideology of the "normal" in education as more than a bad or unjust idea that merely needs to be debunked. It is a deeply ingrained social and material practice that permeates almost every aspect of education and is manifested in a web of interrelated pedagogical policies, practices, and structures. This makes resistance to the normal curve an aporetic (Derrida, 1993) endeavor. Everyday acts of resistance will require educators to navigate seemingly indissoluble contradictions. Constructive resistance must go beyond a utopian critical rhetoric for a more democratic society and even beyond reasonable calls for teachers to be trained to treat differences differently than deficits. While important, these arguments often remain overly abstract and removed from the real world of classrooms. However, thoughtful teachers have strong intuitive understandings of how the idea of the normal is a reductive, insufficient, and counter-productive way of understanding student potential. What is needed are specific and local accounts of how educators resist the normal curve to enact more democratic educational arrangements.

Practitioner research, with its emphasis on the intimate relationship between knowledge and practice (Cochran-Smith & Lytle, 1999, 2009), is uniquely suited for this conceptual and material project. Practitioner researchers theorize from the thick of things, from actual educational contexts that they shape daily. These pedagogical acts help create the conditions to think about the world—and the people in it—anew, which in turn informs new educational possibilities for students. Like disability studies theorists and activists, practitioner researchers are concerned with the relationship between the created, built world and social identity and agency. Both frameworks challenge medical models for diagnosing and individuating identities and emphasize how material structures and social practices stigmatize differences and curtail access to fuller human flourishing. These perspectives also suggest alternatives. As a methodological stance on classroom practice, practitioner research provides a framework for working against deficit notions of student identity and achievement, and working toward re-envisioning the "normal" in classrooms as intersections of students' multiple worlds of knowledge, culture, experience, and potential. We draw on our own work and the work of other practitioner researchers to describe three ways educators resist the normal curve—counter-practices that enable students to create new opportunities for themselves. Through a disability studies lens (e.g., Siebers, 2008; Snyder, Brueggemann & Garland-Thomson, 2002), we analyze how these kinds of resistance, although interrelated and all necessary, characterize different but overlapping understandings of educational access with their own contradictions and possibilities. We end on a hopeful note about the role of practitioner research in creating spaces for teachers to cultivate more varied understandings of students' academic abilities and identities.

The Ideological and Material Apparatus of the Normal Curve

As practitioner researchers and teacher educators, we have been skeptical about deterministic notions of intelligence and in favor of a more radically egalitarian understanding of student potentials and variance. This entails regarding each student not as an irreducible quantum of ability, but rather, as evolving constellations of capacities, needs, desires, and interests. Furthermore, these constellations are situated within a larger universe: school and classroom communities where the thriving and well-being of each student is ineluctably connected to the flourishing of the whole and, conversely, the devaluing or exclusion of any one individual compromises everyone's cognitive and ethical growth. An alternative educational project, therefore, would have resonances with the vision eloquently phrased by the Zapatistas, which serves as an epigraph of our chapter: "To create one world that encompasses many worlds." To carry the metaphor further, we believe in educators sustaining a sense of awe and wonder at our students' creative and intellectual plenitude, as one would experience gazing at the night sky. With a preservation of their mystery and capaciousness comes our own humility as educators, a reluctance to claim that we finally "know" our students, their limits, or their likely trajectories. We expect that they will surprise us and will continually transcend our expectations.

This is not to deny the sway of belief in a more or less fixed individual intelligence that falls along a bell curve. It has achieved the status of common sense, being deeply embedded in both professional and popular discourse. Worse, it can provide a sense of fatalistic comfort that may assuage our personal and collective sense of failure as educators. If students do not do as well as we would like, maybe it is ultimately because they have exhausted their natural capacities.

Like all teachers, we have each differently experienced the ways that deterministic notions of intelligence often settle into institutional rationales for school failure. For example, as a first-year teacher Gerald encountered bell-curve ideology in the form of a diagnostic protocol for students referred for extra resources in his primary classroom. The six-year-old children were given two tests: one to measure "cognitive capacity" and the other to evaluate subject-matter proficiency. If there was no disparity between how the students performed on, e.g., the math diagnostic and what they were measured to be innately capable of, they did not qualify for extra support. Gerald recalls advocating for a girl who had endured significant trauma in her short life that had clearly impacted her schooling. After going through the referral process, Gerald was informed by the school psychologist that although his student did not qualify for additional support—little surprise in a district that was severely under-resourced—as her regular classroom teacher he should be proud because the tests revealed that she was performing "beyond her abilities." Such a claim demonstrates the absurdity of the process.

We believe that it is urgent to resist this type of cynical resignation. Even if, somehow, the existence of something like an IQ that could be distilled to a score could be proved, it would be better to choose a more egalitarian vision of human variance and growth over this truth for a number of pedagogical and ethical reasons. Fortunately we do not need to make that choice. Over the past decades scholars from a range of disciplines have dismantled the idea of the bell curve, especially in its relation to intelligence. For example, biologist Steven Jay Gould (1981) debunks racist iterations of the bell curve, arguing that variance within groups trumps variance across them, though this analysis kept the idea of IQ intact. In *Mindset*, Stanford psychologist Carol Dweck (2007) synthesizes decades of research for a popular audience on the personal dynamics of success. She argues that ability is an achievement that happens over the course of one's life that has more to do with individuals' attitudes toward labels and experiences of success and failure rather with innate capacity. Sociologist Pierre Bourdieu (1992) has developed thunderous critiques of intelligence through his interrelated concepts of field, social capital, and habitus, making links between academic success and personal merit tenuous at best. In the popular press, Malcom Gladwell (2008) has observed that exceptional outliers are not really outliers at all. According to Gladwell, their success may have less to do with talent and more to do with some combination of spatio/temporal fortune (being at the right place at the right time), cultural legacy (cast in somewhat essentializing terms), and opportunities for good-old hard work (where Gladwell might have explored social justice issues with more depth and critical nuance).

In our own field, an industry has developed around the idea of "multiple intelligences" (Gardner, 2008), which is often used to articulate more specific understandings of student abilities and potentials, though each kind of intelligence might, presumably, also be distributed along a demographic bell curve. Mike Rose's (2005) groundbreaking work emphasizes the cognition skills inherent in working-class jobs, thereby disrupting the exclusive relationship between academics and intelligence. These insights about the bell curve and individual capacity are not lost on educators. A group of progressive elementary teachers and parents associated with teachers applying whole language (TAWL) issued a bumper sticker that reads: "My child is not a test-score." The incisive slogan critiques the metonymic logic that is often used to dehumanize individuals and groups by having one aspect, quality, or representation stand in for the whole of their existence and value.

Irrespective of whether a critique of bell-curve ideology appears on a bumper sticker or in an academic journal, resistance to its influence is easier said than done. Althusser (1971) famously described the ways that ideology is not external to political and social reality—not a realm of "imaginary constructions"—but rather embedded in systems and political apparatuses. In other words, ideology is concretized in, and coextensive with, material experience. Beliefs such as the normal curve are not merely abstractions—they are instantiated and actualized in institutional and material formations. Practice is ideological (Street, 1984); ideology is material. In the tradition of Althusser, Žižek (1989) has contradicted the image of ideology as "false consciousness," either an invisible, unconscious force or a mask for reality. He argues instead that ideology structures reality and reminds us that it is not enough to be skeptically aware of ideology's machinations. Such consciousness may even be part of its power. Knowing an injustice is taking place may make us feel all the more helpless without a productive avenue of resistance.

In schooling, the ideology of the normal curve animates a complex material and pedagogical apparatus that supports specific conceptions of individual aptitude, standards, curricula, tracking, assessment, and ideas of so-called "best practices." These concepts and their attendant structures have significant impact on the lives, learning, and well-being of students. They function to "hail" or *interpellate* (Althusser, 1971) individuals as particular kinds of students, which can shape their self-conceptions as learners, their performances on various measures that claim to objectively depict their learning or competency, and ultimately their life chances. Some common educational policies and structures are manifestations of the normal curve in more obvious ways, such as grouping, whether organized at the level of districts (magnet schools), schools (tracking), or classrooms (leveled readers). Other policies reinforce the ideology of the normal curve in more subtle ways. For example, in the wake of *No Child Left Behind* (NCLB), there has been an almost ubiquitous push in public schools for instruction that is based on what has been termed "scientifically based reading research" (SBRR). If a district has adopted instructional "best practices" that are "scientifically proven" and implemented with "fidelity" and certain students still underperform, as many categorically will given the fact that high-stakes assessment measures are designed to produce results along a normal curve, then the logic of SBRR dictates that it must be the students' fault. Further, it implies that educators may absolve themselves of additional responsibility or deeper inquiry into what it means to teach better—precisely what is required to speculate about and create alternatives to the normal curve paradigm.

Resistance as Counter-Practice: Theorizing from the Thick of Things

Activists and theorists within disability studies (e.g., Siebers, 2008; Snyder, Brueggemann, & Garland-Thomson, 2002) have strenuously countered the prevailing idea that disability should be individuated as personal defects requiring curing. Alternatively, they have theorized disability as a minoritized identity, one formed in part by socially produced injustices. This has provided grounds for constructing more nuanced understandings of disabled persons and has also formed the basis of more activist agendas: calls for substantive changes to systems of negative representation and exclusion as well as changes to disabling social and built environments. Disability studies provide a compelling example of how troubling notions of the "normal" at the level of ideas is not enough to counteract dehumanizing practices. Claiming disability as a positive social identity, as those within disabilities studies have effectively done, is a theoretical and political move. It is also a counter-practice, one squarely aimed toward improving the quality of life for disabled persons. As this idea of counter-practice suggests, challenging notions of "normal" ableness and incumbent structures and practices, which construct and pathologize disability, requires a counter-theoretical, but also a material and collective, social response.

Analogously, statistical norms in education are predicated on the assumption that students can be understood, metonymically, in terms of ability—as represented by scores and outcomes, narrowly constructed—and by extension that students' prior performances equip teachers with necessary knowledge of students' capacities as learners. Recalling the bumper sticker slogan we mentioned earlier, in school practices shaped by normal curve ideology, students are often ascribed an institutionally sanctioned identity. The assumption in these systems is that students can be known by their individual accomplishments (and, of course, their failures). In a normal curve model, teaching is often constructed as an "antidote," an intervention intended to move "struggling" students closer to a mean.

A practitioner research stance, by contrast, begins with the assumption that there is much that we don't know about students. Like theorists and activists who have highlighted the importance of regarding disability as "a social location, complexly embodied" (Siebers, 2008, p. 14) rather than an individual pathology, practitioner researchers take social location—their own and their students'—seriously. The normal curve model is by nature generic rather than local: students are regarded and charted from a distance. Reconsidering the normal from the vantage point of the classroom allows for cultivating more egalitarian variations of students' educational accomplishments and capacities—"intelligence," "ability," "academic success," or "high performance"—as well as more nuanced understandings of students' needs and struggles, without reducing them to distal categories or lowest common denominators. Disability studies has opened ablest ideologies to critical interrogation by theorizing from experience and activating critique at the level of social practice. Similarly, practitioner researchers construct counter-understandings of who students are and what they are capable of from the thick of daily classroom experience.

Rather than viewing teaching as an intervention, practitioner research entails educators taking what Cochran-Smith and Lytle (2009) have called an inquiry stance, a means by which classrooms can more systematically become sites of ongoing learning for teachers, for and with their students. Unlike other research paradigms, practitioner inquiry is embedded in daily practice. As the notion of "inquiry as stance" connotes, it is an iterative, reflexive, and deeply invested methodology. For example, practitioner research questions are rarely generated *a priori*, and commonly emanate from the daily life of the classroom. For practitioner researchers, generating new understandings is inseparable from the well-being of their students.

Practitioner research often originates in particular classrooms, but it is frequently connected to nested communities of practice, within and across classrooms, schools, neighborhoods, or universities. This aspect has led some to claim practitioner research shares many qualities of social movements (e.g., Campano, 2009; Cochran-Smith & Lytle, 2009). For example, local or national teacher research networks like the Bread Loaf Teacher Network or the National Writing Project mobilize and connect teacher researchers to broader conversations and projects. More locally, action oriented university/school collaborations, such as an inquiry community Gerald participated in with teachers from a local urban school district, link university-based practitioner researchers with community-based efforts to improve life chances of urban students. Practitioner research is deeply social and often takes place in local communities, for example, an inquiry community Rob participated in over several years with in-service and student teachers in Philadelphia (Zeiders et al., 2007) that provided a locus for teachers to actualize more resistant understandings and teaching identities.

As these examples suggest, practitioner researchers attempt to understand and improve their practices while simultaneously developing new forms of social understandings and social relationships. For example, in the process of surfacing and addressing aporetic (Derrida, 1993) and uncertain aspects of practice, practitioner researchers often construct more nuanced portraits of students and their potentials, which are not fixed or encompassed by narrow measures. Unlike paradigms of research (and practice) that focus predominantly on outcomes, practitioner researchers, like researchers within some action research or participatory action research traditions (e.g., Herr & Anderson, 2005), typically regard their work as both a means to achieving some new outcome or understanding, as well as a productive end in itself (Cochran-Smith & Lytle, 2009; Campano, Honeyford, Sanchez, & Vander Zanden, forthcoming; Simon, 2009).

Practitioner research that is not resistant

Not all forms of practitioner researches are resistant or critical. Cochran-Smith and Lytle (2009) have described how inquiry in increasingly prevalent school- or district-based professional learning communities (PLCs) is often embedded within discourses of accountability and outcomes. While to some degree collaborative, PLCs are often directed toward learning from assessment data, predicated on structured cycles or models, which are sometimes employed as a means of helping teachers—who are considered to be "lacking" necessary professional knowledge—toward achieving the end of increasing student performance. Projects like these can serve to reify the normal curve's authority.

For example, in a previous teaching context, Gerald was required to participate with other teachers in his grade level in a professional learning community whose purpose was to analyze school data and investigate student achievement. During one meeting, the agenda included this request:

Please bring the following to the meeting:

Your list identifying the five students (within one or two points from the next band) ready to move to the highest [quintile] band

1.   List the intervention strategies implemented in your room to move these students to the targeted band

2.   Bring samples of these strategies to share with your grade level

Also, we will address: Test taking strategies for the state exam.

The request to identify particular students and interventions for moving them to higher quintile bands is presented in this memo as both desirable and purely pragmatic. It may be useful, however, to characterize this agenda as a mechanism of what Žižek (2008) has described as "post-political bio-politics," a form of ideology that disavows its ideological nature by placing emphasis on the practical "management and administration" of human lives (p. 40). Who could argue with increasing student achievement and raising test scores? It is not a conservative issue or a liberal issue (hence post-political). The agenda does not invite heated discussion. It is rather about pragmatically and efficiently addressing a problem— low student achievement—using a hyper-rational approach that appeals to common sense and invokes the authority of strategies that are (implicitly) understood as "scientifically proven" to work.

In this instance, the PLC is not concerned with the generation of new knowledge about and for teaching, learning, or students. Rather, it encourages teachers to help their students more efficiently navigate state exams and to use test data to slot students into pre-fabricated social and bureaucratic types. Professional development in this case centers entirely on test performance and preparation; increased proficiency on standardized measures is subsequently thought to demonstrate effective "data-driven instruction," with data understood only in terms of scoring. Students are objectified, both in terms of their lack of particularity (Carini, 2001) and their lack of agency or action. In this respect students are regarded, to borrow from Martha Nussbaum's (1995) notion of objectification, as inert objects to be propelled over the cusp of quintile bands through an outside force—and *fungible*—interchangeable with other students of similar classification or type. Students are acted upon, but they are represented as lacking self-determination. Their individual histories remain unmentioned and unaccounted for; similarly absent are counter-narratives about students' needs, capacities, and complex relationships to schooling. The purpose of this type of practitioner research is to promote "data-driven instruction," with both data and instruction narrowly construed. Through a medical model, teachers prescribe and implement the appropriate strategies that will ostensibly "intervene" on behalf of students' welfare.

Tests are supposed to inform curriculum and instruction. They are—ideally—one of many representations of teaching and student learning that might include more contextually sensitive narrative and observational accounts from teachers, parents, caretakers, and students themselves. In the case of the bell curve, akin to what philosopher Baudrillard (1994) might call the simulacrum, the representation supplants reality and structures educational dynamics: test scores synecdochially stand for students themselves; test preparation becomes curriculum; and, the complexity of school culture gets distilled to "upticks" or "downticks" (Kozol, 2005) on a school's annual yearly progress. These "data driven" PLCs are often about the power of appearances, where an almost fetishistic belief in numbers begins to trump discourse about actual human lives. For instance, it is not uncommon for expulsion rates to increase as high-stakes testing approaches. In the aforementioned example, it is revealing that the only students "targeted" for intervention are those on the cusp of moving into higher quintile bands. What about the rest of the students? In the context of this particular PLC, an aggregated and abstracted representation becomes more important than the educational growth and histories of the students' themselves.

Practitioner research that resists the normal curve

Practitioner research is sometimes appropriated to serve reductively instrumental agendas, utilized to shore up rather than countervail institutional apparatus, as in the case of professional development targeted to improve test scores. However, this does not represent the more progressive and critical strands of practitioner research, which are often dedicated to the project of humanization. In this section, we examine three examples which illustrate practitioner inquiry as resistance to the normal curve: counter-narratives which demonstrate how a synergy between culturally engaged curriculum and student legacies can enable young people to alter their educational trajectories; inquiries into re-designing existing school structures; and the construction of alternative school communities that redefine stigmatized and criminalized youth identities.

Example 1: Resistance as Creating Counter-Narratives Many teacher researchers do not buy into the logic of the normal curve. They recognize that students' existences and potentials cannot be contained by the ascriptive categories used to explain them and take as a point of departure for their inquiries the insight that labels often fuel social reproduction. "Remedial" students are made, not born, through the deficit-based pedagogical policies and practices meant to address their circumstances. This type of practitioner research, often inspired by traditions of critical literacy and culturally responsive teaching, offers educational counter-narratives that question the normal-curve's authority. Instead of viewing students as problems to be "fixed" through a medical model of diagnosis, they provide accounts of how students are active agents who—if provided a supportive educational environment—will draw on their own rich experiential and cultural knowledge to critique and navigate inequitable conditions in the process of self-determination.

Gerald has documented this form of resistance to the normal curve. For example, he has written of a former fifth-grade student, Ma-Lee, who was sorted in the lowest quintile band of student performance, according to testing (Campano, 2005). In a curriculum that recognized and built off her familial refugee experience, Ma-Lee was able to employ personal narrative to address intergenerational trauma and create a more empowering academic identity for herself. For Ma-Lee, coming to critical political consciousness about her community's history was an ineluctable part of her educational development. Gerald has also written of another student, Virgil, who had been involved in the criminal justice system and labeled a "juvenile delinquent" (Campano, 2009). In the resistant literary spirit of Richard Wright, ten-year-old Virgil was able to find, through writing, a cultural release for his (quite rational) oppositional impulses toward authority. He penned a number of powerful essays on political corruption and the vulnerability of young people in society. Both Ma-Lee and Virgil went on to garner academic accolades as well as make exceptional gains on their standardized tests.

The success of Ma-Lee, Virgil, and so many other students documented and not documented in the teacher research literature undermines the auguries of bureaucratic ascriptions, such as the "struggling learner" or the "child in poverty." Their stories expose the tragedy of remedial standardized curricula that homogenize experience by making sure that "every student is on the same page." If Ma-Lee and Virgil were beholden to such a conformist model that suppresses difference, they may never have been able to distinguish themselves through literacy practices that drew on their singular experiences and enact their unique forms of culturally based knowledge and insight.

The possible limitation of this form of resistance to the normal curve inheres in how it might be read by others. Many teacher researchers provide triumphant narratives of students superseding obstacles and injustices in order to defy expectations and become exceptional. It is important to keep in mind that these narratives of personal transformation, by resisting conformity, are quintessentially American, part of our shared national mythos. In this way, the story of students like Ma-Lee and Virgil can be read through the lens of iconic figures such as Lincoln, Carnegie, Malcolm X, or Barack Obama (it is often a male tale). Superseding injustice seems to be the American way. What these stories often leave unexamined is the very notion of bourgeoisie individualism and with it, the normal curve. Students who re-position themselves on the curve—even dramatically—leave the curve intact. The more they have struggled to overcome injustices, the more their stories may be read by others as a moral tale: through an exertion of individual will, anything can be changed, whether the vision of change is critical or reactionary. The flipside to this triumphalism is the suspicion that others who are not "able" to overcome obstacles and injustices may really not be that deserving anyway. They "lack" the discipline, virtue, will, talent, perseverance, vision, temperament, or whatever other vague traits are used in accusatory discourse to stigmatize those most vulnerable in society.

It is therefore important to make several distinctions as we continue our discussion of the normal curve. First, there is a difference between superseding injustices and trying to pull them out at their roots, even though the two often go hand-in-hand. Second, the most effective forms of resistance will always be collective in nature, involving the coordinated efforts of a multiplicity of people working in solidarity toward an ever-fallible vision of social justice.

Example 2: Resistance as Interrogating and Redesigning Structures Many teacher researchers have taken the very constraints of the normal curve as the subject of critical inquiry with students. In the process, they have attempted to root out the structures that level students and to create an alternative. The English educator Joan Cone (2002), e.g., was disconcerted by the "caste-like" academic placement of students in her California high school. Most students in her "low" ability ninth grade class were African American males, even though they did not represent a majority of the school's population. Cone and her colleagues decided to take action to address this inequity by creating heterogeneous classes and making the twelfth grade AP honors open to any student with the desire to enroll. The mere dismantling of tracking did not instantly lead to a more egalitarian educational arrangement. Cone's scholarship traces the changes in pedagogy as well as profound soul-searching into the faculty's perception of students needed to accompany the structural change. Ultimately, she analyzes how both student "failure" and student "achievement" are social constructs, not individual pre-dispositions. One of the most important outgrowths of Cone and her colleagues' collective teacher research was a dramatic rise in the number of African American and Latina/o students who qualified for the University of California and California State entrance requirements.

Vivian Vasquez (2004) offers another compelling example of how students themselves can challenge the idea of levels, even ones associated with the taken-for-granted developmental trajectories of grade levels, where "batched" (Anderson-Levitt, 1996) children of a specific age are thought to exhibit the same intellectual and social limits and needs. As a teacher researcher in a pre-school classroom, Vasquez invited four-year-olds to adopt a critical inquiry stance in their lives. The students developed an "audit trail" (Harste & Vasquez, 1998), which represented the evolution of their investigations into issues such as gender normativity, advertising, and environmental concerns. In resistance to developmental frameworks, Vasquez demonstrated that four-year-olds were not "too young" for a critical curriculum and, further, that young students could act collectively to make changes in their lives. Rather than the teacher implementing a top-down curriculum, she followed the students' leads and their emerging sense of justice and fairness. In one powerful example, Vasquez recounts how her students noticed that they were excluded from the "French Café," a school language club for the older grades. The students collected data to determine who had been invited and who of those excluded wanted to participate, and then used this information to collectively petition the school for access.

In another case, Gerald worked with a student teacher, Angelica, to create pedagogical experiences that valued collaborative intellectual labor through a drama project by El Teatro Campesino, political theater of the migrant labor camp (Medina & Campano, 2006). The students wrote and improvised plays that challenged the ideology of individual authorship and distinction. The plays were often multilingual and addressed issues that were immediately relevant to their lives, such as school tracking, racial profiling, and community histories that had been buried in the regular school curriculum. The performance group, Dancing Across Borders, garnered recognition in the state of California, and the children even performed at Stanford University, but one would never be able to predict which students in the group had been pejoratively labeled "learning disabled," "limited English proficient," or "gang banger." Through drama, the students turned these negative ascriptions around, and their previously stigmatized identities became a source of critical knowledge and insight, or what philosophers (Mohanty, 1997; Moya, 2000) might call "epistemic privilege." For example, in their play titled *What the Teacher Didn't Know*, the students drew on experiences of being labeled (academically, socially, ethnically, linguistically) to deconstruct the structures that had oppressed them.

These examples occurred in contexts where the normal curve was a dominant ideology, reminding us that even within constraining circumstances there are always opportunities for resistance. On a cautious note, however, we cannot underestimate the ways the normal curve can reassert itself, creating an ever-receding "horizon of expectation." For example, if all the children in the California school mentioned at the beginning of this chapter were accepted into gifted and talented programs, one can imagine that the elite will find ever-newer ways to distinguish themselves. In fact, that is exactly what happened in the midwestern district introduced at the beginning of this chapter. As more students received the prized designation, a new category of gifted and talented, the "highly/profoundly gifted," was created, which appropriated the ostensibly egalitarian notion of multiple intelligences to create new classifications of supposed individual aptitude. This raises the possibility that if all students had access to an AP English classroom, maybe a higher placement would be created to accommodate those with more power and privilege. If children gain access to the French Café, maybe a "Latin Bistro" will crop up exclusively for the upper grades. The structures may not be this obvious. In fact, recalling Žižek (1989), the more imperceptible they are, the more insidious. This is the case with intellectual work that is deemed "extracurricular" or "enrichment," such as the performance troop, Dancing Across Borders, which gets relegated to the margins of the school day and becomes uncompensated labor. It only gets recognized if it "gets recognized" by an important audience—but it is not considered a central part of the curriculum.

Example 3: Resistance as (Re)imagining Alternative School Communities As the above examples illustrate, much resistant practitioner research takes place within (and often against) mainstream institutions informed by dominant ideologies. This work frequently is driven by individual teachers' willingness to call common practices or understandings into question, often in collaboration with colleagues and students. Joan Cone's (2005) investigation into the co-construction of low achievement began by wondering what messages are hidden within class rosters and lists, "What, for example, do lists of honor roll students, suspended students, students excused for forensics tournaments, seniors repeating algebra, ninth graders in physical science, ninth graders in honors biology reveal about the school?" Our final example suggests how practitioner inquiry can support revising the fundamental "grammar" of schooling (Tyack & Cuban, 1995) represented by the hierarchical groupings in Cone's question, and other ways of labeling students across their academic lifespans. As this example illustrates, practitioner research has supported the creation of alternative school environments oriented toward more equitable understandings of ability, achievement, potentials, and life chances of disenfranchised youth.

Rob has documented his work in the creation of Life Learning Academy (LLA), a 60-student alternative high school for adolescents who were involved in or deemed "at risk" of involvement in the criminal justice system (e.g., Simon, 2005). Life Learning Academy began as a part of a coordinated inquiry into the San Francisco juvenile justice system and relevant support services led by the Mayor's Office of Criminal Justice and Delancey Street Foundation—a resident-run, self-help rehabilitation facility for former convicts and drug addicts, which president Mimi Silbert has referred to as the "Harvard of the Underclass" (Mieszkowski, 1998)—involving over 400 community-based organizations. The school was publicly chartered to create an alternative for the growing numbers of students falling through the cracks of San Francisco high schools, attempting to address the needs of urban adolescents who had experienced prolonged school failure.

The Life Learning Academy curriculum was intended to be project-based. The first project was the construction of the school itself, built from the ground up on a reconstituted military base on Treasure Island by Delancey Street residents and LLA students and staff. It remains a work in progress: Subsequent groups of LLA students re-design, re-decorate, re-paint, and build additions to the school, such as an organic community garden, a bike repair shop, or a student-run café, the operation of which was integrated with Math and English curricula. This built environment shapes how students conceive of themselves. The process of constructing the building was a literal manifestation of the school ethos, intended to bond disparate individuals—most of whom had never viewed school as a place where they felt supported, understood, or even welcome—into a community. From Delancey Street, LLA appropriated the idea of school as an "extended family," where individuals felt connected to a collaborative endeavor. Teachers were oriented to viewing Life Learning students as individuals of significant promise rather than risk or failure. This philosophy was supported by integrated, project-based curriculum that cut across vocational and core subject areas, constructing "success" as multidimensional—personal, interpersonal, ethical, as well as cognitive or academic—and deeply relational, as the success of any one member of the community was acutely linked to the success of all.

The school did not emerge fully formed. Rather, it required ongoing tinkering, a quality suggested by the school motto: "*The important thing is this: to be able, at any moment, to sacrifice what we are for what we could become.*" LLA evolved from (and continues to involve) ongoing inquiry, recurrent revision, and daily work. From the start, teachers and staff took up fundamental issues of learning and inherited understandings of schooling as subjects for inquiry and constructive resistance. For example, like Joan Cone, Life Learning teachers were deeply concerned about legacies of school tracking present in their own rosters and organizing impulses, as well as those imposed upon them by the state university system and the local school district. Rob and other teachers arranged—and re-arranged—classes heterogeneously, intentionally grouping students across ages, abilities, and interests, and created opportunities for students to assume leadership, mentoring, counseling, and even administrative and teaching roles within the school. These arrangements presented new possibilities for students like Monica, a fourteen-year-old Latina who had been deemed such a significant threat by her middle-school administration that they not only expelled her in eighth grade, but banned her from campus, refusing to allow her to attend her peers' graduation. After eight months at LLA, Monica gained three grade-levels in reading fluency, reading comprehension, and math (LaFrance, 2004). She also did not miss a single day of school in ninth grade. Monica came to view the school as a place where she felt known, where she could move beyond the institutional ascription of "drop-out."

Third-party assessment has demonstrated Life Learning Academy's "success" by multiple measures (LaFrance, 2004)—including significantly lower rates of criminal recidivism, absences, and dropouts, and increased grade-point averages, graduation rates, and passing statewide exit exams. At the same time, the school is not a utopic paradigm. These intentional realignments and challenges to normative understandings continually create new challenges, questions, and dilemmas, including in some cases new hierarchies that re-inscribe differences and divisions. While collectively drawing upon stigmatized or negative social experiences, categories, and labels to construct an alternative community identity in school, many LLA students struggled to work against negative influences outside the school. At the same time, assumptions about normality and aptitude often reasserted themselves—internally, for example in renewed prospects of academic ability assigned to students who previously bore lower expectations; and externally, e.g., in matching up LLA students' "performances" to state expectations or needing to align an intentionally different course of study to district requirements for scope and sequence of courses. Further, while working to undermine such categories as "at risk," mainstream norms can re-surface, as in the premium placed on becoming "productive citizens," where citizenship can have a valence of conformity rather than critical engagement and dissent.

As Life Learning Academy demonstrates, school-based inquiry necessitates a collective response and is often inter-organizational and connected to broader reform. Elsewhere, small school projects like New York's Harvey Milk High School, designed to support the learning of "at-risk" gay, lesbian, bisexual, transgender, and questioning adolescents, present other examples of how school-based practitioner research can support counter-practices that present opportunities for communities of students and teachers to learn together about what counts as school—and to intentionally construct more nurturing, ethical, and egalitarian alternatives.

Conclusion

One of the contributions of disability studies is that it reminds social constructivists to be more literal, what Michael Bérubé (2002) characterizes as closer attention to the "oscillations between social constructionism and critical realism" (p. 343). Constructivism is not merely a metaphor for how discourse operates, but also an ideology that inheres in material reality. Practitioner researchers are uniquely positioned to attend to these realities, as they analyze material structures such as classroom space, school segregation, labeling, tracking, and testing. In the process, they also create new material realities—and with them, new worlds—for students to thrive.

In this chapter, we may have presented the ideology of the normal curve as an ostensible Gordian knot of structures, policies, and pedagogies which can feel almost deterministic. This sentiment has merit, because we live in a classification society fueled by deep political and economic interests. Education has been rightly critiqued as an instrument of social reproduction. However, because the normal curve is a social practice, not an aspect of nature or merely notional, educators can take direct action on its deleterious effects on students through counter-practices. As our examples suggest, such resistance is an ongoing process: a working ideal rather than a state of arrival, an aspect of a critical inquiry stance. This work invariably takes place in the messiness of the everyday. It involves contradiction and often our best judgments in the moment. It is that messiness that the ideology of the normal curve tries to repress, by abstracting one aspect or one moment as somehow representative of a student's potential across contexts and prescribing instruction accordingly. We can therefore define resistance to the normal curve as a situational ethic of practice and a practice of ethics—a commitment to making a more capacious and varied understanding of human potentials "the norm."

Authors' Note

We would like to thank Maria Paula Ghiso for her thoughtful feedback for this chapter.

References

Althusser, L. (1971). Ideology and ideological state apparatuses. In *Lenin and philosophy and other essays*. New York: Monthly Review Press.

Anderson-Levitt, K. M. (1996). Behind schedules: Batch-produced children in French and U.S. classrooms. In B. A. Levinson, D. E. Foley, & D. C. Holland (Eds.), *The cultural production of the educated person: Critical ethnographies of schooling and local practice*. Albany, NY: State University of New York Press.

Baudrillard, J. (1994). *Simulacra and simulation* (S. F. Glaser, Trans.). Ann Arbor, MI: University of Michigan Press. (Original work published in 1981).

Bérubé, M. (2002). Afterword: If I should live so long. In S. L. Snyder, B. J. Brueggemann, & R. Garland-Thomson (Eds.), *Disability studies: Enabling the humanities* (pp. 337–343). New York: The Modern Language Association of America.

Bourdieu, P. & Wacquant, L. (1992). *An invitation to reflexive sociology*. Chicago, IL: University of Chicago Press.

Campano, G. (2005). Ma-Lee's story. In A. Lieberman (Ed.), *Going public: Teachers writing about teaching* (pp. 237–242). New York: Teachers College Press.

Campano, G. (2007). *Immigrant students and literacy: Reading, writing, and remembering*. New York: Teachers College Press.

Campano, G. (2009). Teacher research as a collective struggle for humanization. In M. Cochran-Smith & S. Lytle (Eds.), *Inquiry as stance*. New York: Teachers College Press.

Campano, G., Honeyford, M., Sanchez, L., & Vander Zanden, S. (forthcoming). Ends in themselves: The methodological implications of fostering horizontalidad in university-school partnerships. *Language Arts*.

Carini, P. (2001). *Starting strong: A different look at children, schools, and standards*. New York: Teachers College Press.

Cochran-Smith, M. & Lytle, S. L. (1999). Relationships of knowledge and practice: Teacher learning on communities. In A. Iran-Nejad & P. D. Pearson (Eds.), *Review of research in education*. Volume 24. Washington, DC: American Educational Research Association.

Cochran-Smith, M. & Lytle, S. L. (2001). Beyond certainty: Taking an inquiry stance on practice. In A. Leiberman & L. Miller (Eds.), *Teachers caught in the action: Professional development that matters*. New York: Teachers College Press.

Cochran-Smith, M. & Lytle, S. L. (2009). *Inquiry as stance: Practitioner research in the next generation*. New York: Teachers College Press.

Cone, J. (2002). The gap is in our expectations. *Newsday*, May 6, 2002.

Cone, J. (2005). *Co-constructing low achievement: A study of a senior English class at an urban high school*. Monograph. Retrieved September 12, 2009: http://gallery.carnegiefoundation. org/collections/quest/collections/sites/cone_joan/jc_monograph_edit.pdf.

Derrida, J. (1993). *Aporias*. Palo Alto, CA: Stanford University Press.

Dweck, C. (2007). *Mindset: The new psychology of success*. New York: Ballantine.

Gardner, H. (2006). *Multiple intelligences: New horizons in theory and practice*. New York: Basic.

Gladwell, M. (2008). *Outliers: The story of success*. New York: Little, Brown .

Gould, S. J. (1981). *The mismeasure of man*. New York: W. W. Norton.

Harste, J. & Vasquez, V. (1998). The work we do: Journal as audit trail. *Language Arts, 75*(4), 266–276.

Herr, K. & Anderson, G. L. (2005). *The action research dissertation: A guide for students and faculty*. Thousand Oaks, CA: Sage.

Kozol, J. (2005, September). Still separate, still unequal: America's educational apartheid. *Harper's Magazine, 41*–54.

LaFrance, S. (2004). *Life Learning Academy student academic performance report, academic year: 2002–2003*. San Francisco, CA: LaFrance.

Medina, C., & Campano, G. (2006). Performing identities through drama and teatro practices in multilingual classrooms. *Language Arts, 84*(4), 332–341.

Mieszkowski, K. (1998). She helps people help themselves. *Fast Company, 15*, 4.

Mohanty, S. (1997). *Literary theory and the claims of history: Postmodernism, objectivity, multicultural politics*. Ithaca, NY: Cornell University Press.

Moya, P. (2000). Postmodernism, "realism," and the politics of identity. In P. Moya & M. Hames-Garcia (Eds.), *Reclaiming dentity: Realist theory and the predicament of postmodernism* (pp. 67–101). Berkeley, CA: University of California Press.

Nussbaum, M. (1995). Objectification. *Philosophy and Public Affairs, 24*(4), 249–291.

Rose, M. (2005). *The mind at work: valuing the intelligence of the American worker*. New York: Penguin.

Siebers, T. (2008). *Disability theory*. Ann Arbor, MI: University of Michigan Press.

Simon, R. (2005). Bridging life and learning through inquiry and improvisation: Literacy practices at a model high school. In Street, B. V. (Ed.), *Literacies across educational contexts*. Philadelphia, PA: Caslon.

Simon, R. (2009). *"We are all becoming teacher/theorists": Collaborative inquiry into the intellectual, relational, and political work of learning to teach*. Unpublished doctoral dissertation. University of Pennsylvania, Philadelphia, PA.

Snyder, S. L., Bruegemann, B. J., & Garland-Thomson, R. (2002). *Disability studies: Enabling the humanities*. New York: Modern Language Association of America.

Street, B. (1984). *Literacy in theory and practice*. Cambridge, MA: Cambridge University Press.

Tyack, D. & Cuban, L. (1995). *Tinkering toward utopia: A century of public school reform*. Cambridge, MA: Harvard University Press.

Vasquez, V. (2004). *Negotiating critical literacies with young children*. Mahwah, NJ: Lawrence Erlbaum.

Žižek, S. (1989). *The sublime object of ideology*. London; New York: Verso.

Žižek, S. (2008). *Violence: Six sideways reflections*. New York: Picador.

Zeiders, M., Willard, E., Simon, R., Rowley, M., McCartney, A., Kreft, J., Greco, K., & Carlough, S. (2007). Collaborative teacher inquiry in trying times. *Presentation at the Ethnography in Education Research Forum*. University of Pennsylvania. February, 2007.

SIXTEEN

Conclusion: Re/visioning the Ideological Imagination in (Special) Education

Alex Gurn

Introduction

This book project began not as an edited book but as an article submission to an academic journal, one that was followed by a resounding rejection letter or more aptly put: an objection letter. The letter cited flaws not so much in the construction of a principled argument about the normal curve but in the nature of the principles underlying the argument, which in the readers' estimation, amounted to an attack on the tradition of science and, more specifically, "positivism." Interestingly, the original article, nearly identical to our Chapter 2, operated in certain ways in keeping with the legacy of positive science, visible in our attempt to construct an overt and discernible research logic about the problem (i.e., explicating a researchable problem, making an assertion or hypothesis, presenting contrasting evidence about the assertion, and discussing these findings in the context of special education research and practice). Even more bewildering, one reader's remarks intimated that s/he was deeply offended by our words, feeling personally attacked. After the rejection, we chose not to resubmit the article to another journal and, instead, with the encouragement of Scot Danforth, one of the co-editors of the series in which this book appears, proposed an edited text in which we would invite a group of researchers and educators to interrogate the ideological foundations of the normal curve, including what it means to be construed as outside the boundaries of "normal."

The myth of the normal curve, which pervades dominant Western-European discourses, is based on the notion that social behaviors and characteristics tend to cluster around an average composite or normal range that can be mapped onto the predictable contours of a bell-shaped curve. Falling outside the boundaries of normal signals something extraordinary (or exceptional) that may evoke reverence (for those on the upper reaches of the normal curve) or repulsion (for those at the lower reaches of the normal curve), a desire to emulate or to remediate. Through the lens of the normal curve, difference is read as deviation from an average or norm, and that which is below average is perceived as inherently deficient, a logic that has served to privilege white, affluent, heterosexual, male dominated, and able-bodied ways of being. Indeed, the ideology of the normal curve is inextricably linked to issues of power, and each chapter in this book addresses the relationship between the social construction of normality and marking privilege and power.

The essays in this volume work to deconstruct the normal curve and normalizing tendencies, as they pertain to diversity and difference in education and to the fields of special education and Disability Studies, in particular. It is, however, not the mere existence of "normal" as a commonsense notion that is most troubling, but the existential realities of living under the lens of normative, deficit models, which pose real consequences for individuals and groups deemed outside of the norm. The authors of this book testify to the deleterious effects on people with disabilities and their families as a result of educational and medical practices predicated on the normal curve, casting light into the often dark and isolating corners of disability and difference. As a whole, the volume seeks to expose the normal curve's "regimes of truth" (Foucault, 1980), which remakes some groups and individuals as abled, smart people and some as disabled, problematic, and in need of fixing. From an array of disciplinary perspectives, the contributors to this text have deliberated on numerous problems associated with unswerving acceptance of normality-based ideologies, scratching at a variety of epistemological, methodological, and moral-ethical dilemmas stemming from this worldview.

This concluding chapter will recapitulate some of the arguments made throughout the book, while drawing on conceptual literature from across our multi-disciplinary, and at times contradictory, field of education. The purpose of this essay is to speak across the volume, to reframe the problem of education, and to envision a more humanizing educational future that expands the ideological imagination in (special) education. This discussion will interweave a reading of current controversies in United States' public education reform, driven predominantly by sweeping federal legislation under the No Child Left Behind Act (NCLB), discussed first, and Individuals with Disabilities Education Act (IDEA), discussed later. Reflecting on these controversies allows us to deconstruct the prevailing discourse that shapes public debates and begin to reconstruct a vision for education that travels beyond the boundaries of normality.

The Controversy of No Child Left Behind

NCLB may be understood as a complex nexus of public rhetoric, research, laws, policies, and recommendations that play out at federal, state, and local levels to varying social, political, and economic impacts. NCLB increasingly promotes reliance on a medical model of educational research and schooling practices (Gallagher, this volume), often through the recruitment of racialized language and symbols (Willis, this volume). It frames the "problem" of education primarily in the language of "gaps." Resolutions to our apparent educational woes and to closing the "achievement gap" are mostly construed as a matter of following means and methods "proven effective through rigorous scientific research" and targeting funding "to support these programs and teaching methods that work to improve student learning and achievement" (U.S. Department of Education, http://www. ed.gov/nclb/overview/intro/4pillars.html). From the perspective of NCLB, student learning = test scores = good teaching. This tendency to equate test scores with learning is not new (Hillocks, 2002). What is new is the institutional power in decision-making attributed to a narrow set of assessment scores. Thus, NCLB exerts a powerful institutionalized force on schooling, operating on an implicit theory-of-change that calls for externally imposed "accountability" requirements based on normative, "standardized" measures to create large-scale, positive educational change to improve curriculum content, instructional practices, and achievement indicators of students. NCLB's main lever for reform is the use of standardized tests for making a variety of high-stakes decisions regarding grade-level promotion and retention of students, teacher salaries (as with *pay-for-performance* schemes being implemented in numerous states), as well as funding streams. The logic of NCLB takes for granted the assumption that reliable judgments can be made about student learning and effective teaching based almost exclusively on information gleaned from high stakes, standardized tests and assessment measures that take root in scientism and discourses of normality (see, for example, Gallagher; Macedo & Sordé Martí; Willis, this volume).

This "achievement gap" frame, acutely reflected in the media sphere, has dominated educational discourse over the past several decades. From this perspective, disproportionate levels of academic "underachievement" among non-dominant youth and families, including those with disabilities, typically gets explained through a deficit model that situates school failure in the minds, bodies, and cultures of individual students. Ladson-Billings (2006) offers an alternative frame, arguing that "gaps" in standardized test scores are more aptly understood as a symptom of what she terms the "education debt," which has accumulated over time through complex social, economic, cultural, and moral lived realities of oppressed groups in the United States. In similar fashion, authors in this volume directly and indirectly problematize the dominant deficit framework and demonstrate myriad ways that educational disparities are deeply embedded in often oppressive social, cultural, and economic conditions that "other" people have historically experienced in this country. Arguably, any interpretation of academic performance or learning disabilities that disregards the legacies of racism, classism, xenophobia, ablism, and other normalizing discourses will never be able to accurately explain the reasons behind certain groups' lower achievement or disproportionate representation in special education. For this reason, we need theoretical frameworks that help us to examine educational realities multi-dimensionally and that explicitly incorporate the role of social and cultural power as a point of analysis.

De/Re-constructing Education

Efforts to expose and deconstruct the nature of normativity carry both scholarly and practical significance for the educational challenges that lie ahead. At the dawn of the 21st century, we live in a historical period marred by persistent—and growing—social and economic inequalities (McLaren, 2007; Mohanty, 2006), in which the dominant media construct narratives of education and opportunity principally through the ideologies of individualism and meritocracy (Valle & Gabel, this volume) that serve to justify the unequal positions of power inscribed in the normal curve (Dudley-Marling & Gurn, this volume). Given the robust nature of the problem, scholars and practitioners must refuse to remain trapped in critique alone. Recognizing the importance of imagining alternatives and dreaming of what could be, stepping beyond the boundaries of past and present injustices, Freire's (2000) words offer insight and remind us that criticism alone is insufficient to effect transformational social change:

> When a word is deprived of its dimension of action, reflection automatically suffers as well; and the work is changed into idle chatter, into verbalism, into an alienated and alienating "blah." It becomes an empty word, one which cannot denounce the world, for denunciation is impossible without a commitment to transform, and there is no transformation without action. (p. 87)

Unsatisfied with simply naming various sources of oppression, Freire's lasting legacy on research and teaching reflects an enduring faith in the pursuit of *skepticism* and *praxis*. Through the ongoing linking of social theory and action, praxis-oriented inquiry aims to actively alter social conditions, while attending closely to questions of applicability and answerability of the research to the very people and groups under study (Lather, 1986). By design, this sort of pedagogy is also intentionally focused on realizing people's full human potential, and thus, on educational futures.

Before returning to the undertaking of re-visioning "normal," let us resituate our discussion of present-day educational conditions in what is a decidedly complex world. Several contributors to this volume attend to this complexity, providing historically situated accounts that critically question the validity of the prevailing, linear-oriented modes of inquiry embedded in normative discourse (Davis & Sumara; Dudley-Marling & Gurn; Gallagher; Gelb). At root, the problem lies in the inability of theoretical frameworks that take normality for granted to accurately understand and explain non-linear phenomena such as teaching and learning. Despite its common sense appeal, human intelligence and educational experiences do not occur in predictable ways that abide by statistically normal distributions. While research has offered ample scientific evidence to challenge the claim that people with disabilities are categorically different than "normal" people, this belief has persisted and proven resistant to critique (see Dudley-Marling & Dippo, 1995). However, the chapters in this book point to an alternate framing of educational discourse, one that sees all people as different (i.e., it's normal to be different). Here normality is a social construct linked to an ideology that affects the distribution of social goods, including status (Gee, 2008). So what would happen if we instead took difference as the norm?

The counter-stance that it is normal to be different does not imply randomness but rather patterned difference within particular social and historical conditions. Davis and Sumara (this volume), who call this tenet structure determinism, underscore the profound educational significance of this principle:

> The learning system is structure determined—it determines what will be learned, not the event or experience that prompts learning to happen. Much in contrast to complicated (mechanical) systems that can be caused to respond in specific ways by external forces, the way that a complex (learning) system adapts to a new situation is rooted in its biological-and-experiential structure—its embodied history.

In other words, the meaning and direction of human learning depend on a complex arrangement of factors, such as, the make-up of the individual, her interests and motivations, her prior knowledge and experiences in conjunction with a range of environmental and historical variables. Despite what packaged, "teacher-proof" curricula imply, learning problems cannot be equated with deficits inherent to the learner, nor can human beings be conditioned to respond in specific and predictable ways through external intervention to overcome those putative deficits. Given the uneven, uncertain, and emergent nature of teaching and learning, teacher discretion and teachers' pedagogical content knowledge are of utmost importance, qualities that are rapidly becoming something of an "endangered species" (Pearson, 2007) amidst the tumultuous political climate in this era of standards and accountability. Writing nearly 100 years ago, John Dewey (1922) conveyed his enduring faith in the transformative potential of a thinking, engaged teaching force exercising political clarity, something that continues to have significant implications for today's educational realities:

> What will happen if teachers become sufficiently courageous and emancipated to insist that education means the creation of a discriminating mind, a mind that prefers not to dupe itself or to be the dupe of others? Clearly they will have to cultivate the habit of suspended judgment, of skepticism, of desire for evidence, of appeal to observation rather than sentiment, discussion rather than bias, inquiry rather than conventional idealizations. When this happens, schools will be dangerous outposts of a humane civilization. (p. 141)

In both Campano and Simon's and Crawford and Bartolomé's chapters, the authors highlight the potential of teachers as these dangerous outposts, as change agents capable of stemming the silencing tide of normative discourse in schools and classrooms. Campano and Simon situate praxis-oriented practitioner inquiry as an ideological stance and methodology for teaching and research whereby "educators can take direct action on (the normal curve's) deleterious effects on students through counter-practices" (this volume). Since practitioner inquiry entails continually analyzing and negotiating cultural spaces with one's students, these transactions implicate the teacher (and his/her historical and cultural baggage) as much as the students in the pedagogical process. With its focus on theorizing and action from the local, a critical inquiry stance (Cochran-Smith & Lytle, 2009) uniquely positions teachers to resist the hegemony of deficit orientations, for instance, through the telling of counter-narratives that recognize the "epistemic privilege" of all youth, particularly those deemed "at-risk" or "low performing" by conventional measures. With the capacity to cross borders between young people's worlds and institutions of power, teachers have the potential to carry out the work of redesigning schooling structures and to (re)imagine alternative school communities for re-dressing deep-seated social and cultural inequities.

Similarly, Crawford and Bartolomé (this volume) highlight the positionality of teachers to challenge "the prevailing use of a unilinear, lock-step, and solely basic skills approach" with students with disabilities, seeking ways to enact more humanizing pedagogies. For example, they cite culturally responsive teaching as a promising approach, which aims "to tap into and build on students' life experiences and their existing knowledge and skills as both a strategy for learning about their students and for 'hooking' students into learning conventional academics" (this volume). The authors demonstrate how this approach, with its focus on continually getting to know students' lived experiences and existing knowledge bases, confronts many teachers' tacit theories that non-dominant students bring nothing of intellectual value or relevance to classroom learning. At the same time, Crawford and Bartolomé point out:

> Culturally responsive pedagogy requires that educators begin with the belief that every child can learn, and with the expectation that they have the knowledge and skills to provide students all that they need, including knowledge of how to use a variety of technologies in order to access and make significant progress in the general curriculum. (this volume)

Their chapter alludes to the critical role that teacher education must play in revisioning schooling for non-dominant youth. While it is vitally important to ensure the technical skill sets and content knowledge of teachers in the work force, emphasizing only these aspects of teaching will fall short of altering chronic inequality within schools. Preparing teachers to teach more effectively does not mean that those teachers will be capable of comprehending the ways in which classroom practices, schools, and society more broadly, structure inequality and failure. For instance, intense top-down pressure created under NCLB has been shown to encourage administrators and teachers toward unethical practices, such as placing disproportionate numbers of poor and minority students in special education programs, nudging low performing students to drop out or focusing schooling efforts on so-called "bubble kids" (e.g., Booher-Jennings, 2005; Nichols & Berliner, 2007). Although high-stakes testing policies may create the facilitative stress that leads to this unethical gaming of the system, we must also recognize that educators draw on deep-seated normative assumptions about race, class, and ability in singling out these students, albeit conceivably through unconscious means. In this volume, Ball and Harry's and Arlette Willis' chapters provide troubling accounts of some of the negative consequences of NCLB's high-stakes testing agenda. While many educational scholars label these impacts of high-stakes standardized testing as "unintended" consequences, they are neither unexpected nor unknown (Darling-Hammond, 2007). To have a reasonable hope of transcending these conditions or re-writing wrongs of contemporary history, we will require dialogue and action that moves beyond the individualist and rational-technical theories that have dominated much of the public and scholarly rhetoric around reforming and re-structuring public education (Skrtic, 1995), while at the same time, remaining open to the possibility that seemingly contradictory ideological positions may not be mutually exclusive.

Untangling the relationships between disability, race, class, and other social constructions entails thinking that invariably questions the nature of ideology and power in education and society. As Macedo and Sordé Martí (this volume) point out, this involves making connections between technical knowledge that schools of education typically seek to impart on future teachers and the socio-historical realities that underlie the so-called achievement gap that leads to persistent school failure among historically oppressed groups. This kind of knowledge, or critical literacy, among teachers and administrators necessitates "courses on the nature of ideology, ethics, and education — courses that are, by and large, missing from the curriculum of schools of education" (Macedo & Sordé Martí, this voume). Administrators are included here because critical traditions in education often overlook official school leaders as possible transformational allies, instead focusing efforts to speak to and influence classroom teachers. This focus stems from principled decision-making regarding where critical scholars' battles are "best" fought. On the one hand, as Skrtic (1995) has asserted, one must acknowledge that "educational administration remains today largely as it was in the 1950s, firmly grounded in functionalism and thus in the theories of organizational rationality and human pathology" (p. 194); consequently, the driving theoretical frameworks of school leadership (and by extension, perhaps the leaders themselves) are incompatible with non-rational and post-structural theories of disability studies and other critical scholarship. On the other hand, critical scholars tend to embody genuine desire to stimulate change from the ground up, in solidarity with those people and groups most often excluded from the privileges of institutionalized power (Freire, 2000). Although principled, we should question whether this emphasis has limited the field's catalytic potential for social justice and seek out avenues to bridge the worlds of teachers and administrators. Although few and far between, there are documented cases of educational administrators and teachers working in tandem to address problems of social justice and equity from the ground-up of classroom practice and top-down of administrative leadership (Caro-Bruce, Flessner, Klehr, & Zeichner, 2007).

Looking ahead, it is clearly necessary for all educators to have foundational knowledge of the complex socio-political dynamics underlying students' struggles to succeed and learn in school, but again, critical talk is not enough to bring about change. For instance, in a recent empirical study of teacher discourse, Dudley-Marling & Paugh (in press) attempted to challenge teachers' language habits as a way of re-thinking the deficit approach and encouraging a more social constructivist approach to difference. However, what the authors found, predictably enough, was that the teachers were able to take up the language of a social constructivist stance when they were talking about children in general, but when they talked about children in their own classrooms they readily defaulted to deficit language. Likewise, in re/visioning education equitably, we need new ways—and language —for talking about change.

We also need collective action on the part of scholar-activists to collaborate and organize with educators, parents, and students who experience the varying effects of normalizing discourses. In her chapter that traces the roots of special education and the interconnection with historically racialized ideologies, Beth Ferri begins to disentangle the persistent and pernicious confluence of racism and ableism. More importantly, her chapter suggests paths of resistance that can simultaneously address multiple forms of oppression. Ferri complicates the notion of coalition building across diverse groups, suggesting an approach that is more inclusive of different visions for change and different motivations for action. Frequently, calls for disparate groups to collectively toil for the improvement of schools take for granted that these groups share common interests and stand on equal footing; however, as Ferri contends:

> What this has often amounted to is the belief that what is good for the majority is also good for the minority, advancing an agenda that uncritically equates the dominant group's interests with what is normal. In other words, what is assumed to be good for white people will necessarily be good for black people is often an unstated assumption operating in calls for coalition. Yet, these groups often operate from different sets of premises and priorities, which can lead to conflicts of interests, rather than shared interests. (this voume)

Thus, the act of building vital coalitions and practicing solidarity pivots on the interests and abilities of people to listen deeply to the "other," to suspend judgement, to respect other's experiences, and to enter into honest dialogue.

There are no simple solutions to the problems presented in this volume, no foolproof resolutions, and no magic bullets. And as Bernadette McCartney's chapter brings to light, resisting normative deficit-orientations in one's daily personal practice is a constant struggle, even for a critical educator. Her essay underscores how personal narratives can provide powerful counter-discourses to prevailing notions of disability that construe individuals through a deficit lens, how "deep understandings can be gained through listening to and reflecting on the diverse voices and experiences of disabled people and their families (who) are uniquely positioned by and position themselves in relation to normalizing discourses" (this voume). However, McCartney's own story reveals that experiencing and recognizing a deficit gaze is a far cry from rupturing its influence on one's life. As McCartney explains, she is explicitly opposed to the underlying philosophy of exclusion and "othering" that relies on the separation of most people as normal and some as abnormal. She has railed against exclusionary practices throughout her professional career. Yet, when it comes to addressing disability as a parent, the tendency is hard to resist. For example, she finds herself comparing her child's development against so-called "normal" peers and framing her worries in relation to average scores. However, as her chapter demonstrates, it is also possible to critically reflect on one's own experiences and to reframe family histories so as to challenge and resist discourses that effectively dehumanize oneself and loved ones.

Engaging and Disengaging the Dominant Culture

Narratives carry the potential for analyzing family and community histories for contradictions and unraveling the influences that push and pull the conflicted lives and contradictory experiences on the boundaries of the normal. But this process does not simply happen through re-telling. Without narratives that run counter to the dominant discourse, families risk remaining "caught in the loop of the hunt for disability…. It can be difficult to recognize that one is in the loop, that one has bought into the myth of normativity and sometimes it is only in retrospect that a mother can see it for what it is" (Valle & Gabel, this volume). Collectively, the essays in this book offer an array of analytical tools for recognizing and interrupting this self-perpetuating loop to begin to transform prevailing discourses of normativity vis-à-vis disability and difference. In taking up the task of envisioning alternatives to normative discourses, we, as educators, must address a dilemma that has long troubled social activists and scholars: From what positionality will this transformation work transpire, from within institutions of power or within communities seeking to navigate those institutions? The feminist theorist Gloria Anzaldua (1987) takes up this question in her classic, visionary text *Borderlands/la frontera*:

> At some point, on our way to a new consciousness, we will have to leave the opposite bank, the split between the two mortal combatants somehow healed so that we are on both shores at once and, at once, see through serpent and eagle eyes. Or perhaps we will decide to disengage from the dominant culture, write it off all together as a lost cause and cross the border into a wholly new and separate territory. Or we might go another route. The possibilities are numerous once we decide to act and not react. (p. 25)

The contributors to this volume have implicitly asked readers to journey into expanding the ideological imagination, challenging taken-for-granted assumptions about the notion of normality and what this entails for students with learning disabilities. At once, this book sees the world through "serpent eyes," entrenched in the everyday realities of lived phenomena and practice and through "eagle eyes," soaring up above to examine historical patterns and social theories that may help explain what is happening on the ground. In re/visioning education, the authors of this text by and large attempt to straddle the "both shores" of the dominant and non-dominant cultures, yet there is considerable variance in the degree to which they choose to engage with or "disengage from the dominant culture."

In their analysis of non-dominant students' disproportionate representation in special education, Ball and Harry (this volume) critically review schools' assessment and placement practices for high-incidence categories and, in particular, schools' established use of the severe discrepancy model to base such decisions. As others have argued (e.g., Donovan & Cross, 2002), Ball and Harry cast doubt on this framework, which searches for statistically significant differences between a student's measured academic achievement and her apparent global ability, as measured by IQ tests. Since IQ, which has been exposed as racially and socio-economically biased, tends to underestimate the intellectual ability of people of color and poor people (e.g., Gould, 1981), the discrepancy model and its underlying normative assumptions "blind us to the power of context and culture both in children's display of their knowledge and in professionals' interpretations of those displays" (Ball & Harry, this volume). Related objections have been raised elsewhere (e.g., Harry & Klinger, 2006) as to the application of the exclusionary clause, a problematic legal stipulation that requires schools to demonstrate that the source of a learning problem inheres in the student and not in his or her environment or experience. In short, scratching below the surface of dominant practices indicates that schooling processes for determining students' special education eligibility is "anything but a science" (Harry & Klingner, 2006, p. 9).

In fact, the federal government has reached similar conclusions. With the passage and re-authorization of the Individuals with Disabilities Education Act of 1997 and 2004 (IDEA, 2006), the U.S. government recommends abandoning discrepancy models. The law instructs that states cannot require a school to use "a severe discrepancy between intellectual ability and achievement" and furthermore, "must permit the use of a process based on the child's response to scientific, research-based intervention and may permit the use of other alternative research-based procedures for determining whether a child has a specific learning disability" [IDEA, 2006, CFR 300.307(a)]. The U.S. Department of Education (2005) also "strongly recommends" that states adopt response to intervention (RTI) models in lieu of the discrepancy model (p. 31). Ball and Harry's chapter underscores the variability in RTI approaches across states and school districts, and acknowledges that the field is rife with contradictions, even misuses. Yet, ultimately, these authors place their faith in the promise of RTI to bring about positive social change in (special) education. They, therefore, keep one foot firmly on the shore of dominant culture.

In contrast to Ball and Harry's hope for RTI, many disabilities scholars believe that RTI is merely a different way of sorting kids. For example, Valle and Gabel's essay (this volume) strongly cautions against RTI for identifying children with disabilities, claiming that these approaches in effect serve to amplify our adherence to the discourse of normativity. They state:

> Once targeted as deficient to the norm, these students are instructed by teachers who carry out "evidence-based practices"—i.e., instruction grounded in scientific studies that (a) identify and control for variables in the classroom and (b) indicate the level of confidence with which outcomes and results can be associated with those variables.... It seems we are bent on creating more opportunities to label children beyond what has been established by special education—a curious choice at best given the well-documented deleterious effects of labeling.

The way ahead is ambiguous and uncertain, underscoring the need to view all of these contested debates with a healthy dose of skepticism. At the same time, one must acknowledge that the creation of categories to make sense out of difference in the world is a deeply rooted human activity, one that is not going to cease. This chapter does not suggest that it should, that we should seek an ideological alternative that sees no difference among human beings. To do so would be naïve and merely serve to reify the privileged positions of dominant groups. Everyone is not the same. Everyone is not constructed or treated equally. In the eyes of society, not everyone can be deemed "normal." Yet, it is not the use of labels per se that is most significant but the consequences of those labels. Thus, as scholars and practitioners, we must work to examine where our educational categories and labels come from and what work these labels do. In other words, what ideology underlies the labeling of people, how does it operate, and who benefits and loses when it is applied?

Looking ahead, educators need to do more than merely deconstruct the, at times, harmful categories of normal. Changing tides takes more than talk and recognizing injustice does not inevitably translate into redistributive justice. Sheer resistance against the normative and competitive sorting mechanisms that underscore NCLB will not ensure educational equality for all students. To only deconstruct, as this chapter has primarily done, leaves our task unfinished. In addition to questions that critique, we must pose questions that alter the parameters of the dialogue and pose alternatives.

One lesson of this book is that pushing beyond the deficit gaze of the normal curve can begin with an essential ideological shift. By moving away from the tendency to view students that do to fit the "norm" as problems and schooling as a means of intervening or correcting those problems, we may better equip ourselves to view the totality of learning as a social endeavor, to reposition the pedagogical lens on individuals and groups situated within complex interactions of institutions and socio-historical realities. In this way, educators would ask questions that inquire what forms of knowledge, skills and experiences students bring to school and push themselves to support their interpretations with observable, discernible evidence. In what ways is a student smart, capable, creative, or inquisitive? What does the student already know and what does she want to know? What kind of a learner is she? How do answers to these questions change based on different contexts or over time? For example, one English teacher that I worked with spent a school year observing and documenting the many questions that her students posed in and out of class time, using this information to both inform classroom learning and pay attention to students' language development. To be clear, starting with these basic questions before asking what students should know or be able to do does not absolve educators of their responsibility to teach. Instead, it provides teachers and students with unique signposts that can be used to bridge what students know and what will be useful for them to know in the future.

In essence, assessment, curriculum and instruction should always remain in dialogue with the complex, patterned, shifting contexts of young people's lives. Furthermore, when educational institutions categorize/label/diagnose a child, we must remember that however functional, however scientific, such classifications are "arbitrary capsules, inherently imbued with historical, cultural, and political contexts" (Stevens & lisahunter, 2009). In other words, while the act of classifying or labeling performs useful social and cognitive functions, this knowledge should be viewed as impermanent and incomplete. For educators to account for this uncertainty, or unknowability, of teaching and learning, it is necessary to attend systematically to matters of description over prediction, closely observing and documenting what a student knows and is able to do over time. Moreover, as Stevens and lisahunter (2009) remind us:

> It is the responsibility of all within the education field to inform its public about the limits of assessment and reporting whilst supporting a richer description of where their students are positioned in terms of the knowledges available to us rather than the arbitrary frames of reference such as Year/Grade 5 or normative benchmarks such as *average*." (p. 102)

However, given the growing dominance of prescriptive curricula, pacing guides, and progress monitoring assessments in public and for-profit schools, descriptive or adaptive approaches to classroom pedagogy are exceedingly difficult to put into practice. In the United States, public educators must contend with federal legislation guidelines that privilege research and schooling designs that focus on questions of effectiveness and prediction in terms of normative performance rather than descriptive accounts of individual learning (Erikson, 2005). Yet this is certainly not uncharted territory. Prior to the current standards movement, one notable example of educators pushing beyond the boundaries of normativity was the Prospect School. The school was founded on the belief that the knowledge and experience of teachers, parents, and children themselves, rather than the knowledge of outside experts or specialists, are uniquely positioned to generate understandings of young learners. Prospect School staff developed and documented school-wide observational and descriptive processes to "bend (their) attention to the children and their works, with care and caringly, and over the span of a child's school life" (Carini, 2001, p. 3). One of these processes, the descriptive review of the child, consisted of the entire school staff engaging in weekly in-depth, non-evaluative discussions "to recognize and specify a particular child's strengths as a person, learner, and thinker, so that as a school (they) could respond to and build upon those capacities" (Carini, 2001, p. 4; see also Himley & Carini, 2000).

Germane to this discussion is the recent research of Elizabeth Moje (e.g., Moje, 2008; Moje et al., 2004). Utilizing sociolinguistic and ethnographic methodologies, Moje and her colleagues have studied the complex patterns in youth everyday (home, community, and peer group) and school-based funds of knowledge and discourses, focusing particularly on Spanish-speaking Latino populations. Through systematic observation of literacy practices that take place both in- and out-of-school, their research illuminates possibilities to integrate young people's existing knowledge and experiences in literacy learning. Action researchers such as Gutierrez (2008) and Morrell (2008) have extended the notion of realigning schooling to reflect youth perspectives, knowledge, and histories by drawing on critical pedagogy to teach students to become critical readers and researchers of the word and the world, thus explicitly taking up matters of equity and social justice that have bearing on students' lives in-and out-of-schooling.

These brief examples are presented not as models for any change agenda. What they offer are possible directions to alternatively frame our educational problems and to think differently about the way forward. I recognize that it is never easy to teach *against* the grain, including for people with deep and abiding commitments to do so. I also recognize that the challenges before us are enormous, but for a great many educators, it is utterly exhausting, or even dehumanizing, to teach *with* the grain. And the stakes are too high for far too many young people not to insert ourselves into the struggle. Education offers a unique opportunity to transform and be transformed, speaking to the dialectic nature of teaching and learning. This is not a simple process or a passing episode. It is a way of life.

Parting Thought

Turning back to the start of this essay and the anecdote of the origin of this book, this project itself disengaged in certain ways with dominant perspectives.

Abandoning our pursuit of a more traditional special education outlet, we forewent potential dialogue within the special education community. Positioned within disability studies, this book thus reflects an ideological and rhetorical niche that may put off or even offend some readers, which assumes, however unlikely, that the text will (necessarily) reach across the boundaries of dominant culture. That said, one notable goal of this volume is to spark debate and dialogue, not only with those who agree with its fundamental assumptions and claims made, but also with those who are skeptical or even distrustful of its ideological motivations. Whether you are at odds or in line with what has been written in this chapter or book, I encourage you to voice your issues, your resistance, your questions, or your solidarity. We will be changed in the process and, in doing so, change the world itself.

References

Anzaldua, G. (1987). La conciencia de las mestiza [Towards a new consciousness]. In G. Anzaldua (Ed.), *Borderlands/la frontera: The new mestiza.* San Francisco: Aunt Lute.

Booher-Jennings, J. (2005). Below the bubble: Educational triage and the Texas accountability system. *American Educational Research Journal, 42*(2), 231–268.

Carini, P. (2001). *Starting strong: A different look at children, school, and standards.* New York: Teachers College Press.

Caro-Bruce, C., Flessner, R., Klehr, M., & Zeichner, K. (2007). *Creating equitable classrooms through action research.* Thousand Oaks, CA: Corwin.

Cochran-Smith, M. & Lytle, S. L. (2009). *Inquiry as stance: Practitioner research in the next generation.* New York: Teachers College Press.

Darling-Hammond, L. (2007). Race, inequality and educational accountability: The irony of 'No Child Left Behind.' *Race Ethnicity and Education, 10*(3), 245–260.

Dewey, J. (1922, October 4). Education as politics. *New Republic, 32,* 139–141.

Donovan, S., & Cross, C., Eds. (2002). *Minority students in special and gifted education.* Washington, DC: National Academy Press.

Dudley-Marling, C. & Dippo, D. (1995). What learning disability does: Sustaining the ideology of schooling. *Journal of Learning Disabilities, 28,* 408–414.

Dudley-Marling, C. & Paugh, P. (in press). Confronting the discourse of deficiencies. *Disability Studies Quarterly.*

Erikson, F. (2005). Arts, humanities, and sciences in educational research and social engineering in federal education policy. *Teachers College Record, 107*(1), 4–9.

Fine, M. (2007). Expanding the methodological imagination. *The Counseling Psychologist, 35*(3), 459–473.

Foucault, M. (1980). *Power/knowledge: selected interviews and other writings,* 1972–1977. New York: Pantheon.

Freire, P. (2000). *Pedagogy of the oppressed* (30th anniversary edition). New York: Continuum.

Gee, J. P. (2008). *Social linguistics and literacies: Ideology in discourses* (3d ed.). New York: Routledge.

Goffman, E. (1974). *Frame analysis: An essay on the organization of experience.* Cambridge, MA: Cambridge University Press.

Gould, S. J. (1981). *The Mismeasure of Man.* New York: W. W. Norton & Co.

Gutiérrez, K. D. (2008). Developing a sociocritical literacy in the third space. *Reading Research Quarterly, 43*(2), 148–164.

Harry, B., & Klingner, J. K. (2006). *Why are so many minority students in special education? Understanding race & disability in schools.* New York: Teachers College Press.

Hillocks, G. (2002). *The testing trap: How state writing assessments control learning.* New York: Teachers College Press.

Himley, M. & Carini, P. (Eds.). (2000). *From another angle: Children's strengths and school standards.* New York: Teachers College Press.

Ladson-Billings, G. (2006). From the achievement gap to the education debt: Understanding achievement in U.S. schools. *Educational Researcher, 35*(7), 3-12.

Lather, P. (1986). Research as praxis. *Harvard Educational Review, 56*(3), 257–277.

McLaren, P. (2007). *Life in schools: An introduction to critical pedagogy in the foundations of education* (5th edition). Boston: Pearson/Allyn and Bacon.

Mohanty, C. T. (2006). *Feminism without borders: Decolonizing theory, practicing solidarity.* Durham, NC: Duke University Press.

Moje, E. B. (2008). Everyday funds of knowledge and school discourses. In Martin-Jones, M., de Mejia, A. M., Hornberger, N. H. (Eds.). *Encyclopdeia of language and education, Second Edition. Discourse and education v3* (pp. 341–355). New York: Springer.

Moje, E. B., Ciechanowski, K. M., Kramer, K., Ellis, L., Carrillo, R., & Collazo, T. (2004). Working toward third space in content area literacy: An examination of everyday funds of knowledge and Discourse. *Reading Research Quarterly, 39*(1), 38–70.

Morrell, E. (2008). *Critical literacy and urban youth: Pedagogies of access, dissent, and liberation.* New York: Routledge.

Nichols, S. & Berliner, D. (2007). *Collateral damage: How high-stakes testing corrupts America's schools.* Cambridge, MA: Harvard Education Press.

Pearson, P. D. (2007). An endangered species act for literacy education. *Journal of Literacy Research, 39*(2), 145–162.

Skrtic, T. M. (1995). Special education and student disability as organizational pathologies: Toward a metatheory of school organization and change. In Skrtic (Ed.). *Disability and democracy: Reconstructing (special) education for postmodenity.* New York: Teachers College Press.

Stevens, L. P. & lisahunter (2009). ReFraming phases in education: Science, reform and quality. *Curriculum Perspectives, 24*(1), 98–106.

U.S. Department of Education (2005). *USDOE commentary and explanation about proposed regulations for IDEA 2004.* Washington, DC: U.S. Department of Education.

Contributors

Eileen Ball, Curry College, Boston, Massachusetts

Lilia I. Bartolomé, University of Massachusetts-Boston, Boston, Massachusetts

Gerald Campano, Indiana University, Bloomington, Indiana

Felicity A. Crawford, Wheelock College, Boston, Massachusetts

Brent Davis, University of British Columbia, Vancouver, British Columbia

Curt Dudley-Marling, Boston College, Chestnut Hill, Massachusetts

Beth Ferri, Syracuse University, Syracuse, New York

Susan Gabel, National-Louis University, Skokie, Illinois

Deborah Gallagher, University of Northern Iowa, Cedar Falls, Iowa

Steven A. Gelb, University of San Diego, San Diego, California

Michael Gill, University of Connecticut, Storrs, Connecticut

Alex Gurn, Boston College, Chestnut Hill, Massachusetts

Beth Harry, University of Miami, Miami, Florida

Bernadette Macartney, University of Canterbury, Christchurch, New Zealand

Donaldo Macedo, University of Massachusetts-Boston, Boston, Massachusetts

Michael Mancini, St. Louis University, St. Louis, Missouri

Rebecca Rogers, University of Missouri-St. Louis, St. Louis, Missouri

Rob Simon, University of Toronto/Ontario Institute for Studies in Education, Toronto, Ontario

Teresa Sordé Martí, Universitat Autònoma de Barcelona, Barcelona, Spain

Dennis Sumara, University of British Columbia, Vancouver, British Columbia

Jan Valle, City College of New York, New York, New York

Arlette Ingram Willis, University of Illinois at Urbana-Champaign, Champaign, Illinois

INDEX

Disability Studies in Education

GENERAL EDITORS: SUSAN L. GABEL & SCOT DANFORTH

The book series Disability Studies in Education is dedicated to the publication of monographs and edited volumes that integrate the perspectives, methods, and theories of disability studies with the study of issues and problems of education. The series features books that further define, elaborate upon, and extend knowledge in the field of disability studies in education. Special emphasis is given to work that poses solutions to important problems facing contemporary educational theory, policy, and practice.

To order other books in this series, please contact our Customer Service Department:

(800) 770-LANG (within the U.S.)
(212) 647-7706 (outside the U.S.)
(212) 647-7707 FAX

Or browse by series:

WWW.PETERLANG.COM